Screening Charles Dickens

ALSO BY WILLIAM FARINA
AND FROM MCFARLAND

Italian Crime Fiction in the Era of the Anti-Mafia Movement (2020)

Saint James the Greater in History, Art and Culture (2018)

The Afterlife of Adam Smith: The Influence, Interpretation and Misinterpretation of His Economic Philosophy, 1760s–2010s (2015)

Man Writes Dog: Canine Themes in Literature, Law and Folklore (2014)

The German Cabaret Legacy in American Popular Music (2013)

Eliot Asinof and the Truth of the Game: A Critical Study of the Baseball Writings (2012)

Chrétien de Troyes and the Dawn of Arthurian Romance (2010)

Perpetua of Carthage: Portrait of a Third-Century Martyr (2009)

Ulysses S. Grant, 1861–1864: His Rise from Obscurity to Military Greatness (2007)

De Vere as Shakespeare: An Oxfordian Reading of the Canon (2006)

Screening Charles Dickens
A Survey of Film and Television Adaptations

WILLIAM FARINA

McFarland & Company, Inc., Publishers
Jefferson, North Carolina

ISBN (print) 978-1-4766-8567-0
ISBN (ebook) 978-1-4766-4786-9

LIBRARY OF CONGRESS AND BRITISH LIBRARY
CATALOGUING DATA ARE AVAILABLE

Library of Congress Control Number 2022039441

© 2022 William Farina. All rights reserved

No part of this book may be reproduced or transmitted in any form or by any means, electronic or mechanical, including photocopying or recording, or by any information storage and retrieval system, without permission in writing from the publisher.

Front cover image: John Howard Davies (left, as Oliver Twist) in *Oliver Twist*, 1948 (United Artists/Photofest); *background*: © Janaka Dharmasena/Shutterstock

Printed in the United States of America

McFarland & Company, Inc., Publishers
Box 611, Jefferson, North Carolina 28640
www.mcfarlandpub.com

*To medical professionals worldwide fighting the good fight.
Your courage and selflessness inspire all of us.*

Acknowledgments

By God's grace I have thus far weathered the worldwide pandemic of 2020–2021. What the future holds, no one can say; however, credit should be given wherever any credit is due. As with all my previous work, no one has contributed more helpfulness to these pages than my life companion, Marion Buckley. In addition to encouraging a rather uncertain original idea, she has repeatedly earned the title of Most Valuable Sounding Board, both for superhuman patience and discriminating judgment. Many thanks to her, and with all with my love.

Also, a shout-out to my friend Jerome Bloom for many helpful insights grounded in his performing Dickens on stage, along with my neighbor Mary Kurz, a retired teacher of Dickens, for loaning me books and giving added encouragement.

Table of Contents

Acknowledgments vi
Introduction 1

1. *The Pickwick Papers* (1836–1837) 9
2. *Oliver Twist* (1837–1838) 19
3. *Nicholas Nickleby* (1838–1839) 30
4. *The Old Curiosity Shop* (1840–1841) 39
5. *Barnaby Rudge* (1840–1841) 48
6. *A Christmas Carol* (1843) 57
7. *Martin Chuzzlewit* (1842–1844) 69
8. *Other Christmas Novellas* (1844–1848) 77
9. *Dombey and Son* (1846–1848) 86
10. *David Copperfield* (1849–1850) 94
11. *Bleak House* (1852–1853) 104
12. *Hard Times* (1854) 112
13. *Little Dorrit* (1855–1857) 120
14. *A Tale of Two Cities* (1859) 129
15. *Travelogues* (1842–1863) 139
16. *Great Expectations* (1860–1861) 147
17. *Our Mutual Friend* (1864–1865) 157
18. *Later Short Stories* (1859–1866) 166
19. *The Mystery of Edwin Drood* (1870) 174
20. Biographical and Apocryphal 182

Table of Contents

Summary   190
Filmography   197
Chapter Notes   203
Select Bibliography   221
Index   223

Introduction

"Dickens's highly visual narrative style and vigorous plots have inspired filmmakers throughout the history of cinema. Indeed, many critics and scholars believe his alternating stories, divided by chapters within a single novel, helped seed the idea of cross-cutting and the development of film editing."[1]

Like countless other stay-at-homes during the worldwide pandemic of 2020–2021, I found myself watching television far more than usual. One of many things learned (or rather re-learned) from this forced leisurely pursuit is that the 19th-century English novelist Charles Dickens (1812–1870) was arguably the greatest storyteller who ever lived. This lofty artistic status of Dickens is supported by, among many other aspects, the simple fact that no other author's works have been adapted for the screen so often—more than 400 are known to date. Indeed, no other writer comes even close in this regard. From a poignant *Bleak House* fragment directed in 1901 by George Albert Smith (*The Death of Poor Joe*), to director Armando Iannucci's rollicking and multiracial 2019 feature film *The Personal History of David Copperfield*, the novels and short stories of Dickens have become nearly synonymous with the history of filmmaking.[2] Some critical observers have gone so far as to argue that Dickens contributed heavily to the technical development of film, even though he lived and died many years before motion pictures were invented (see epigraph). In addition to this stylistic influence, no one can deny that Dickens has handily provided future filmmakers with an embarrassing wealth of dramatic material, a legacy consistently exploited by them for more than 120 years.[3]

The main purpose of this study is neither literary criticism nor literary biography, although elements of both will be incorporated into the analysis. Rather, the primary goal is to present a less than comprehensive, contemporary survey of video adaptations taken from works of Charles

Dickens, and above all, to do this in an entertaining manner.[4] For extra measure, discussion of the surprisingly few biographical films or documentaries based on his recorded life will be included as well. Perhaps the most notable of these latter items are *The Invisible Woman* from 2013, a critically acclaimed effort starring and directed by British celebrity actor Ralph Fiennes, as well as *The Man Who Invented Christmas* (2017), a star vehicle for Dan Stevens plus a bevy of famous supporting players. For the chapters based on individual works by the novelist, some of these will obviously be longer or shorter than others, but varied chapter lengths can also have several advantages. To give one example, the ubiquitous *A Christmas Carol* has over the centuries proven to be endlessly recyclable for commercial storytelling purposes and, as a result, has an extremely long list of film interpretations, possibly more than any single literary work of fiction. Accordingly, multiple versions for this most overexposed of all tales by Dickens can be critically highlighted and compared within more manageable parameters of commentary.

At the opposite end of this spectrum, Dickens' later (but often skillful and engaging) short stories have been surprisingly underserved by modern filmmakers, and therefore a shorter chapter length for this category need not dwell too long on things that might have or should have been. Although a selected (but not fully complete) list of Dickensian video works is included in the filmography, and as noted elsewhere in this survey, a comprehensive critique for all movie interpretations of, say, *A Christmas Carol* could easily fill a book by itself, and in fact have. By contrast, some of the novelist's previous or subsequent (but far lesser known) Christmas tales, such as *The Chimes*, *The Cricket on the Hearth*, and *Mr. Pickwick's Christmas*, have also received several interesting film treatments, including some as silent features or more recent animated shorts. Separate narrative chapters can thus be completely devoted to these other Dickens holiday stories that are not nearly as much part of the modern consciousness as his most famous work. Thus, both the relatively known and unknown Charles Dickens tales of Christmastime may be closely examined using the format of separate chapters. Chapters of slightly different lengths for different works or different categories of works will more easily and effectively allow all bases to be covered, in a manner of speaking.

The overarching theme uniting both the fiction of Dickens and most of the films based upon his stories is the traditional (and impossible to avoid) Dickensian sympathy for the common man, the poor, and the oppressed of society, especially in the face of cruelty and adversity. This affectionate sympathy for the common man appears to be more relevant than ever in today's unstable world of a declining middle class. Charles Dickens knew all about poverty, both from personal experience and from the early industrial urban environment he later worked and prospered within. Nevertheless, Dickens was himself in fact a deeply troubled personality, as more recent biographers have highlighted, upsetting the old image of the iconic novelist as a strictly benign, jovial, and benevolent fatherly figure. As it turns out, Dickens knew all too well about human frailty, beginning with himself. Perhaps this is how he was able to write about the poor with such believable and bracing empathy. Arguably, this is the Charles Dickens (as a storyteller) that our contemporary world most responds to: a ferocious social critic, yet deeply sentimental and deeply flawed as an individual human being. It is therefore fitting that each generation, including those yet to come, deserve their own dramatic interpretations of his work, both in printed criticism and, more influentially, on film.

There have been surprisingly few direct surveys like this in this past. Probably the most extensive effort to date has been by the British amateur enthusiast Michael Pointer, whose excellent *Charles Dickens on Screen: The Film, Television, and Video Adaptations* (Scarecrow Press, 1996) may still be located on some library shelves. This worthy effort, however, is currently more than two decades old, during which time there have been numerous movie adaptations of Dickens, many of which are outstanding in quality.[5] Moreover, the 1996 publication of this older book predated a wealth of new material appearing in 2012 around the bicentenary of the novelist's birth year, in the immediate aftermath of the revisionist and highly controversial biography by noted British author and scholar Claire Tomalin.[6] A few years earlier, in 2001, *The Cambridge Companion to Charles Dickens* (Cambridge University Press) included a fine essay by academic Joss Marsh titled "Dickens and Film" along with several other good essays touching upon the same topic by other writers.[7] While far from comprehensive, the essay by Professor Marsh did underscore the tremendous historical importance of the creative partnership between British film director David Lean and a still-unknown Alec Guinness during the late 1940s following World War II. In hindsight, it was the Lean-Guinness collaboration that transformed the Dickens movie adaptation into a serious art form, a lofty status it has easily held ever since. Directors and actors, both American and British, continue to be inspired by these adaptations, which have been often emulated but rarely surpassed.

Sixteen years after the book by Michael Pointer, the 2012 bicentenary saw several visual projects with similar themes, such as the previously quoted exhibition at MoMA and a (currently unavailable) BBC documentary, *Dickens on Film*, directed by British auteur Anthony Wall. More recently, on June 13, 2020, *The Guardian* published another fine article by film critic Guy Lodge, "Streaming: The best Dickens Adaptations"—hinting at the potentially broad appeal for an expanded study on the same idea during these times of stay-at-home entertainment.[8] Though prompted by the latest 2019 film adaptation of *David Copperfield*, Lodge's all-too-brief survey suggests that more and more viewers are turning to the iconic Dickens for quality entertainment. Since the foreseeable future may well involve more pandemics and more stay-at-home mandates (and, consequently, more stay-at-home video entertainment), this book will hopefully offer useful guidance for the growing legions of Charles Dickens fans both reading the books and, probably more numerous, those watching the movies based on his unique brand of serialized fiction graced with a keen social conscience.

A good overview of various problems associated with Dickens film adaptations may be had by examining those few videos based on Dickens' early short works, *Sketches by "Boz," Illustrative of Every-day Life and Every-day People* (1833–1836), a miscellaneous collection first bringing the young novelist to public attention and later emboldening him to seek a full time living as a professional storyteller. Vividly illustrated by the accomplished engraver George Cruikshank and published as a complete two-volume set by John Macrone of London in 1836, *Sketches by Boz* fully established Dickens as a popular humorist with a prodigious gift for descriptive detail a full year before Queen Victoria came to the English throne in 1837. Cruikshank, along with Dickens' other illustrators throughout his long career, did much to visualize the eccentric characters of the novelist (with active involvement by the novelist), so much so that these same images were often employed by filmmakers when the silent movie era began some seven decades later. The biggest problem is that many of these early silent shorts are now irretrievably lost. For example, in 1913, following the Dickens birth centenary year, the historic American Vitagraph company produced a silent short for *Mr. Horatio Sparkins*, drawn from the *Sketches by Boz*, and directed by the prolific Van Dyke Brook (1859–1921).[9] The previous year (in 1912), Brook, who seems to have been drawn towards Dickens' more obscure works, also directed a pair of silent shorts, *Mrs. Lirriper's Lodgers* and *Mrs. Lirriper's Legacy*, now both lost as well.[10] No other video versions of these Dickens stories were ever made, and, in this case, the rare adaptations that were completed can no longer be screened. Thus, any aficionado screening the works of Charles Dickens must first face up to the unpleasant fact that many of the earliest adaptations, and in some cases, the only adaptations, are now forever unavailable, barring any future sensational discovery of lost prints.

One would think that by the post–World War II, television era of the 1950s, this problem of disappearance would have subsided. Quite the contrary. For example, on March 6, 1956, the classic NBC live series *Matinee Theater* ran a one-hour episode (in color) titled *The Mating of Watkins*

Tottle, also based on a short story from Dickens' *Sketches by Boz*.[11] Directed by Emmy–winning Lamont Johnson (1922–2010) and hosted by the affable, recognizable John Conte, the series itself is now widely considered one of the best of its kind from the era, and this particular episode is the only one known to have been made from this specific Dickens work. Like many other broadcasts from the same period, however, the kinescope for this intriguing TV episode is thought to be now lost and is certainly not available any longer for public viewing. The exact same frustrating problem applies to many other television productions of the 1950s (and some even later) that were based upon Dickens source material, not to mention others as well. We know that these broadcasts occurred from records easily accessible on the Internet or other publicly accessible sources, and frequently have many details preserved from other data bases, including photographic publicity stills. On the other hand, and as with all officially lost video productions, there remains a remote hope that recordings of these will one day somehow surface. In the meantime, we can only speculate and guess as to their overall quality or search for surviving critical reviews from the period to obtain more clues about them.

The next (and possibly last) notable video work to incorporate picturesque elements from *Sketches by Boz* was the one-hour 1967 ABC television special titled *Mr. Dickens of London*, a part-documentary, part-biographical dramatization harking back to the Dickensian promotional travelogues of the early silent era.[12] Directed by Barry Morse (1918–2008) and hosted by Juliet Mills, daughter of distinguished British actor John Mills (who played Pip in David Lean's historic production of *Great Expectations* from 1946), *Mr. Dickens of London* also featured Michael Redgrave, patriarch of the famous English acting family, portraying the novelist come back to life as a London tour guide. Problematically, and despite its relatively late date (1967) combined with headline-quality performers, the production is today impossible to find or screen in any platform. Whether any recording still exists is unknown. Although reportedly not very good and overshadowed at the time by political-military events in southeastern Asia, the unavailability of this artifact for screening is frustrating because it no doubt would shed some light on public attitudes, especially American public attitudes, towards Dickens during that pivotal moment in history. According to Michael Pointer, *Mr. Dickens of London* also contained elements drawn from the novelist's nearly unknown holiday short story, *The Seven Poor Travellers*, first published in 1854 for the Christmas edition of Dickens' periodical *Household Words*.[13] Broadcast for the one and only time on December 12, *Mr. Dickens of London* hinted at another important side of the novelist's style: his longstanding penchant for telling Christmas tales in a manner generally considered offbeat and frequently unorthodox in their message.[14] Thus, three short film works utilizing *Sketches by Boz*, respectively dated 1913, 1956, 1967, illustrate many of the irregularities often associated with screening the fictional works of Charles Dickens the novelist by modern-day television or movie audiences.

Throughout this survey, repeated reference is made to the six "core" works of Dickens, which is a purely subjective classification on the part of this commentator. These six core works include *Oliver Twist*, *The Old Curiosity Shop*, *A Christmas Carol*, *David Copperfield*, *A Tale of Two Cities*, and *Great Expectations*. The designation is used mainly to identity books that were hugely popular during the novelist's own time and have, to varying degrees, remained so ever since. Although few contemporary readers still delve into the pages of *The Old Curiosity Shop* (or even recognize the title), nearly all Dickens fans are familiar with the tragedy of Little Nell, the book itself was a true sales blockbuster at the time of its publication, and filmmakers have frequently turned to the story for inspirational material. For that matter, these six novels taken as a group represent an overwhelming majority of all Dickens film adaptations—especially *A Christmas Carol*, which has probably been adapted in various movie guises more than any single work in all English literature. This does not necessarily mean these six books are considered Dickens' best creations, only that they are the most popular (and bankable) for purposes of video portrayal. As pure literature, strong cases for masterpieces can be made for many other novels by Dickens, including *Bleak House*, *Little Dorrit*, *Dombey and Son*, *Nicholas Nickleby*, *The Pickwick Papers*, and *Our Mutual Friend*, all of which have their adherents and indeed have all enjoyed several very fine movie versions made in recent decades.

Dickens and filmmaking have always been closely associated, even though the novelist died 27 years before the first known adaptation of his work appeared. The idea is itself not new and was noticed by many others during the previous century, even before the era of sound. American-born pioneering director D.W. Griffith (1875–1948), often rightfully credited with helping to invent the modern motion picture, is Exhibit A in this regard. Griffith, a man not given to extravagant praising of others, openly and early on cited Dickens' fiction as a prime influence on his own cinematic work. Specifically, the basic film technique known as cross-cutting or alternating story plots within a single narrative format was expressly attributed by Griffith to the serialized novels of Dickens. One of Griffith's earliest works as a director, a silent short adaptation of Dickens' *The Cricket on the Hearth* (1909), utilized the then-groundbreaking method, and all of Griffith's subsequent work maintained an undeniably Dickensian flavor. In short, one cannot talk meaningfully about Griffith, or filmmaking in general, without also mentioning Dickens' earlier contribution of storytelling style. By the era of sound, another enormous figure in the world of directing, and one given more to written theorization, the Russian-born auteur Sergei Eisenstein (1898–1948)—a younger contemporary of Griffith—articulated the same principle in his classic 1944 essay, "Dickens, Griffith and the Film Today," later becoming a touchstone for filmmakers of the post–World War II generation, including David Lean.[15] By the late 1940s, what had begun as instinctive creativity with Griffith and later transformed into written gospel by Eisenstein had then become a full blown arthouse viewing experience as practiced by Lean and his followers, some of these mere imitators but others even more bold and original in vision.

In addition to his undeniable stylistic impact on filmmaking, Dickens must also share primary credit for giving movie entertainment a thematic social conscience, combined effectively with irresistible sentimentality. More impressive still is the ongoing popularity of the novelist's work despite a continual onslaught during the postwar era against outdated Victorian social attitudes and Dickens' adult personal life which can be charitably described as messy. Recent biographers have been especially critical, yet Dickens the storyteller, despite these extensive criticisms, fully maintains his lofty reputation both on video and the printed page.[16] Possibly the biggest artistic charge leveled against him in recent years is that of having a chauvinistic attitude towards women in his storytelling. There can be no denying that many—perhaps too many—of Dickens' heroines often appear weak and colorless, both on film and in print; moreover, modern critical biographies have certainly revealed that, as a man, Dickens had pronounced elements of male chauvinism in his own personality. Nevertheless, there are good counterarguments in his favor, and modern audiences seem to grasp these, instinctively if nothing else. First and foremost are the characters themselves. Miss Havisham from *Great Expectations* (one of the most riveting characters in all English literature) and Betsey Trotwood from *David Copperfield* are female creations both strong and memorable, as well as eccentric. There are more. Minor female characters such as Jenny Wren from *Our Mutual Friend* or the Marchioness from *The Old Curiosity Shop* (among others) are anything but weak and colorless. If many of Dickens' female characters appear sometimes too submissive that is mainly because such characterizations were the commercially acceptable literary convention of the time, and Dickens was, above all else, a professional storyteller who paid close attention to the prejudices and expectations of his Victorian reading audience.

Male chauvinism is not the only serious charge recently brought against Dickens the storyteller. The pages of his beloved novels, unfortunately, abound with stereotypes of race and White Anglo-Saxon nationalism. For example, East Indians and Native American characters are sometimes portrayed as inferior beings. More troubling was the novelist's mixed attitude towards human slavery—unquestionably the burning issue of the 19th century. Although officially and unapologetically against human slavery both before and after the American War Between the States, Dickens still opted on occasion to fictionally portray African Americans in a near cartoonish manner, as one might expect from any Dead White Man—for example, in his notoriously anti-American novel *Martin Chuzzlewit*.[17] As with outdated attitudes towards gender, British Victorian readers would have expected hardly anything less coming from their most famous and successful novelist. This was a pre–Civil War era in which the British Empire still looked down upon the United States, both politically and culturally. Interestingly, however, in recent years several prominent film productions have considerably blunted this vexing problem by casting actors of color into famous Dickensian roles, as well as using non-white non-male directors and screenwriters. We have little doubt that Dickens as an artist would have approved such updated but unconventional employment. In any event, the results have been impressive and will be covered within this survey.

Never in any doubt, on the other hand, then or now, was the indefatigable imagination and endless originality of the novelist. It is no wonder that Charles Dickens was known during his own time as The Great Inimitable. Obviously, the stories he shared remain easily accessible in book form for everyone so inclined to read and explore. Excluding all that has been lost in video form, or is no longer accessible to general audiences, the surviving adaptations based on these novels still comprise a stunningly extensive and diverse body of work. These stories continue to engage, entertain, and instruct, even for those viewers knowing little or nothing about the person who authored them, or who have never voluntarily picked up a book to read and never intend to. The achievement is indeed impressive, especially coming over two centuries after his birth, as his tales continue to be visually adapted for newer and younger audiences of film. In a very real sense, the ongoing popularity of Dickens' novels on film is akin to Samuel Pickwick teaching and helping his younger associates—with a little streetwise help from one of those associates, Sam Weller—on how to live well and make living worthwhile, all the time maintaining a genuine compassion for and active charity towards the less fortunate in life. The lesson is timeless and continues to find widespread resonance, especially during this contemporary age of pandemic selfishness and fear. And oh yes, it is also a fun message to hear and watch, one that entertains those of us otherwise finding little to agree about.

1

The Pickwick Papers (1836–1837)

> "'The happiness of young people,' said Mr. Pickwick, a little moved, 'has ever been the chief pleasure of my life. It will warm my heart to witness the happiness of those friends who are dearest to me, beneath my own roof.'"[1]

The first monthly installment for *The Posthumous Papers of the Pickwick Club* appeared in late March of 1836, published by Chapman & Hall of London, edited by "Boz" and, as added by the frontispiece emphatically, "WITH ILLUSTRATIONS."[2] The maiden issue of the series sold modestly well. Thus, inauspiciously began perhaps the most famed storytelling career trajectory in all English and world literature. By the time the *Pickwick* series concluded in November 1837, it had become an unprecedented commercial success, forever changing the book publishing industry, making its surprised printers wealthy in the process, and establishing its youthful creator as a marketable brand name on the street. Accordingly, a bound complete edition of *The Pickwick Papers* soon arrived in retail outlets, proudly advertising its author as Charles Dickens, rather than Boz. A newly-coronated, 18-year-old, fashion-setting Queen Victoria read the novel and became a fan. During his creation of *The Pickwick Papers*, Dickens was a 24-year-old freelance journalist on the make, recently married, aspiring to be a full-time writer, and striving to maximize unit sales as best he knew how. *Pickwick* captured the watershed process of a previously unknown Dickens transforming himself from the pseudonymous Boz into Charles Dickens the world-famous novelist. Before the *Pickwick* series was completed, however, it's now well-known author began producing yet another serialized work (*Oliver Twist*) that would bring to him even greater heights of fame, along with a degree of notoriety.

Within the context of film history, the literary origins of *Pickwick* are significant because these beginnings were in fact (strictly speaking) not

American comedian John Bunny as Samuel Pickwick in *The Pickwick Papers* (1913).

literary, but rather visual and illustrative. Dickens, then flush with recent success as Boz the humorist, was initially approached by Chapman & Hall merely to provide accompanying prose sketches for pre-made illustrations making fun of English sporting clubs composed mostly of bumbling male misfits. Instead, the aspiring novelist created a continuous, unified storyline, and in the process, the first true Dickens novel. This same storyline gradually came to generate the illustrations, rather than vice versa. These now-iconic images from *Pickwick* thus slowly became subservient to the text, with Dickens the writer going further still by taking a very hands-on approach to their visual development, working in tandem with hired illustrators.[3] Sales skyrocketed as the series progressed. The publishing house of Chapman & Hall, its initial concept thwarted by the novelist's originality, no doubt cried all the way to the bank. Later, by the end of the 19th century, as the fledgling motion picture industry enthusiastically adapted all Dickens' novels (including *Pickwick*) for the big screen, much of its stylistic, pictorial inspiration would come directly from these same original illustrations that the author had earlier taken such pains to ensure accurately represented his text. Thanks to Charles Dickens and early filmmakers' enthusiasm for his literary legacy, the modern "costume" film drama was born almost simultaneously with the movie industry itself.

Dickens' brilliant transformation of lead character Samuel Pickwick from an object of cruel ridicule into a widely admired figure of heroic, Dionysian proportions (despite Pickwick's privileged class naivete and unimpressive physical appearance) proved an early indicator of the novelist's innovative genius. Nearly all readers could relate to Samuel Pickwick in a manner of speaking, since who among us has never been judged by their appearance?[4] Next came the novel's midstream introduction of Pickwick's cockney sage and street-smart protector, Sam Weller, along with his formidable working-class father, Tony Weller. The other Pickwickians stayed truer to their satirical conception: Snodgrass, a self-proclaimed poet who writes nothing; Winkle, a would-be sportsman (and duelist) with no experience in firearms; and Tupman, the aspiring ladies' man who ends his days a confirmed bachelor. Mr. Jingle is a zany stock character straight out of commedia dell'arte, ultimately saved and redeemed by Pickwick's beneficence, as is the Widow Bardell, whose misguided but successful lawsuit against Pickwick (for alleged breach of promise to marry) is repaid with forgiveness and financial relief, even from within the depths of the London Fleet debtors' prison. The attorneys—Buzfuz, Perker, Snubbin, Phunky, Dodson, Fogg—all are portrayed ranging from benignly ineffective to unapologetically villainous. Pickwick's dramatic trial and initiation to the gross injustices of the English legal system, at the literal center of the storyline, remained a personal favorite for Dickens to the very end of his days, and would later be a recurring source of staged dramatic material for film producers of the early 20th century.[5]

As the first full-length and commercially viable Dickens narrative, *Pickwick* served as a convenient template for the novelist's future productions. All the basic building blocks of storytelling considered quintessentially Dickensian are to be found within the pages of *The Pickwick Papers*, including its dazzling diversity of thematic material. With action expressly dated to the years 1827–1828, *Pickwick* has a decidedly pre–Victorian (before 1837) and post–Waterloo (after 1815) English setting during the late Industrial Revolution, concurrent with the same period in which the upstart United States of America was seriously beginning its own divisive political debate and violent internal conflict over slavery. These earlier dates were also important formative years for the teenage Dickens, who in 1827, at age 15, left the drudgery of a London shoe-blacking factory and, with temporary support from his father, briefly resumed his formal education. It marked an important turning point in his life and career. All subsequent works after *The Pickwick Papers*, to varying degrees, seemed to hark back towards this nostalgic past with an irresistible combination of ferocious social criticism and soft-hearted sentimentality. Lawsuits, prisons, country landscapes, city slums, holiday cheer, a parade of eccentrics, discarded English combat veterans of the Napoleonic Wars, digressive interludes into fantasy and mystery—all these basic elements are found within the storyline of *The Pickwick Papers* and continued to appear plentifully within Dickens' imaginative fiction for the next 33 years.

Outside the core group of Dickens' six most popular novels (see Introduction), *Pickwick* has proven itself in modern times to be a surprisingly close runner-up in terms of sheer quantity for film inspiration and adaptability.[6] The reasons for this are at least twofold. First, Samuel Pickwick himself is one of Dickens' most endearing adult characters for audiences and performers alike. Based alone on his ridiculous appearance (for all to see in the series' illustrations), Pickwick is initially dismissed by readers; not only because of his farcical physique, but also for his self-defeating honesty, philosophical sanity, and childlike innocence.[7] Then this same lead character, so lacking in outward impressiveness, is gradually transformed (along with readers' opinions of him) as he journeys from the rural English countryside of Rochester's Dingley Dell to the urban nightmare of the capital city, with its dysfunctional courts of law and illogical debtors' prisons, surviving all personal trials with dignity and considerable hired help from his world-wise footman.[8] The novel ends with three weddings or betrothals: Sam Weller to the serving girl Mary, Winkle to Arabella (with Pickwick securing a hesitant father's blessing), and Snodgrass to Emily (under Pickwick's own roof), just as Dickens had himself been recently married to Catherine Hogarth in April of 1836. Pickwick proclaims his satisfaction in helping young people towards happiness (see epigraph), which he does with notable success throughout the second half of the novel, while remaining blissfully single himself. The story concludes with an aside that Mr. Pickwick, by 1837, was more advanced in years but still a highly respected member of the community, reminding readers that the fictional plot previously related took place in an older England, with Napoleon already defeated on the battlefield, but a full decade before Queen Victoria had assumed the reins of the English monarchy.

It should therefore not be surprising that Dickens' eponymous hero found himself immediately portrayed at the dawn of the motion picture era when in late 1901, *Mr. Pickwick's Christmas at Wardle's*, a now-lost silent short, was produced in London by British film pioneer Robert W. Paul (1869–1943), directed by Paul's longtime associate Walter R. Booth (1869–1938).[9] The episode, drawn from Chapter XXVIII of the novel, represented Dickens' first youthful essay on the Christmas holidays, one that he would repeatedly return to in the future. Some five years later, a somewhat more mature, 30-year-old Dickens began his memorable series of Yuletide novellas with *A Christmas Carol* (1842). In a similar manner, it appears that *Christmas at Wardle's* was Paul and Booth's practice run for their longer, more ambitious, and still-extant *Scrooge: or Marley's Ghost*, also dating from late 1901. One could thus easily postulate that *Pickwick* proved a starting point for the modernized, fictional celebration of Christmas, *à la* Charles Dickens, both on the Victorian printed page, and for the fledgling movie industry of the early 20th century. In the novel, the charming Christmas Eve celebration at Wardle Manor of Dingley Dell serves as a lengthy prelude to Pickwick's unfair trial, unjust imprisonment, and ultimate vindication in the eyes of almost everyone concerned, with assistance from his cheeky sidekick Sam Weller. Although Pickwick is teased by other guests at Wardle's party for his comically festive appearance and demeanor, he then proceeds to make himself the life of the party, as well as a useful morale booster for the elderly and infirmed mother of his host Mr. Wardle.

Other side-story interludes from *The Pickwick Papers* provided convenient material for early silent shorts, although many of these now appear lost to the ravages of time, like so many other silent films of that era. In 1904, Scottish auteur James A. Williamson (1855–1933) directed *Gabriel Grub the Surly Sexton*, drawn from Chapter XXIX of *Pickwick*, the title character of Grub being a clear predecessor to Dickens' much better-known Ebenezer Scrooge.[10] *Gabriel Grub*, however, did not see its U.S. release until 1908, after which it was soon followed (in 1909) by the prolific Edison Company's *A Knight for A Night* (also now lost), based on Chapter XLIX of *Pickwick* and its dream-sequence "Story of the Bagman's Uncle."[11] Both *Knight for A Night* and *Gabriel Grub* likely attracted early film directorial attention at least in part for their visually fantastical and supernatural elements, especially the former, in the process paying a respectful, more Anglicized homage to the novel's Quixotic literary roots, as well as offering memorable illustrations (among many), produced for these two particular chapters in *Pickwick* by Hablot Knight Brown (1815–1882), aka "Phiz."

This initial flurry of movie activity centered around *Pickwick* by filmmakers during the first decade of the 20th century was fully sustained in the years leading immediately up to the Great War. Following its *Knight for A Night* from three years earlier, came the Edison Company's 1912 production of *Mr. Pickwick's Predicament*, the first known filming of the famous trial scene from Chapter XXXIV.[12] More ambitiously, in 1913 came a sweeping three-reel dramatization, *The Pickwick Papers*, produced by the seminal Vitagraph Studios of Brooklyn, New York, directed by Laurence Trimble (1885–1954), and starring celebrity comedian John Bunny (1863–1915) in the lead role, who in the process helped to lead the charge of established stage actors onto the film sets of early silents.[13] That same year (1913) also saw two now lost silent shorts produced by the British Clarendon Film Company, both directed by Wilfred Noy (1883–1948), both based on the same and another well-known episode from the Dickens novel, respectively titled *Pickwick Versus Bardell* and *Mr. Pickwick in A Double-Bedded Room*.[14]

In the immediate aftermath of the Great War, as the film industry resumed normal operations, came a feature-length *The Adventures of Mr. Pickwick* (1921), directed by the prolific British Dickensian specialist Thomas Bentley (1884–1966). This effort represented an ambitious attempt to fully dramatize *Pickwick* on the big screen with a much longer running time.[15] Sadly, like many others, this major work has long been considered irretrievably lost, although it received good notices during its initial release, and film afficionados remain on the lookout for a surviving copy possibly resurfacing. Still preserved and available for screening, however, are several silent newsreels made by the British Pathé company, beginning in 1927, capturing enthusiastic costume re-enactors and civilian crowds celebrating the centenary of the fictional Pickwickian stagecoach ride to Rochester and Dingley Dell, complete with anachronisms such as motorized vehicles and utility power lines.[16] A few years later (in 1928), on the other side of the Atlantic Ocean, just as the silent era was coming to a close, the suburban Chicago Pickwick Theatre, located in Park Ridge, Illinois, had its grand opening. As fate would have it, the mayor of Park Ridge at the time, William H. Malone, was an enthusiast for Dickens' novel and was given the honor of naming the new movie palace within his jurisdiction. Designed by architects Roscoe Harold Zook, William F. McCaughey, and Alfonso Iannelli in a grandiose Art Deco style with distinctive flourishes of Native American (Mayan) décor, the Pickwick Theatre still ranks as one of the most unique venues for the performing arts in the Chicagoland area. Today, the renovated 900-seat main auditorium, along with several attached smaller theaters, is listed on the National Register of Historic Places, and proudly maintains its longstanding tradition, even during the current pandemic, as a large-scale metropolitan showcase for first-run features, arthouse films and live stage shows.

The idea of setting Dickens' *Pickwick Papers* to music appears to have been pursued long before talking movies became the new commercial norm by the early 1930s.[17] Less widely known is the well-documented fact that the infancy of television dates from around this same period. Amazingly, by November of 1936, less than two weeks after the BBC began to regularly schedule TV broadcasts, the start-up London Television Service presented excerpts from the world's very first televised opera, this signal honor going to none other than the obscure music drama titled *Pickwick*, composed by relatively unknown British conductor Albert Coates (1882–1953).[18] This now forgotten work had been originally staged at Covent Garden, broadcast subsequently from the London Alexandra Palace, and then promptly vanished from public awareness. No images from the broadcast are known to have survived. In the immediate wake of this music video extravaganza, came in 1938 another TV production, this one strictly staged as a play with no music, of the inexhaustibly popular courtroom drama, *Bardell Against Pickwick*, later rebroadcast post–World War II (in 1946) with an expanded edition of the same title, and like the opera before it, live from London's Alexandra Palace.[19] Also like the opera telecast, no known images have survived. The ambition of turning *Pickwick* into a hit musical, however, was far from over, as the second half of the 20th century would vividly demonstrate.

Meanwhile, the 1950s saw an unprecedented surge in non-musical *Pickwick*-related film activity. A 1952 feature film, *The Pickwick Papers*, was aggressively condensed into a two-hour viewing experience, directed by naturalized American citizen Noel Langley (1911–1980), along with a British-born all-star cast led by James Hayter (1907–1983) in the title role.[20] Somewhat surprisingly, this production remains the only talking cinematic version (in terms of movie theater release format) of the Dickens novel to date. Following hard on its heels was a 1952–1953 BBC-produced television series, *The Pickwick Papers*, running seven episodes and over six hours in total length, with respected Shakespearean actor George Howe (1900–1986) playing Samuel Pickwick.[21] It holds the unusual distinction of being the very first known TV series based on a Charles Dickens novel, establishing an episodic format that PBS *Masterpiece Theatre* would later fully exploit during the 1970s. Unlike the 1952 movie version, the original BBC serial of *Pickwick* appears to be lost or is not currently available for viewing. As if all this were not enough, 1952 also saw an American, specially produced TV episode by CBS for *The Trial of Mr. Pickwick*, adapted for the small screen by the very same Alistair Cooke (1908–2004) who later went on to become better known as the original introductory host for *Masterpiece Theatre*.[22]

Anglo-American television of the 1950s, however, was far from done with *The Pickwick Papers*. In 1955, British Independent Television (ITV) launched its short dramatic series with the ever-reliable subject matter of *Bardell v. Pickwick*, drawing upon a similar cast from the 1952 BBC serial, including Shakespearean stalwart Donald Wolfit (1902–1968) as Sergeant Buzfuz and Dickensian specialist Edna Morris (1906–1972) as the Widow Bardell.[23] This production later reached American viewing audiences in 1956 as a regular installment of ABC's *Lilli Palmer Theatre*.[24] That same year (1956) saw the first colorized film of a Dickens work, *A Charles Dickens Christmas*, a short British TV dramatization of Pickwick's holiday party at the Wardle Manor of Dingley Dell, and still available for viewing on YouTube, among other platforms.[25] Finally, in 1959, the ABC network and British producer Harry Alan Towers (1920–2009) unveiled their *Fredric March Presents Tales from Dickens*, with four full episodes drawn from *The Pickwick Papers*.[26] These included new productions of the well-known holiday (*Christmas at Dingley Dell*) and trial (*Bardell Versus Pickwick*) scenes, plus less familiar material (*Mr. Pickwick's Dilemma*, followed by *Sam Weller and His Father*).[27] In general, excerpts or images from these specific episodes of *Tales from Dickens* are not known to have survived. Early television broadcasts, like early silent films, have suffered more than their share of permanent archival losses.

With the 1960s, the idea of setting *The Pickwick Papers* to music was revived with gusto, especially after the 1960 blockbuster success of Lionel Bart's *Oliver!* (based on Dickens' *Oliver Twist*) in London's West End, along with its subsequent 1963 triumph on Broadway. *Pickwick* the musical, with a book by playwright Wolf Mankowitz, music by conductor-composer Cyril Ornadel, and lyrics by Leslie Bricusse, successfully premiered to British acclaim, initially in provincial Manchester, then in London's West End, for the 1963 season. Soon afterwards in 1965, however, celebrity-producer David Merrick brought it to Broadway, where it bombed. *Oliver!* it was not. Popular Welsh singer-comedian Harry Secombe, who later played Bumble in the film version of *Oliver!*, starred in the title role of *Pickwick* and managed to record a hit song drawn from the show, dubbed "If I Ruled the World." This song soon became a hit recording for Tony Bennett, Sammy Davis, Jr., James Brown, Stevie Wonder, Tom Jones, Robert Goulet, Diana Ross, and Nancy Wilson, to name a few. Today, millions of listeners enjoy these recordings without having the slightest idea that the song's initial inspiration came from a Charles Dickens novel. Although *Pickwick* failed to gain traction on Broadway during the mid–1960s at the height of Beatlemania and the British Invasion, the BBC later saw fit in 1969 to present a condensed version of the same musical as a TV movie, again featuring Secombe in the lead.[28] In addition, the original Manchester production likely spurred BBC's northwest regional rival Granada Television to present its own *Mr. Pickwick* as a straight, non-musical teleplay around the same time period in late 1963.[29]

By this time, Dickens' *Pickwick* seems to have also become a European continental phenomenon for video entertainment. From France came a short film, *Affaire Bardell Contre Pickwick* (1962), and a serial, *Les Adventures de M. Pickwick* (1964), while in Italy a TV series appeared, *Il Circolo Pickwick* (1968).[30] Meanwhile, back in Great Britain and the original language of Dickens, the turbulent decade concluded in somewhat unlikely fashion with a film short titled *Uneasy Dreams: The Life of Mr. Pickwick* (1970).[31] The director for this unusual work was a then-rather young, future music documentarian of note, the late Jeremy Marre (1943–2020). Sponsored in part by the British Film Institute, Marre's video presented an imaginative and surreal backstory for the rather illusive character of Samuel Pickwick, a unique personality in literature somehow

1. The Pickwick Papers (1836–1837)

combining cultural sophistication, good intentions, and childlike innocence. It seemed a bizarre yet appropriate way to end an era. After this intensive display of Pickwickmania during the 1950s and 1960s, however, filmmakers went pretty much silent on the same subject matter for about the next 15 years.

Finally in early 1985, at the high watermark of Thatcherism in Great Britain, the BBC produced a 12-episode, nearly six-hour miniseries of *The Pickwick Papers*, starring stage and screen veteran Nigel Stock (1919–1986), along with a distinguished cast of mostly male British character actors.[32] The miniseries effectively combined the many lessons learned over the past century by the film industry for converting literary works of Charles Dickens into palatable home video entertainment. Like the earliest silent versions of *Pickwick*, this latest miniseries was visually influenced by the Phiz illustrations from the original 19th-century editions of the Dickens novels. As such, the 1985 BBC production must still be considered the gold standard for *Pickwick* adaptations to date. Like the novel, it starts slowly, then picks up considerable speed as Dickens the consummate storyteller begins to reshape his material throughout the first third of the tale. By the time that the Pickwickians reach Dingley Dell's Wardle Manor for a festive Christmas celebration, only the most insensible viewers have failed to catch the holiday spirit. Then follows Pickwick's stern education in the courts and prisons of pre–Victorian England. From this psychological trial of endurance, he emerges older, wiser, and spiritually triumphant, more than ever ready to do good in a world badly in need of his help. For Nigel Stock (portraying Pickwick), the BBC miniseries also represented a fitting apotheosis to his long and fondly remembered acting career.

Before leaving this rather expansive topic, it would be remiss not to survey the bumper crop of Pickwick-related animated features that appeared with little advance notice during the mid to late 1980s. The first of these arrived in 1985, the same year as the watershed BBC miniseries, produced by the short-lived Burbank Films Australia.[33] After completing full-length animations of the six most popular of Dickens' novels between 1982 and 1984, Burbank continued this series with releases of the less popular *Nicholas Nickleby* and *The Pickwick Papers*, both dating from the following year of 1985. Burbank's animated *Pickwick* delves into some of the more obscure aspects of the novel, including a number of digressive, sidebar interludes, while downplaying more adult themes, such as Pickwick's alleged breach of promise to marry the Widow Bardell and its sordid aftermath. More impressive still, in 1987 came *Charles Dickens' Ghost Stories* by pioneering animators Jean Mathieson and Al Guest of Emerald City Productions in Dublin, Ireland.[34] *Ghost Stories* draws upon three supernatural diversionary tales from *The Pickwick Papers*, and like the Burbank animation preceding it, culminated with a strikingly grotesque portrayal of Gabriel Grub ("The Goblin and the Gravedigger"). With its jarring, *Simpsons*-like visual aesthetic, stentorian voiceovers, and serious thematic undercurrent, *Ghost Stories* possibly best captures the dark and childlike vision of *Pickwick* in its own peculiar way.[35] Like the animated *Pickwick Papers* of 1985, *Ghost Stories* harks back to the early silent film era's fascination with this dark side of Dickens' genius, just as Dickens would himself later return to tales of mystery and suspense during the final period of his prolific writing career.

Although the Dickensian film revival of the late 20th and early 21st centuries has apparently had nothing more to offer on *The Pickwick Papers* since 1987, the present day may be ripe for a younger generation's latest take on this intriguing but lesser-known classic. The 24-year-old Dickens had originally conceived *Pickwick* as a young man's vision of virtuous old age. He certainly succeeded in this endeavor and, in the process, became the first modern English-speaking celebrity storyteller. In our own troubling, contemporary era dominated by voices of cynical and malevolent old age, perhaps what many of us need is Samuel Pickwick as a role model—representing a more desirable, alternative state of being—if nothing else, one presented on the pages and flatscreens of fictional entertainment, with good moral lessons drawn from the not-so-distant past. Pickwick is, by the end of the fable, a successful businessman who comes to realize there is far more to life than business. Dickens would have surely approved, and he was known to have been openly proud of his early handiwork. Even before completing *The Pickwick Papers*, however, this consummate storyteller began to fully exert his extraordinary talents for narrative and plot, as he simultaneously worked on a new serial, transporting amazed readers directly into the horrors and hardships of the early 19th-century English workhouse, the late Industrial Revolution, and above all, the burgeoning urban jungle of London town.

2

Oliver Twist (1837–1838)

> "'That is no excuse,' replied Mr. Brownlow. 'You were present on the occasion ... and indeed are the more guilty of the two, in the eye of the law; for the law supposes that your wife acts under your direction.'
>
> 'If the law supposes that,' said Mr. Bumble, squeezing his hat emphatically in both hands, 'the law is a ass—a idiot. If that's the eye of the law, the law is a bachelor; and the worst I wish the law is, that his eye may be opened by experience—by experience.'"[1]

To date, *Oliver Twist, or the Parish Boy's Progress* ranks second only to Dickens' *A Christmas Carol* in overall popularity with filmmakers; hence, it is the most adapted full-length novel in history, not only for Charles Dickens, but for any novelist.[2] As such, it is a difficult work to meaningfully write about within a confined space such as this. We will do our best, however, always bearing in mind that new discoveries and insights are constantly being made with respect to this unassailable masterpiece. Written when its author was 25 years old and flush with confidence over burgeoning success from *The Pickwick Papers*, Dickens' *Oliver Twist* first appeared in serial form (in early 1837) while the *Pickwick* series was still ongoing, then as a bound novel (in late 1838) even before its own serialization concluded in early 1839. Like *Pickwick*, *Oliver Twist* first appeared under the pseudonym "Boz" but finished under the author's real identity, Charles Dickens—by then a fully marketable household name. Unlike *Pickwick*, *Oliver* took things to an entirely new level in just about every respect, including a thundering critique of early capitalism that would have landed many a less-talented writer in jail or serious hot water with the ruling classes, a critique in the form of fiction that later left even the likes of Karl Marx awestruck.

The precise origins of the artistic impulses creating this cultural

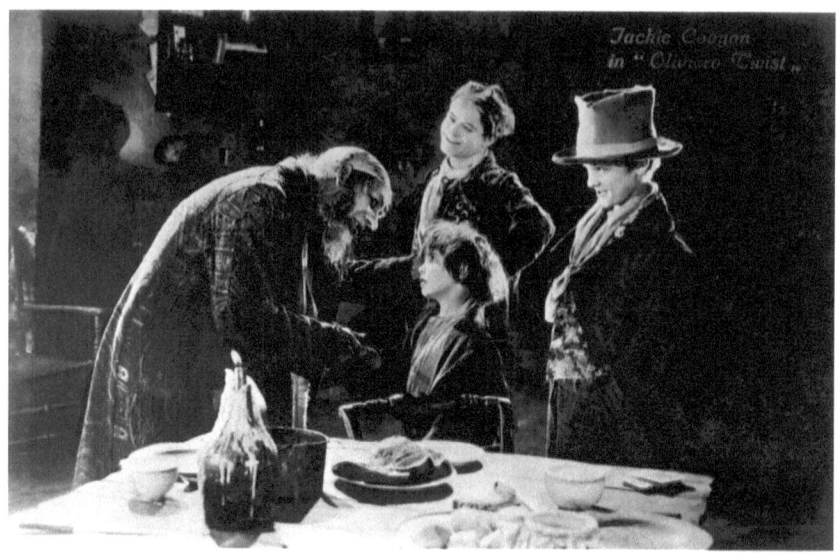

Lon Chaney as Fagin (left) and Jackie Coogan as Oliver in Frank Lloyd's *Oliver Twist* (1922). Charley (Taylor Graves, behind Coogan) and the Artful Dodger (Edouard Trebaol) look on.

landmark are difficult to pinpoint as well, but a few general, frequent observations are worth repeating. The notorious New Poor Law of 1834 had temporarily legitimized the infamous English workhouse institutions for orphans, so damningly portrayed in the novel, and crafting of this legislation was likely witnessed by Dickens firsthand as a Parliamentary reporter long before he became a celebrity novelist. Dickens was so deeply disgusted by the entire process and end-result that he ever after declined to enter English politics, even though several real opportunities were later presented to him. He felt he could do far more for society by telling a good story, a conviction which he then proceeded to put into spectacularly effective practice. In the novel, Oliver, a nine-year-old village orphan, after an emotionally cold but secure rural upbringing, enters a hellish, legally empowered workhouse, only then to be cast out after reluctantly asking for more gruel. Thus Dickens once again, as he would continually do, places the fictional action back in the mid–1820s and mid–1830s of his youth, writing from personal experience in a manner that was, to put it mildly, bracingly convincing.

More recent research has demonstrated that Dickens as a young adult lived in close proximity one of London's more seamy workhouses likely to have heard of its many horrors, and perhaps barely avoided being sent to one himself, thanks to a financially irresponsible father. Later in early 1837, under the pseudonym of Boz, Dickens produced a short story titled *Public Life of Mr. Tulrumble-Once Mayor of Mudfog*, highlighting a provincial English workhouse in that fictional locale.[3] This story was printed by the prominent London publisher Richard Bentley, who fully appreciated Dickens' talents and then engaged him to write two complete novels. Instead of producing more humorous sketches, however, Dickens pivoted and immediately began the *Oliver Twist* series with its searing indictment of the English workhouse as a social model. Dickens' alarmed publisher Bentley fortunately decided not to reign in the fiery young novelist (but only when he saw serial sales immediately skyrocket), while all English literature simultaneously learned yet again that skillful shock value oftentimes sells prodigiously to the general reading public.

Before briefly surveying some of the more famous film interpretations of *Oliver Twist*, it is useful to summarize Dickens' distinctive character development within the novel. Designated parish beadle and workhouse enforcer Mr. Bumble, while omnipresent in the text, is often reduced in film versions to the status of a casual side joke or sometimes even less. The more powerful dramatizations of *Oliver*, on the other hand, tend to avoid this frequent mistake, and in the process have attracted highly accomplished character actors to the role. In the text, it is Bumble who christens the orphan "Oliver Twist" after his mother dies, Bumble who first intimidates Oliver, ordering him to "bow to the board," then shuffling his reluctant charge to and from abortive apprenticeships with a chimney sweep and undertaker. It is Bumble who then connives with and marries the venal Mrs. Corney, conspires with her and Oliver's evil half-brother Monks (Dickens' first stock villain) to conceal his genteel parentage, and finally, after being exposed for his misdeeds and dressed down by the virtuous Mr. Brownlow, convincingly proclaims near the end of the story that "the law is a ass" (see epigraph). Bumble may be a failure as a human being, but he is also human enough to be disconcertingly recognizable by most readers, and thus becomes indispensable for effective dramatization. In contrast, Dickens' colorful cast of labeled criminals—Fagin the Jewish fence, Sikes the ruffian burglar, Nancy the prostitute, and Dodger the pickpocket (all speaking in dazzling, authentic cockney slang)—at the time many fan-readers of the earlier *Pickwick Papers* were taken aback by this realistic but ambiguous portrayal of urban depravity. Sanctimonious and profiteering workhouse board members, it was suggested, were far worse societal offenders than the murderous thieves of London town.

Oliver Twist the novel also benefited enormously from illustrations etched by Dickens' arguably most distinguished collaborator, caricaturist George Cruikshank (1792–1878), the same artist creating memorable etchings for Dickens' earlier hit collection, *Sketches by Boz* (1836). Before falling out with Dickens over personal egos and differing lifestyles, Cruikshank also supplied illustrations for Dickens' *The Mudfog Papers* (1837–1838) and *Memoirs of Joseph Grimaldi* (1838), after having become so feared as a caricaturist that the British royal family allegedly paid him off not to attack them with political cartoons. Cruikshank's striking images for *Oliver Twist*, like those of Hablot Knight Browne (aka "Phiz") for *The Pickwick Papers*, both helped to sell Dickens' early works, as well as provide direct visual models influencing early filmmakers following in their wake. Over a hundred years after publication of the novel, directors the caliber of David Lean and Roman Polanski would still turn to Cruikshank's work for inspiration in establishing their own cinematic styles for *Oliver Twist*. This would prove especially true with respect to Dickens' repulsive urban den of thieves (Fagin, Sikes, Dodger, Charlie, etc.), beginning with the overtly anti–Semitic but profoundly tragic figure of Fagin himself.

Given such a pedigree, it should be no wonder that the legacy of Dickens' *Oliver Twist* and the history of motion pictures are nearly synonymous. As early as 1897, during the infancy of the film industry, a silent short, titled *Death of Nancy Sykes* [sic], was produced by the American Mutoscope and Biograph Company of Manhattan, only two years after that historic enterprise's founding in 1895.[4] This now-lost work was based upon one of Dickens' most shocking and favorite dramatic scenarios, the brutal, horrific murder of Nancy by Bill Sikes, drawn from Chapter XLVII of *Oliver Twist*. This is the earliest known film adaptation of a Dickens work, and it is early indeed. Great Britain wasted no time in catching up. The following year (in 1898), pioneer producer Robert W. Paul and director Walter R. Booth, released a silent short (also now lost) titled *Mr. Bumble the Beadle*, depicting the comic courtship between Bumble and Mrs. Corney.[5] Even before the end of the 19th century, silent picture shorts had thus latched on to *Oliver Twist*, both for its breathtaking criminal violence, as well as comic relief provided by one of its more important yet undervalued characters, Mr. Bumble.

Interestingly, the second decade of the movie industry began in 1906 with two different competing silent features based on *Oliver Twist*, now both lost, but reportedly successful at the time. In France, the Gaumont Film Company, the first of its kind in the world and following its recent (1903) success adapting a segment from Dickens' *Nicholas Nickleby*, released its own version of *Oliver Twist* to English-speaking markets. Simultaneously, the American Vitagraph Studios reportedly attempted to reset Dickens' pre–Victorian tale in early 20th-century New York City with *The Modern Oliver Twist: or the Life of a Pickpocket*.[6] Then three years later, Vitagraph upped the ante by rebooting the same plot with *Oliver Twist* (1909), this time with a Dickensian period setting. A large fragment of this later version still survives, available for viewing. Directed by Vitagraph founder J. Stuart Blackton (1875–1941), the 1909 *Oliver* featured silent screen stars Edith Story as a female actor portraying the orphan male lead, Elita Procter Otis as a very melodramatic Nancy (previously having made this role famous, as the subtitles inform us), and William J. Humphreys as a completely unsympathetic, ultra-treacherous Fagin.[7] The 1909 Vitagraph update briefly restores (mainly as comic relief) the role of Bumble, which, based on old subtitles, had been eliminated in the shorter versions (less than 10 minutes each) of the earlier 1906 films.

The years immediately leading up to World War I saw multiple silent film versions of *Oliver Twist* produced in France and Italy (1910–1911).[8] Then in 1912, the centenary year of Dickens' birth, came two major productions from the U.S. and U.K., respectively. The 1912 American *Oliver Twist*, now partially lost, was produced by the Crystal Studio of the General Film Publicity and Sales Company in the Bronx. It featured the distinguished stage actor Nat C. Goodwin as Fagin and was perhaps the first major film production fully grasping that role's importance to the story.[9] Goodwin had recently made his portrayal of Fagin famous on the theatrical stages of New York City, and surviving stills of his performance suggest human tragedy behind the stereotype. At five reels, it was reportedly the longest Dickens film adaptation to date thus far. Later that same year (1912), the British responded with their own *Oliver Twist*, now lost, by the noteworthy team of producer Cecil Hepworth and director Thomas Bentley. Although Bentley later expressed second thoughts artistically, the venture was commercially successful and enabled later Dickensian productions by the same highly accomplished duo.[10] The following war years, as one would expect, experienced a dearth of filmmaking, with one notable exception.[11] In 1916, before the U.S. entered the conflict, yet another American *Oliver Twist* was filmed, directed by the famed Jesse L. Lasky (1880–1958) and featuring another female actor as Oliver, Marie Doro (who earlier starred on stage with Nat C. Goodwin), as well as character specialist and stage veteran Tully Marshall as Fagin. Tragically, this film is lost, but surviving stills of the production suggests that it was visually striking, in addition to reputedly being unsettlingly realistic in its portrayal of criminal violence.[12]

In English-speaking markets, the post-war era began with another American attempt at modernizing the *Oliver* story by transporting it to New York City with *Oliver Twist Jr.* (1921), along with two short features by British-based Master Films, *Nancy* (1922) and *Fagin* (1922), all now lost.[13] Of more interest from the same period, however, was Charlie Chaplin's *The Kid* (1921), widely considered one of the greatest silent films ever made, and helping to launch the lengthy careers of both Chaplin and American child star Jackie Coogan. Although a non–Dickens story, *The Kid* was reportedly conceived by Chaplin as a homage to *Oliver Twist*, his favorite novel. Chaplin, apart from his own Oliver-like escape from English poverty in his early personal life, was also a self-admitted fan of Marie Doro, who had convincingly portrayed Oliver on both stage and screen in the recent past. As for Jackie Coogan, his next major film project would be none other than *Oliver Twist* (1922), directed by Scottish jack-of-all-trades Frank Lloyd (1886–1960), and co-starring master-of-disguise extraordinaire Lon Chaney as a visually terrifying Fagin.[14] The prolific and underrated American actor James A. Marcus played Mr. Bumble. Nearly a century later, the 80+ minute silent film still makes for a compelling experience, especially with respect to the two lead performances by the eight-year-old Coogan and the 39-year-old Chaney. Although sound films were only six years away, this fine work would set the standard for all *Oliver Twist* film adaptations over the next quarter century.

Though not the first Dickens sound adaptation, nor the most famous, nor (by far) the best, California-based Monogram Pictures' low budget *Oliver Twist* (1933) was the first time this endlessly popular novel was made into a talking motion picture.[15] Compared to the excellence of Jackie Coogan 11 years previous, the lead performance by child actor Dickie Moore is painful to watch (and listen to), while the overall production looks stodgy, cheap, and slow-paced next to the bracingly crisp silent classic of 1922. Nevertheless, the 1933 Monogram *Oliver* is not without merit. Presented as a Depression-era, allegorical tragedy, the criminal gang of Fagin, Sikes, Nancy, Dodger, and crew seem to embody the temporary demise of American organized crime after the end of Prohibition and beginning of the New Deal. Some of the individual performances are noteworthy as well. The striking portrayal of Bill Sikes by William "Stage" Boyd (1889–1935) as a violent alcoholic is delivered with uncomfortable realism, especially given the short-lived Boyd's known personal struggles with alcohol and substance abuse. American stage veteran Irving Pichel (1891–1954) somehow amplifies Fagin's menace by understating his performance, while British journeyman Lionel Belmore (1867–1953) delivers both comic relief and unintentional wit as Mr. Bumble. The 1933 Monogram production vanished from American viewer radar shortly after its initial release, was forgotten for nearly half a century, and then reappeared during the revivalist 1980s as Charles Dickens–based films began returning to fashion.

After a 15-year hiatus in *Oliver*-themed filmmaking (due mainly to World War II, its lengthy prelude, and aftermath), the year 1948 saw a landmark movie version of *Oliver Twist* by British directorial genius David Lean (1908–1991). Lean's pathbreaking collaboration with a young Alec Guinness (1914–2000) had begun two years earlier with the equally magnificent *Great Expectations* (1946), and now found an even more radical cinematic outlet with Dickens' inescapable second novel.[16] Then 34-year-old Guinness' Fagin is one for the ages. Throwing post–Holocaust restraint to the winds, Guinness plays up every anti–Semitic stereotype lingering in the addled public imagination, yet somehow firmly maintains some audience sympathy for this tragic character.[17] In the movie, when the mob of Jacob's Island yells at Fagin to yield "In the King's name," Fagin later responds with "What right have they to butcher me?"—a profoundly unanswered question echoing throughout the ages.[18] The all-British cast of this indispensable classic was rounded out by John Howard Davies as Oliver (playing a gaunt and all-too-believable workhouse orphan), and the inimitable Francis L. Sullivan as Mr. Bumble, whose importance to the story was clearly recognized by Lean and co-writer Stanley Haynes. Noted 20th-century Irish composer Arnold Bax provided a memorable film score. It would be nearly another four decades before the lofty status of this production was surpassed in any respect, and many perceptive critics argue plausibly that the Lean-Guinness version of 1948 is still definitive.

The prodigious achievement of Lean and Guinness appears in hindsight to have stunned competing movie versions into several decades of inactivity. During the late 1950s, however, things began to shake loose. In 1959, a modestly successful, 29-year-old British pop songsmith named Lionel Bart (1930–1999) convinced himself that the time was right for an Anglo-American blockbuster stage musical based on a Charles Dickens novel, specifically *Oliver Twist*. Bart was musically illiterate—he could neither read nor write music nor play a musical instrument—but he had a formidable, natural gift for creating catchy tunes. After taping a short demo, he went about trying to sell his big idea to major producers and was met with across-the-board, snobbish rejection until impresario Donald Albery (1914–1988) agreed, half out of pity, to produce Bart's still uncompleted opus at the New Theatre in London's West End for a bargain basement budget price of £15,000.[19] Albery normally staged works by serious playwrights but apparently saw something in Bart's unique vision of Dickens adapted for 1960s mass audiences. Then Bart, still desperate for cash, reportedly sold his musical rights in *Oliver!* to British entertainer Max Bygraves (1922–2012) for the obscenely low price of £350. Casting began while Bart was still finishing the songs. A still unknown, 27-year-old Michael Caine (born Maurice Micklewhite in 1933), prepared for, desperately wanted, and auditioned for the role of Sikes, but was passed over in favor of then-better-known professional boxer Danny Sewell. The role of Fagin was offered to, and declined by, the likes of Rex Harrison, Sid James, and Peter Sellers, before a relatively obscure Ron Moody landed the part. Finally, *Oliver!* opened during the summer of 1960 and was such a tremendous hit with adoring audiences that by 1963 the musical had reached American Broadway with similar widespread acclaim. It has never since stopped being revived with notable success.

Five years after its international triumph, *Oliver!* became a major motion picture and the toast of the 1968 Academy Awards, including winner of Best Picture.[20] Unfortunately, among all the accolades and excitement, the original spirit of *Oliver Twist* the book, one written as a risky, revolutionary work of fiction by a 25-year-old firebrand novelist, had all but vanished. Even at the height of this commercial success, however, there were some naysayers pointing out, among other things, that *Oliver!* borrowed a number of direct departures from the novel taken from the David Lean film some 20 years earlier.[21] British commentator Michael Pointer was among those especially objecting to the respectable re-interpretation of Fagin as "a picaresque old rogue ... scampering off down the road at the end in a Chaplinesque image of which director Carol Reed should have been ashamed."[22] Thus a good part of Dickens' cautionary tale was stripped of its tragic pathos by the musical and film, except for the doomed pair of Nancy and Sikes, toned down but still left partially intact. In a curious bit of nepotism, director Carol Reed (1906–1976) cast his nephew, British bad-boy heartthrob Oliver Reed (1938–1999), into the role of Sikes, resulting in perhaps the film's best performance, and maybe providing a glimpse of what Michael Caine would have brought to the original stage role had he been hired for the purpose.

With all the hype over *Oliver!* and its massive infiltration into the popular consciousness, several other important productions around the same time went nearly unnoticed and are today unjustly forgotten.[23] As if anticipating the musical, in 1959 American TV celebrity producer David Susskind brought a 90-minute version of *Oliver Twist* to *The DuPont Show of the Month* for the CBS network.[24] *The DuPont Show* specialized in serious literary adaptations and typically featured serious acting and directorial talent for their projects. Reportedly, its 1959 *Oliver* was no exception in this regard, although it is unknown if any kinescope still survives. Two years later (in 1961), as if in reaction to the alleged saccharine qualities of the musical, the BBC offered up a gritty, 13-episode, six-hour-plus miniseries, *Oliver Twist*, faithfully adapted for television by the venerable playwright Constance Cox (1912–1998), whose skillful adaptation of Dickens' *Bleak House* for the BBC had turned heads in 1959.[25] This true-to-the-text production of *Oliver Twist* featured an extensive Anglo-Irish cast of classically trained character actors, serving as a distant forerunner for a similarly high-quality BBC reboot of *Oliver Twist* in 1985. Notwithstanding numerous video competitors, the 1962 *Oliver* remains available today as a UK-only DVD set.

With *Oliver!* the musical and film completing "the jollification of Dickens" (Michael Pointer) for mass audiences, the next logical phase of interpretation was inevitable—film animation.[26] The initial step in this gradual process began in 1974 with *Oliver Twist*, produced by Disney-alum Hal Sutherland and featuring a brand new collection of songs, with the role of the Dodger voiced and sung by former Monkees rock star Davy Jones, who previously played the same role both on Broadway and London's West End.[27] The film received wide distribution through Warner Brothers but made a poor impression on both audiences and critics; however, it is still available. Faring much better was the animated *Oliver Twist* of 1982 by Burbank Films Australia, beginning that company's notable run of no fewer than eight Charles Dickens adaptations between 1982 and 1985. Next came the Irish-based Emerald City Productions animated version of *Oliver Twist* (1986), more sinister and foreboding in mood than its predecessors.[28] After that, things started to get weird. A corporate decision-maker at Disney had the idea to produce an animated *Oliver & Company* (1988), in which the action is transported to modern New York City (not a new concept), change the plot (again, not new), but to turn most of the main characters into orphaned or abandoned pet animals, then for good measure, hire big names such as Billy Joel, Robert Loggia, and Dom DeLuise to do voiceovers.[29] The result is still widely available for viewing. Encouraged by this precedent, Saban Entertainment, itself destined to be acquired by Disney in 2001, produced *Adventures of Oliver Twist* (1996–1997), an animated television series in which the anthropomorphic aspect receives greater emphasis while the human tragedy of Dickens' original story is downplayed to the point where Oliver (a talking puppy) is no longer an orphan but merely lost in the streets. In this manner, 20th-century animation of *Oliver Twist* came to a startling conclusion.

Parallel with the animation trend came several more serious, albeit less financially profitable, but more humanized productions. In 1982, CBS via its Hallmark television series, presented *Oliver Twist* with a fine Anglo-American cast led by George C. Scott (as Fagin), alongside other notables such as Tim Curry (Sikes) and Timothy West (Bumble). This TV movie was directed by Clive Donner (1926–2010), who earlier in life had been a film editor for the classic *Scrooge* (1951) featuring Alistair Sim, as well as later working with Alec Guinness.[30] Then in 1985, the BBC updated its own *Oliver Twist* with a classy 12-episode miniseries, utilizing mostly lesser-known stage actors, and with a screenplay written by respected British novelist Alexander Baron (1917–1999), this time taking pains to follow the original Dickens text.[31] The impressive results are Shakespearean in dramatic effect, thought probably not as appealing to general viewership. One common thread between the 1982 Hallmark and 1985 BBC productions are performances by Lysette Anthony (b. 1963), in 1982 as Oliver's doomed mother Agnes and later in 1985 as Oliver's more fortunate Aunt Rose.

Appearing almost like atonement for its previous animated departures, Disney's relatively straightforward production of *Oliver Twist* (1997) still managed to commit the fatal error of eliminating Bumble as a character.[32] The 1997 Disney *Oliver* did feature, however, some impressive names, including Richard Dreyfuss as Fagin and a 16-year-old Elijah Wood (b. 1981) as Oliver, before he later went on to much greater fame as Frodo in *Lord of the Rings*. Meanwhile, British ITV responded with its own miniseries *Oliver Twist* (1999). For this production, Dickens' text was substantially rewritten by Liverpool-native Alan Bleasdale, adding a lengthy backstory, several new characters, and most controversially, redemption of the villain Monks at the end of the story. Perhaps the most memorable performance came from a pre-famous Keira Knightley (b. 1985) as Oliver's Aunt Rose. This offbeat version aired the following year in 2000 as part of the PBS 30th season for *Masterpiece Theatre*. Along with numerous spinoff versions of *Oliver Twist*, these movies represented a rather bizarre ending to the 20th century for more conventional—if conventional is the right word—film adaptations.

The new century brought more cinematic surprises, not all of which were bad. Director Roman Polanski (b. 1933), rolled out his highly anticipated and incredibly dark-visioned *Oliver Twist*, allegedly made for his own children, in 2005. Visually striking, this film includes a star-worthy performance by Ben Kingsley (Fagin), a fitting swan song by Edward Hardwicke (Brownlow), the always excellent Alun Armstrong (Fang), and a stately soundtrack composed by Rachel Portman.[33] Unfortunately, while streamlining the plot, Polanski opted to eliminate Oliver's backstory (transforming his benefactors from long-lost relatives into enlightened philanthropists), while reducing the role of Bumble to an opening footnote. The result is to blunt the novel's storytelling punch even while this same quality is indirectly enhanced by a distinctive style. Better yet was the five-episode miniseries *Oliver Twist* (2007), the third such produced by the BBC since the 1960s, with character actor virtuoso Timothy Spall firmly re-establishing the overt Jewishness of Fagin from the original text, after this quality had been consistently suppressed ever since Alec Guinness amplified it back in 1948.[34] Coky Giedroyc (b. 1962) became the first female director of a major *Oliver* film, and along with screenwriter Sarah Phelps, brought an authentic period feel to the entire enterprise. Welsh comedian Rob Brydon did a wonderful turn as Magistrate Fang, the versatile Edward Fox highlighted the gullible side of Brownlow, and RADA-graduate Sophie Okonedo gave a refreshingly restrained but effective interpretation of the too often melodramatized tragic heroine, Nancy. Between Polanski and latest BBC miniseries, it appears that the built-in seriousness of Dickens' *Oliver Twist* has now been placed firmly front and center for a whole new generation of audiences.

The latest, and possibly most poetic chapter in the long history of *Oliver Twist* on film, came in 2019 when it was announced by British Sky-Comcast that a new movie version of the Dickens classic (in a modern London setting) would be released in late 2020, titled *Twist*, directed by Martin Owen (b. 1973), and starring an 86-year-old Michael Caine in the role of Fagin.[35] Other innovations will reportedly include female transpositions for the crucial characters of Sikes and Dodger, played respectively by *Game of Thrones* star Lena Headey and British hip-hop artist Rita Ora. The role of Oliver will go to Rafferty Law, son of British matinee idol Jude Law.[36] The film will also surely have special significance for Caine, who some 60 years ago was rejected to play Bill Sikes in the original West End production of *Oliver!*, and who much later, after becoming the toast of the film industry as a leading man, described that particular rejection as one of his biggest career disappointments. As the old saying goes, no matter how successful one becomes in life, it is still the isolated defeats that are always remembered with absolute clarity.

As previously suggested, the preceding survey barely scratches the surface for *Oliver Twist*-related videos. For example, it does not include countless spinoffs, prequels, sequels, and imaginative side-riffs having little to do with the original text but still borrowing heavily from its iconic characterizations and themes. For example, one could easily write an entire book focusing solely on the silent movie versions of *Oliver Twist*, many of which have vanished over the last century, never to be seen by anyone again. Herein we have merely attempted, among other objectives, to simply remind readers that Dickens' novel was a viable film franchise long before talkies transformed the entertainment industry after 1928. As for Dickens, a one-of-a-kind storytelling genius, by 1838, while still completing the serialization for *Oliver Twist*, he apparently realized that much of his commercial power and appeal as an author came from his unique ability to critique English social institutions, while reaching into the recent English past, and in particular his own recent personal past. Accordingly, he began working on yet another serial novel, this one taking a deeper dive into the tricky, fictional universe of semi-autobiography.

3

Nicholas Nickleby (1838–1839)

"There is only one other point, on which I would desire to offer a remark. If Nicholas be not always found to be blameless or agreeable, he is not always intended to appear so. He is a young man of an impetuous temper and of little or no experience; and I saw no reason why such a hero should be lifted out of nature."[1]

After achieving nearly unqualified acclaim with *The Pickwick Papers* and *Oliver Twist*, Dickens turned to writing his third serialized novel in 1838, at roughly age 26. Whereas *Oliver* had presented to readers a child hero typically at the mercy of his adult companions (often in conflict with one another), *Nicholas Nickleby* gives us a vivid portrait of the artist as a young man (to quote James Joyce), painted by the young artist himself. This literary self-portrait is surprisingly unflattering. Then again, the novelist gives readers notice of this revelation with an Author's Preface (see epigraph). Nicholas is intelligent, strong, good-looking, and has good intentions, but he is also impetuous, occasionally violent, gullible, sheltered, and frequently baffled by the rapidly changing environment surrounding him. The hero of his own life (to paraphrase from *David Copperfield*) is likable enough but deeply flawed. Only after many adventures filled with hardships and challenges does Nicholas seem to emerge victorious and somewhat wiser. While writing his third novel, Dickens was popular and confident but also overextended with work and far from financially secure. American critic and academic Robert L. Patten aptly summed up this work: "*Nickleby* is the culmination of Dickens's early career."[2]

The Life and Adventures of Nicholas Nickleby first appeared as a serial between April 1838 and October 1839, with illustrations by "Phiz" (aka Hablot Knight Browne), and published by Chapman & Hall of London, the same firm earlier achieving spectacular sales figures with Dickens' *The Pickwick Papers*. Like *Pickwick* and *Oliver* before it, *Nickleby* began

3. Nicholas Nickleby (1838–1839)

Steerforth (Cecil Mannering) and Little Em'ly (Edna May) elope: A scene from the film *David Copperfield* (1913), directed by Thomas Bentley and produced by Cecil Hepworth.

its public life pseudonymously "Edited by Boz" but concluded under the name "Charles Dickens"—this time with an added published bonus of the author's portrait painted by Daniel Maclise in 1839.[3] As in previous novels, the action in *Nickleby* is antedated to the pre–Victorian mid–1820s, a troubled period in the life of the young novelist during which his father was cast into debtors' prison while the son was temporarily forced to work as a child drudge in a London shoe blacking factory. About 15 years later, in 1838, after having forever and rightfully ruined the public reputation of the English child workhouse in *Oliver Twist*, Dickens targeted substandard, provincial boarding schools. Traveling incognito with his illustrator Knight Browne while pretending to be a potential customer, Dickens personally visited such institutions, including the Bowes Academy of Yorkshire, whose one-eyed headmaster William Shaw had been convicted in 1823 of gross negligence by allowing abused students to suffer under his watch, but was nonetheless allowed to carry on as headmaster.[4] In *Nickleby*, Dickens' villain Wackford Squeers is obviously a composite, but some elements representing Shaw are clearly included. In his own journals, Dickens described Shaw as a "scoundrel" and admitted finding inspiration for the doomed character of Smike from the gravestones of former students in the cemetery adjacent to Bowes Academy.[5]

Specific literary influences also appear in *Nickleby*, doubly significant in that many carry over into subsequent film versions. These influences begin with an intense friendship between Dickens and William Macready (1793–1873), one of the leading British actors of the 19th century, who by 1838 had become a kind of stand-in father figure for Dickens.[6] In early

1838 Dickens witnessed Macready perform the lead in a restored version of Shakespeare's *King Lear*, bringing the role of Lear's tragic fool back into prominent view.[7] Parallels abound between Lear with his fool and Nicholas with Smike in the novel.[8] In *Nickleby*, Nicholas' father is dead, whereas in real life, Dickens' father was very much alive, though neither reliable nor esteemed, while Macready was by contrast revered. The traveling troupe scenes from *Nickleby* are likely an homage to Macready as the irrepressible Vincent Crummles, with Nicholas and Smike allowed by Crummles to have salaried roles in Shakespeare's *Romeo and Juliet*. More troubling is the novel's portrayal of Nicholas' mother as vacuous, weak-minded, and disloyal—by Dickens' own later admission, an unfavorable depiction of his own mother who, to his dismay circa 1824–1825, had encouraged him being employed continuously as a child laborer in the London blacking factory.[9] As in *Pickwick*, there is also an element of *commedia dell'arte*, with the romance between Nicholas and Madeline almost thwarted by parental machinations in pursuit of monetary wealth.[10] Though not strictly a literary source, Dickens' fast, passing friendship with his then-portrait painter Daniel Maclise seems to receive a nod as well with the vivid and sympathetic character delineation in *Nickleby* of miniaturist painter Miss La Creevy.[11] It is La Creevy who befriends the penniless family of Nicholas when they first arrive in London, especially Nicholas' sister Kate, who in Chapter 10 has her portrait painted by La Creevy (as illustrated by Phiz), just as Dickens had his own portrait painted by Maclise around the same time period.

At the dawn of the 20th century and the silent film era, *Nicholas Nickleby* was one of the earliest Dickens novels to be tapped for episodic movie material. One such scene comes from Chapter 13, illustrated with gusto by Phiz, depicting Nicholas' physical rebellion against his cruel employers at Dotheboys Hall, standing up for an abused Smike, and beating Squeers senseless before the eyes of students and Squeers' despicable family. Nicholas' provoked outburst is reminiscent of Oliver Twist violently turning on a surprised bully (Noah Claypool) from Dickens' previous novel, in which audiences surely took delight. As early as 1903, the famed Gaumont Film Company of France, shooting in England with comedian Alf Collins (1866–1951) as director, released a two-minute silent short titled *Dotheboys Hall: or Nicholas Nickleby*, still preserved with the British Film Institute.[12] Somewhat longer in length and probably similar in content, but now lost, was another silent short produced in 1910 by the American Edison Company titled *A Yorkshire School*, directed by Canadian-born James Henry White (1872–1944).[13] Thus it transpired that the very first scene from *Nicholas Nickleby* the novel, repeatedly transferred to film, also went to the heart of Dickens' social criticism, namely, outraged dramatic exposure of cruel and inept provincial English boarding schools. Every movie adaptation of *Nickleby* since the early silent shorts has featured this same energetic scene as an opening attention-getter for paying audiences, and rather effectively so.

The year 1912 marked the centenary of Dickens' birth and was distinguished by several ambitious silent film productions of his work, including one of *Nicholas Nickleby* by the famous Thanhouser Company of New York City.[14] This approximate 30-minute visual essay is still widely available for viewing and is indeed impressive for its time. American-born Edwin Thanhouser (1865–1956) must be counted as a true pioneer of the silent film industry, to which he fortuitously brought vast personal experience in the dramatic and theatrical arts. He was particularly fond of Charles Dickens' novels and produced no fewer than six Dickens adaptations between 1911 and 1913, one of which is now lost. *Nicholas Nickleby* was his fifth Dickens-related effort, and possibly his best. The cinematic style of the Thanhouser *Nickleby* is gritty and realistic, with superb attention to period detail. Slapstick, bombast, and melodrama—all so typical of other films from that era—are jettisoned or reduced to a minimum. The acting performances are mostly serious. American silent film icon Justus D. Barnes, who starred in the classic Western prototype, *The Great Train Robbery* (1903), portrayed the villainous (Uncle) Ralph Nickleby. Other notable stage and silent screen stars such as Victory Bateman and Ethyle Cooke were brought in to play minor character roles. Among many impressive qualities, the Thanhouser *Nickleby* somehow manages to condense a long novel with a complicated plot and numerous characters into a short but coherent cinematic experience. This was due in no small part to Edwin Thanhouser's extensive stage background before he turned to moviemaking. The results were not widely appreciated at the time but hold up still extremely well in artistic terms over a century later.

After the signal achievements of Thanhouser, there were no more films of *Nickleby* for the next 35 years, silent or sound. Then in 1947, following World War II, from England came *The Life and Adventures of Nicholas Nickleby*, directed by Brazilian-born Alberto Cavalcanti (1897–1982) for London's prestigious Ealing Studios.[15] Considering the stellar creative team that was assembled by Ealing for this project, the results must be viewed in hindsight as a disappointment, especially in light of what would follow a few decades later. Cedric Hardwicke (father of Edward Hardwicke) played a compellingly sinister Ralph Nickleby, while stalwart British actors such as Stanley Holloway (Mr. Crummles) and Sybil Thorndike (Mrs. Squeers) were brought in for minor roles; however, this adaptation ultimately comes across as clumsy, garbled, and hard to follow, despite nearly a two-hour running time.[16] The 1947 *Nickleby* also had a convenient cast overlap for the 1952 film version of *The Pickwick Papers*, with James Hayter playing both the Cheeryble twins, as well as Mr. Pickwick four years later. This seems fitting, since the Cheerybles of Dickens' *Nicholas Nickleby* frequently come across as twin Pickwicks in their jovial benevolence. Although British production of the 1947 *Nickleby* was likely driven by acclaim for the landmark 1946 *Great Expectations*, both this *Nickleby* and the 1952 *Pickwick* pale in overall quality comparison to the David Lean-Alec Guinness Dickens collaborations of 1946–1948.[17] Today, audiences may still judge for themselves on a modest pay-per-view basis.

As if to acknowledge the relative failure of the 1947 *Nickleby* to effectively compress Dicken's novel into a coherent two-hour feature film, the BBC went into action for the next several decades, repeatedly trying to tell the same story as an episodic television series, and thus more similar to the original work in pacing and detail. The first one arrived in 1957 (re-televised in 1958) with a 10-episode *Nicholas Nickleby*, totaling five hours, starring (as Nicholas) William Russell, later going on to greater fame during the 1960s as science teacher Ian Chesterton in the British hit show *Doctor Who*.[18] Next came a 13-episode, five-hour *Nicholas Nickleby* in 1968, starring Martin Jarvis with a screenplay written by Irish playwright Hugh Leonard (1926–2009).[19] An expanded edition of Leonard's adaptation was repeated in 1977 (and again in 1978) with six one-hour episodes and a mostly new cast led by Nigel Havers as Nicholas.[20] For the 1977–1978 BBC production, British director Christopher Barry (1925–2014) had a significant *Doctor Who* connection as well, and would have known William Russell from the 1957 series, although Russell did not participate in later TV versions of *Nickleby* scripted by Hugh Leonard. All the BBC productions between 1957 and 1977 met with respectful receptions but failed to make commercial headway beyond the United Kingdom.

Such was the popularity of the novel *Nicholas Nickleby* that theatrical adaptations, some with plot endings quite different from the book, began appearing in London even before Dickens completed the original serial in 1839. A full-scale musical based on *Nickleby*, however, was not attempted until the early 1970s, following in the wake of international acclaim for the movie version of *Oliver!* circa 1968. Finally, in 1973, came *Smike*, a television production by the ever-enthusiastic BBC, written by Roger Holman and Simon May.[21] The problem was that the plot presented in the musical has little or nothing to do with Dickens' novel other than taking suggestions from character names, personalities, and one setting, the notorious Dotheboys Hall in Yorkshire. Most of the story, as re-imagined by its creators, addresses the toxic environment at the school, long before Nicholas violently turns on and against his sadistic employers. This outburst is not suggested in *Smike*, which instead emphasizes the good-natured optimism of its put-upon namesake in the face of cruelty and adversity with songs such as "Don't Let Life Get You Down." Former Franco Zeffirelli leading man Leonard Whiting was cast as Nicholas. It is not known whether a video of this broadcast has survived, but various song recordings may still be found on YouTube, given the show's ongoing appeal to a cultish and mostly British audience of a certain age group.

Following modest success of the 1977 BBC serial broadcast, a much more ambitious English stage project took shape, one to later prove quite far-reaching in its theatrical influence. In preparation for an expansive and large-scale 1980 production in London's West End, the Royal Shakespeare Company (RSC) retained British playwright David Edgar (b. 1948) to transform Dickens' long novel into a nine-hour, all-day stage extravaganza, with Trevor Nunn, then Artistic Director of the RSC, lending a directorial hand. The late Roger Rees (1944–2015) was brought in to play the energetic lead role, along with an oversized rotating cast. Edgar's lengthy redaction is to date probably the truest reading of Dickens' original text. The resulting tour de force, *The Life and Adventures of Nicholas Nickleby*, proved a big audience hit and usually (but not always) a critical hit as well. The staged play was then filmed live at the Old Vic Theatre and first broadcast in 1982, before conquering Broadway and reaching American television audiences in early 1983, then rebroadcast later that same decade.[22] It is still widely available for viewing, despite its somewhat dated trappings and conventions. The show represented an American breakthrough for *Nickleby*, as well as a major achievement for Roger Rees, with Dickens' Nicholas now receiving much wider recognition as an earlier, biographical prototype for both David Copperfield and Pip from *Great Expectations*. This show's substantial impact was felt across the English-speaking world of live stage, including the vibrant Chicago theater scene of the time.

After the international triumph of the RSC live show, animation was the inevitable but logical next step. In 1985, following the animated series of Dickens' six best-known novels by Burbank Films Australia, came its feature production of *Nicholas Nickleby*, almost concurrent with its 1985 animated version of *The Pickwick Papers*. This choice of a Dickens work previously neglected by comparative standards was surely influenced by the rousing acclaim of the RSC stage version between 1980 and 1983. It remains the only animated *Nickleby* to date but must be considered a worthy effort showcasing Burbank's early knack for tackling this kind of project. One major change in the film from Dickens' text is that a distracted Uncle Ralph, stricken with guilt after learning the recently deceased Smike was in fact his biological son, is killed in a street accident, as opposed to hanging himself, the latter scenario obviously considered unacceptable for younger, more sensitive viewers. Such story changes, however, still underscore the inherent darkness and adult content within the novelist's original text, even for his best sellers created for general Victorian-era audiences.

After these relative high points, the last 15 years of the 20th century passed quietly with no new video interpretations of *Nickleby*. Then, beginning in early 2001, things began to move again, reinterpreting the now-familiar tale for a new generation of millennial-fan viewers and readers. First came a British ITV-produced *The Life and Adventures of Nicholas Nickleby*, directed by the highly talented but short-lived Stephen Whittaker (1947–2003), a protégé of John Schlesinger and another *Doctor Who* alumnus in the *Nickleby*-to-film postwar saga. The distinguished cast included a 25-year-old James D'Arcy as Nicholas, the formidable Charles Dance as a magnificently malevolent Ralph Nickleby, and a supporting host of English character actors with well-known or soon-to-be-well-known marquee names. Among the latter group was a young Tom Hiddleston (b. 1981) in one of his first minor screen appearances while still a student attending the University of Cambridge, and Sophia Myles (b. 1980) as Kate Nickleby and who, despite her youth, had already made a major Dickens film appearance in the 1999 *Oliver Twist* as Oliver's young mother Agnes. In addition to many fine performances and a sensitive re-scripting of the text (at over three hours running time), the 2001 *Nicholas Nickleby* displayed an ominously dark-hued color-palette for its sets, whether supposedly in London or Yorkshire, very much in keeping with the authentic and somber Dickensian spirit of the tale.[23] The film also deservedly earned BAFTA and RTS Awards for its distinctive costume designs by Barbara Kidd, yet another veteran of the *Doctor Who* series. Overall, a good argument can be made that this movie is the best cinematic *Nickleby* to date.

Not to be outdone by British television, however, a joint Anglo-American feature film production, *Nicholas Nickleby*, was released the following year in 2002. Condensed even further into a total running time of slightly over two hours, the 2002 *Nickleby* succeeded where the somewhat shorter 1947 version repeatedly failed, in no small part due to its tremendous star power and glossy presentation.[24] Also helping was sharp, concise screenwriting by American director Douglas McGrath (b. 1958), combined with an accessible and attractive soundtrack by prolific British film composer Rachel Portman (b. 1960). Leading the stellar cast was a 73-year-old Christopher Plummer as Ralph Nickleby, his nuanced portrayal of Dickens' tragic antagonist making a favorable comparison with that of Charles Dance from the previous year's film. For that matter, the 2002 production appears to have been viewed as a chance for ambitious actors to participate in the Dickens classic, at least for those who missed out in 2001.

Newcomer Charlie Hunnam was cast as Nicholas, while Anne Hathaway, fresh from her 2001 breakout role in *The Princess Diaries*, played Madeline. Other notables cast effectively into secondary roles included Jim Broadbent (Wackford Squeers), Nathan Lane (Vincent Crummles), Edward Fox (Mulberry Hawk), Tom Courtenay (Newman Noggs), Timothy Spall (Charles Cheeryble), Jamie Bell (Smike), and Alan Cummings (Folair). Interestingly, the 2002 film also featured Australian comedian Barry Humphries, better known to most international viewers as Dame Edna, in the role of Mrs. Crummles, continuing a longstanding Anglo tradition of cross-dressing stage roles.

While both *Nickleby* films of 2001–2002 attempted and succeeded, to varying degrees, by staying true to original settings and trappings of Dickens' novel, a 2012 serial adaptation from Northern Ireland, irreverently dubbed *The Life and Adventures of Nick Nickleby*, took an opposite approach. Filmed in contemporary Belfast on a shoestring budget with a relatively unknown local cast and presented by the BBC as a daytime soap opera, *Nick Nickleby* transposed Dickens' old plot into a modern setting with surprisingly few alterations, all within the space of five episodes and less than four hours. Critics and connoisseurs were impressed, but daytime television audiences not so much.[25] Uncle Ralph's long-suffering clerk Newman Noggs, played by Jonathan Harden, did effective double duty as a narrator. Uniquely, Smike is transformed into an institutionalized, abused elderly woman (Mrs. Smike), a role taken by Linda Bassett, probably better known to many viewers as Nurse Phyllis Crane from the hit TV series *Call the Midwife*. Dotheboys Hall becomes Dotheolds Hall. Ralph Nickleby was more than competently portrayed by Adrian Dunbar, one of the few other performers in the show with public name recognition of any significance. Although the 2012 *Nick Nickleby* failed to attract the audience that it deserved, it succeeded in demonstrating that the storytelling genius of Charles Dickens still easily adapted to present-day settings, and likely did so in ways that most viewing television audiences can hardly imagine.

Returning to the early Victorian era, the literary conclusion of the *Nicholas Nickleby* series in October of 1839 also saw the birth of Dickens' youngest daughter, and reportedly his favorite child, Catherine Dickens, later known as the painter Kate Perugini (1839–1929). During the early 20th century, Kate would prove to be an invaluable source of biographical information on the private life of her father, as well as indirectly giving considerable insight into his distinctive art of storytelling. The notable post–World War II surge in popularity for *Nickleby*, especially on film, would immediately follow these revelations, suggesting that better biographical insight into Charles Dickens' personal life was necessary for a wider public appreciation of his literary output. Did Dickens see his own life as a story to be told publicly, if not obliquely through the art of fiction? The autobiographical and picaresque aspects of *Nickleby* certainly anticipate the more mature (and circumspect) assessments later offered through *David Copperfield* and *Great Expectations*, as well as the critical social commentaries of *Bleak House* (disguised parentage) and *Little Dorrit* (debtors' prison). These unique qualities all easily transferred to film for later generations. *Nickleby* displays a confident youthful optimism, with Nicholas getting the girl, rescuing his sister, defeating a malicious relative, and above all, dismantling a hated Yorkshire boarding school. In real life, Dickens most certainly helped to accomplish the last item, writing that shortly after *Nickleby*, this type of English institution had severely declined in number and reputation.[26] And yet *Nickleby* was fiction, not real life. By this time, the novelist also had learned that killing off youthful characters such as Smike or Nancy (from *Oliver Twist*) could translate into brisk sales for his books. The tragic death of Smike in Chapter 58 of *Nickleby* is gloriously sentimental, but also convenient for the other characters and, above all, a commercially viable narrative device. For his next work, Dickens would become even more audacious in killing off a main character, this time a 13-year-old girl, done slowly and deliberately within the plot to maximize reader interest and sympathy.

4

The Old Curiosity Shop (1840–1841)

> "In the Destroyer's steps there spring up bright creations that defy his power, and his dark path becomes a way of light to Heaven."[1]

With the completion of *Nicholas Nickleby* in late 1839, Dickens had firmly established himself as the most popular novelist of his generation, though far from the wealthiest, and with a growing family to support. In typical fashion for him, Dickens had tried to branch out into magazine editing with his very own *Master Humphrey's Clock* (edited under the pseudonym "Boz"), first appearing in April of 1840, published by Chapman & Hall of London. The idea was to primarily edit and sell the works of other writers, including for safe measure, the beginning of his own latest original work, likely intended as a short story, titled *The Old Curiosity Shop*. Yet again, however, things did not go as planned. In the succinct words of recent Dickens biographer Claire Tomalin, "Sales crashed."[2] The London reading public was not interested in works by other writers—they wanted to know what was going to happen to Dickens' newest star character, Little Nell. Not for the first or last time during a long career, Dickens was forced to pivot, and he immediately began to improvise a full-blown novel, seemingly out of thin air. By the end of 1841, *The Old Curiosity Shop* had been regularly serialized and published unambiguously under the authorial name of Charles Dickens, with illustrations by Phiz and Dickens' friend George Cattermole (1800–1868). Once again, Dickens had produced a massive best seller (on both sides of the Atlantic Ocean), and today, nearly two centuries later, the novel remains one of his most popular.

With respect to the literary version of *The Old Curiosity Shop*, two things stand out in distant hindsight. The first is that the work was apparently created on a spur of the moment, with little planning or precedent, and this chaotic genesis is reflected by a rather haphazard plot and one-dimensional characterizations, excepting the grandfather who comes across as a sympathetic but tragically flawed figure. The second is that the novel was, despite its heavy improvisation, hugely successful and clearly struck a deep chord somewhere within the Anglo-American mass consciousness. Dickens accomplished this impressive feat, as in previous works, by reaching deep into his own personal past, antedating the novel's story back to his teenage years of the mid–1820s.[3] The lingering death of the novel's main character, 13-year-old Little Nell Trent, strongly suggests a reference to the unexpected passing of Dickens' 17-year-old sister-in-law, Mary Hogarth, on May 7, 1837, who died in the grief-stricken novelist's arms about three years before he began writing *The Old Curiosity Shop* in early 1840.[4] Shattered by Mary's death, Dickens for the first and only time in his career missed monthly deadlines for *The Pickwick Papers* and *Oliver Twist*, on which he was working simultaneously at the time. Suggestively, when he resumed writing a month later, he produced respective dark episodes in which Pickwick enters Fleet Prison (Chapter XLI) and Oliver

Modeling for bronze statue *Dickens and Little Nell* (1891) by Francis Elwell (right), drawing inspiration from *The Old Curiosity Shop*. After winning a prize at the 1893 Columbian Exhibition in Chicago, the statue was later moved to Clark Park in Philadelphia.

4. The Old Curiosity Shop (1840–1841)

meets Fagin's gang (Chapter IX). Then two years later, while writing *Nicholas Nickleby*, Dickens gives Nicholas' teenage cousin Smike a gloriously sentimental and melodramatic death. Finally, a year later with *The Old Curiosity Shop*, Dickens wears heartfelt sorrow on his sleeve with the final demise of Little Nell, an event literally stretched out over two full chapters in the book. Meanwhile, an entire generation of early Victorian-era readers, including distant Americans, Aussies, and other English-speaking societies, willingly and ostentatiously joined this shared grief over the premature passing of a completely fictional character who never existed beyond the novelist's own vivid imagination.

To contrast with this deep literary pathos, Dickens presents his usual large cast of side characters and subplots, the most noteworthy of which may be the unlikely romance between a startlingly-named Dick Swiveller—an associate of Nell's dissolute brother—and the nicknamed Marchioness, initially a nameless, slave-like servant to the embittered Mrs. Sally Brass, and later christened Sophronia Sphynx at the end of the novel after Nell's untimely demise.[5] Swiveller, like Jingle from *Pickwick*, is a stock "zany" character drawn from Dickens' beloved traditions of *commedia dell'arte*. Significantly, the Marchioness is given the same age as Nell (13 years old), but a happier, brighter future, eventually escaping from her oppressive keepers, receiving a formal education, and marrying her generous and good-hearted benefactor, Swiveller. Better film interpretations of *The Old Curiosity Shop* would later recognize the importance of the Swiveller-Marchioness subplot, acknowledging its overall importance to the general tone and direction of the story, while inferior film versions would tend to omit or downplay this same crucial facet. In addition to this optimistic sidebar, a cruel money-lending dwarf, Daniel Quilp, must rank as one of Dicken's most exuberant villains, though it is Nell's own grandfather, along with his insatiable gambling addiction, who sets the tragedy in motion and propels it to an unhappy conclusion. This was also the first appearance in Dickens' fiction of a biological father figure (Grandfather Trent), and the portrait presented by the novelist is indeed disturbing. It is well known that Dickens' own biological father struggled with unpaid financial debt for most of his adult life (to the serious detriment of his family), and widely assumed that an addictive gambling habit was part of this persisting problem.

Given its fame and reputation as the ultimate tearjerker, it comes as no surprise that *The Old Curiosity Shop* received numerous silent film treatments at the beginning of the 20th century, although sadly, little has survived from these early efforts. Reportedly first (in 1906) came the retitled silent short *Little Nell* from the pioneering Gaumont Film Company of France, followed in 1909 by a slightly longer *The Old Curiosity*

Shop by the Essanay Studios of Chicago.[6] Both works are now considered lost. Also lost is another silent short, *The Old Curiosity Shop*, from 1912 by Britannia Films of London.[7] Still reportedly surviving for the most part, however, but difficult to screen beyond specialized festivals, is a single-reel 1911 version of *The Old Curiosity Shop* by the venerable Thanhouser Company of New York City, directed by Barry O'Neil, aka Thomas McCarthy (1865–1918). Little Nell was portrayed by Marie Eline, one of the better-known child stars from the early silent era, and only nine years old at the time of this production. This was the first of six Thanhouser-Dickensian film efforts produced between 1911 and 1913 around the 1912 centenary of the novelist's birth.[8] Given Edwin Thanhouser's acknowledged expertise in the dramatic arts, this group of silent shorts, five of which have survived the ravages of time, must be considered central to the early silent era's canon of quality cinematic adaptations for Dickens' most popular works.

In Great Britain, the nearest equivalent to the American Thanhouser as a quality filmmaker during this same period was Dickensian specialist Thomas Bentley (1884–1966), and who like Thanhouser, supplemented his skills as a movie director with considerable live theater expertise. The *Old Curiosity Shop* seems to have particularly attracted Bentley's interest, as he directed two silent features of the same title, first in 1914 and then a longer remake in 1921, both films now unfortunately lost. This is a shame because Bentley's work was praised at the time by silent movie critics.[9] Then a decade later in 1934, Bentley had the distinction of directing the very first sound version of *The Old Curiosity Shop*, with Ben Webster as Grandfather Trent, Hay Petrie as Quilp, and a 14-year-old Elaine Benson as Little Nell Trent. For those who saw Bentley's earlier silent versions, his 1934 talkie has been declared the best of his interpretations for this particular novel, and some continue to feel that Webster's portrayal as Grandfather Trent has never been surpassed.[10] Crucially, Bentley also recognized the importance of the Swiveller-Marchioness subplot within the novel and was careful to include it in his feature-length work. Nevertheless, this film, though still surviving, is difficult to find outside of United Kingdom import circles. It is well possible that, given the dominating achievements of Bentley and Thanhouser during the first half of the 20th century, other competing full-length, English-language features based on *The Old Curiosity Shop* were non-existent, simply not caring to follow in their immediate, imposing wake.[11]

When new video interpretations of the novel finally began to appear during the post–World War II era of television, the first one of significance opted to focus on the entertaining side-story of Swiveller and the Marchioness, versus the tragic and occasionally maudlin tale of Little Nell. In

1955, the American NBC network assigned a 60-minute time slot for its *Alcoa Hour* to a production titled *The Small Servant*, a reference to Dickens' own designation for the Marchioness before she is nicknamed by her unlikely benefactor.[12] The new teleplay had the added advantage of featuring in its leading roles two promising British actors, Laurence Harvey and Diane Cilento, both appearing for the first time before large TV audiences. The show was well received by viewers. It also served as a reminder that *The Old Curiosity Shop* was not all doom and gloom, but rather offered hope for the future as well, hope sometimes deriving from the same tragedy that seems to constantly surround the Trent family. *The Small Servant* was then picked up and repeated by UK Granada (later ITV) in early 1960, receiving a similar, favorable reception.[13] Then during the winter of 1962–1963, the BBC produced an ambitious 13-episode, three-hour miniseries for *The Old Curiosity Shop*, representing the first time that Dickens' novel had been given a serious, full-length dramatic treatment for a wide general audience. British playwright Constance Cox, having notable success earlier that same year with her BBC presentation of *Oliver Twist*, was brought in to do the screenplay, while a relatively-unknown Joan Craft (1916–1999) was hired as director and would go on over a long career making a specialty of literary film adaptations, especially for the works of Charles Dickens.[14] Formally trained character actor Patrick Troughton was cast as villain Daniel Quilp, later referring to this performance as his favorite role in a very lengthy and impressive resumé. Troughton would soon afterwards achieve much greater fame (during the late 1960s) in the *Doctor Who* TV series but surviving stills of him in makeup as Quilp suggest a compelling portrayal. Unfortunately, kinescopes of these early television broadcasts are not known to have survived, although intriguing publicity shots for the same productions can be found in the public domain.

Attempts at adding songs to *The Old Curiosity Shop* may extend back as far as 1906 and Gaumont's silent *Little Nell* (now lost), which reportedly had a primitive gramophone recording accompanying its presentation.[15] A few years later in 1916, the relatively obscure Italian composer Lamberto Landi (1882–1950) wrote an opera titled *Nelly*, based on Dickens' tale, but this was not performed until 1947 (in Lucca), and no commercial video or audio recordings are known to exist. Then during the 1970s, following the worldwide smash sensation of Lionel Bart's *Oliver!*, musical adaptations were attempted for a number of other Dickens novels. Amazingly, *The Old Curiosity Shop* was no exception in this regard. In 1975, both British and American television broadcast a two-hour Reader's Digest production titled *Mister Quilp*, thus assigning top billing and plot emphasis to Dickens' repulsive villain rather than Little Nell.[16] Unlike then-recent Dickensian musical fiascos such as *Smike* and *Pip*, the musical

Mister Quilp featured a soundtrack by one of Hollywood's most distinguished composers, Elmer Bernstein (1922–2004), along with (for the most part, at least) a surprisingly well-qualified creative team. The title role of Quilp was taken by the talented British journeyman actor Anthony Newley, who mugged and flayed his way through a frenzied, hunchbacked performance still painful to watch. Critics and audiences alike were left at best confused, and at worst, bored; moreover, a good case can be made that the soundtrack represents some of Bernstein's most forgettable music, among a substantial oeuvre that more typically was bracing and unforgettable. Although a complete recording of this musical is apparently nowhere to be found, miscellaneous preserved excerpts and promotions may still be seen on YouTube, all confirming the negative impressions originally left on almost all viewers nearly half a century ago.

The resounding failure of *Mister Quilp* represented the nadir of this novel's fortunes on film. Then things slowly turned around, or at least became less misguided. Four years later in 1979, the BBC presented a nine-episode, eight-hour miniseries dramatization of *The Old Curiosity Shop*, still widely available for viewing on DVD.[17] With a sensitive screenplay by Irish novelist William Trevor (1928–2016), the potentially maudlin elements of the story were kept in check while important subplots and many minor characters were restored, including that of Swiveller and the Small Servant-Marchioness. In a nod to its acclaimed 1962–1963 production, the BBC once again initially cast a (by then) somewhat older Patrick Troughton into the role of Quilp, but had to replace him with stage and television stalwart Trevor Peacock when Troughton's fragile health began to fail him early in the filming.[18] Noted Anglo-American composer Carl Davis (b. 1936) provided a musical soundtrack. The 1979 *Old Curiosity Shop* also benefited from participation of seasoned British actors the high caliber of which included Sebastian Shaw as Grandfather Trent, Margaret Courtenay as Mrs. Jarley, and Wensley Pithey as the Single Gentleman. In Dickens' original text, the latter character assumes the role of a sympathetic narrator, Grandfather Trent's estranged younger brother, and later, outside of the text, is identified as Master Humphrey, the eccentric namesake of Dickens' edited journal in which the serial was initially published.[19] Later film productions of this same novel would demonstrate the potential aesthetic risks and theatrical downside of attempting to alter or omit seemingly small details such as these provided by the novelist in his published text.

Five years after this stellar miniseries by the BBC came an animated version of *The Old Curiosity Shop* in 1984 by Burbank Films Australia. Clocking in at a little over one hour, the Burbank film is the only animated version of Dickens' novel to date. It came as part of a memorable

4. The Old Curiosity Shop (1840–1841)

series of eight animated Dickens classics made by Burbank during the early to mid–1980s, in many respects paving the way for more animated Dickens-sourced movies coming soon afterwards. Though streamlined by necessity, the basic plot and essential characters are left intact by Burbank, with some interesting details included. For example, the opening sequence depicts a lost Little Nell wandering the ominous nighttime streets of London, until assisted and led safely home by a kindly Master Humphrey, somewhat acting as an explainer of events to young audiences. This is perhaps the only video interpretation in which Dickens' narrator is interposed by name into the plot, and under the name that the novelist originally devised for that narrator. The result is surprisingly effective. Master Humphrey, as narrator of the tale both in sound and vision, gains immediately eyewitness credibility, as well as developing a sympathetic viewpoint for the audience towards both Nell Trent and her hapless, gambling-addicted grandfather. Impressively, and despite the hyper-compressed action, important minor characters such as Swiveller, the Marchioness, Mrs. Jarley, and Schoolmaster Marton are all given their proper due. Accordingly, the film remains imminently watchable for both adult and child viewers.

Far less effective—rather disappointing, in fact, given the star power employed—was a 1995 Disney-Hallmark TV production of *The Old Curiosity Shop* spanning no fewer than four episodes over three hours in total running time. Gorgeously filmed in Ireland, with top notch acting talent employed, including costume drama virtuoso Tom Courtenay as a very un-dwarflike Daniel Quilp, and a recently knighted Peter Ustinov as Grandfather Trent, the end-result nevertheless presents a case study in how a few injudicious changes to Dickens' plot can seriously undermine the power of his story. The problems begin with complete elimination of Nell's more fortunate parallel, the Marchioness, and a confused reduction of Swiveller to multiple roles of comic relief, frustrated suitor, and by the end, redeemed fortune seeker. Long gone is the zany stock figure drawn by Dickens from the old conventions of *commedia dell'arte*, used by the novelist to rescue the Marchioness from a tragic fate like that of Nell's. More surprising still is the pronounced emphasis of the Single Gentleman (played ably by James Fox) as the estranged younger brother of Nell's grandfather, rescuing Trent from insanity in a coda that is rather hard to believe, even for a Disney film. Thus, in the place of salvation for the Marchioness at the end of the story is substituted an unlikely moral reform of Grandfather Trent and his gambling addiction (coming after Nell's demise), along with repeated half-baked platitudes of Nell's saintly goodness living on in the memories of others left behind long after her death. With these missed opportunities for utilizing serious talent and attractive backdrops, a thorough Disneyfication of Dickens reached its crescendo during the mid–1990s.

After this comparative letdown, the new 21st century began on a much more promising note. In 2007 (repeated in 2008), British ITV unveiled a lavish production of *The Old Curiosity Shop*, starring the excellent Derek Jacobi as Grandfather Trent, completely lovable when played in Jacobi's normally good-guy persona but terrifyingly real when in the disruptive throws of his gambling habit.[20] Fifteen-year-old Irish actor Sophie Vavasseur portrayed Little Nell, opposite her 15-year-old counterpart George MacKay as the likeable but easily manipulated shop assistant, Kit Nubbles. Twelve years later MacKay would go on to major stardom as the leading man in Sam Mendes' 2019 epic war drama, *1917*.[21] Clocking in almost precisely at two hours, the 2007 *Curiosity Shop* was ably directed by Brian Percival (b. 1962), who would himself soon go on to much greater fame as the director and co-creator of the PBS international hit series *Downton Abbey* (2010–2012). Other key roles, both major and minor, in the 2007 *Curiosity Shop* were skillfully cast from the repulsive Daniel Quilp of Toby Jones to the jovial Mrs. Jarley of Zoë Wanamaker. Between the concise cinematic drama of the 2007 film and the faithful expansiveness of the 1979 miniseries (both produced in Great Britain), the authentic spirit of Dickens' *The Old Curiosity Shop* has been adequately served on video over the last half century. These are in addition to the earlier notable achievements of Edwin Thanhouser and Thomas Bentley, as well as the presumably lost kinescope for the 1962–1963 BBC miniseries adaptation by Constance Cox.

The latest appearance of Dickens' Little Nell in mainstream video may also be one of the strangest. In December of 2015, BBC-Netflix presented its miniseries mash-up *Dickensian*, cancelled after only one season but still available for viewing on Amazon Prime. There is little that is truly Dickensian about the series, other than a prolific use of character names and settings from over a dozen novels.[22] Likely intended as an homage to the novelist by multiple screenwriters, this combined and messy plot, over the course of 20 half-hour episodes, left many viewers merely confused, and most critics divided at best. The new plot is too clever for its own good, forgetting the sage advice of Constance Cox from a previous generation to keep things simple.[23] One positive aspect of the series was the appearance of many fresh British acting faces to the small screen, including an age-appropriate Imogen Faires (b. 2002) as Little Nell Trent from *The Old Curiosity Shop*, interacting with numerous, otherwise familiar characters (played by unfamiliar actors) from other famous novels by Charles Dickens. Some judicious exceptions to the mostly youthful cast of *Dickensian* were Ned Dennehy as Scrooge (from *A Christmas Carol*), Anton Lesser as Fagin (from *Oliver Twist*), and perhaps most notably, seasoned Irish actor Stephen Rea (b. 1946), playing Inspector Bucket from *Bleak House*, also one of the earliest detective characters in all of English literature, an important innovation for which Dickens rarely receives any credit.[24]

Presently, perhaps the most famous sculpture of Charles Dickens in the United States, if not the world, is to be found in Philadelphia, Pennsylvania. Created by Francis Edwin Elwell in 1890, then later exhibited at the Chicago Columbia Exhibition of 1893, *Dickens and Little Nell* is today on public display in Clark Park of Philadelphia's vibrant Spruce Hill neighborhood. The sculpture presents a highly sentimentalized and idealized image of Dickens accompanied by possibly his most famous fictional creation, one sculpted slightly more than two decades after his death. Nonetheless, the work was highly praised in its own time by the otherwise critical likes of Lorado Taft and continues to draw favorable public attention despite its dated style and dead-white-man cultural baggage.[25] The novelist himself would have surely appreciated the tribute. If Little Nell's tragic, untimely demise in *The Old Curiosity Shop* indirectly leads to the rescue of the Marchioness by Swiveller, thus fulfilling the narrator's observation that a "dark path" can sometimes become "a way of light" (see epigraph), then the same may be said about Ewell's statue and Dickens' novel in general. A fictional, tragic conceit gave rise to a permanent legacy in the popular imagination, still on full view in the American City of Brotherly Love, despite all our current civic discord. The final irony is that by 1841, Dickens was himself ready to fully break from what had been thus far a tremendously successful formula for literary fiction. The first of his great literary experiments, though not entirely successful, was about to begin.

5

Barnaby Rudge
(1840–1841)

> *"To surround anything, however monstrous or ridiculous, with an air of mystery, is to invest it with a secret charm, and power of attraction which to the crowd is irresistible."*[1]

On September 21, 1832, the world-famous 62-year-old novelist Sir Walter Scott passed away in his native Scotland, leaving behind arguably the greatest literary legacy of his generation, having for all practical purposes invented and popularized the genre of English-language historical fiction. At that time, an unknown Charles Dickens was 20 years old and working as an underpaid freelance journalist in London, probably feeling grateful to have escaped abject poverty and the financially precarious household of his family upbringing. The other great English novelist of the early 19th century, Jane Austen (1775–1817), had been dead for over a decade and not yet widely read. Austen was also a purveyor, if not inventor, of an entirely different fiction genre, and in her own day was considered an acquired taste, mainly for literary connoisseurs. Her unique style likely held little interest for the young Charles Dickens. Walter Scott, on the other hand, probably represented everything that Dickens aspired to become—sophisticated, famous, admired, respected, and above all, widely read by both the high and the low. It might well be said that the long shadow of Walter Scott hung over any writer circa 1840—English language or otherwise—hoping to make a name for himself, even the (by then) well-established Charles Dickens.

Like *The Old Curiosity Shop* before it, *Barnaby Rudge: A Tale of the Riots of 'Eighty*, was first published by Chapman & Hall as a serial in the short-lived journal edited by Dickens, *Master Humphrey's Clock*, between 1840 and 1841, initially under the pseudonym "Boz" and later concluding under the express authorship of Charles Dickens, with illustrations by Phiz (aka Hablot Knight Browne) and George Cattermole.[2] Soon after the complete *Barnaby Rudge* was published in book form during late 1841, the journal folded. Paying readers were primarily interested in Charles Dickens, not other writers—the latter being the original intent of the journal. As for *Barnaby*, the critical consensus over the last two centuries was recently well summed up by biographer Claire Tomalin: "It [*Barnaby*] was the least popular of his books at the time, and has remained so."³ This judgment, though widely held and narrowly accurate, is still a bit harsh. Charles Dickens operating at a fraction of his ability as a novelist was still far better than most other writers. *A Tale of Two Cities* it certainly was not, but *Barnaby Rudge* still holds considerable interest for those willing to delve deeper into the novelist's early development. Above all, *Barnaby Rudge* was a major creative departure, in that it represented an initial foray into the realm of historical fiction à la Walter Scott, as well as Dickens' first attempt at setting a story outside his own lifetime, with semi-historical events in the novel taking place during the years 1775–1780, two full generations before Dickens' birth in 1812.

Painting of *Dolly Varden* (1842) by British artist William Powell, now in the Victoria and Albert Museum, inspired by the same character from Dickens' *Barnaby Rudge* (© Victoria & Albert Museum, London).

Unlike Dickens' previous novels and, for that matter, unlike most of his future ones, *Barnaby Rudge* explores the world of Dickens' grandparents circa the late 1770s. This period witnessed the height of the British Enlightenment, as well as the revolution of the American colonies and birth of the United States. Notwithstanding the halcyon days of post–Napoleonic Great Britain inhabited by the fictional likes of Samuel Pickwick and Nicholas Nickleby, many Englishmen believed that something had gone fundamentally wrong with the British Empire when it lost its 13 American colonies and immediately afterwards found itself isolated on the world stage. Particularly ugly were the so-called Gordon Riots of 1780, not typically taught to American-born history students, but keenly on the radar of Charles Dickens and politically likeminded Englishmen of those times.[4] During these riots, which preceded the 1781 defeat of Lord Cornwallis at Yorktown, Virginia, by combined American and French military forces, angry London mobs chanting anti–Catholic slogans assaulted any opposition in their path (including the government citadel of Newgate Prison) before being violently suppressed by royally authorized troops.[5] This context becomes the backdrop for otherwise ordinary or not-so-ordinary life dramas within Dickens' storytelling framework. The novelist as narrator dwells at some length on the often-irrational mystique driving mob violence (see epigraph), while maintaining his customary sympathy towards the common man, as seen through the eyes of his main adult character, the simpleton Barnaby Rudge Jr., as well as Dickens' usual sharp criticism for all social injustice, especially any social injustice citing religious dogma as an excuse.

Charles Dickens appears to have had a personal stake in this obscure bit of 18th-century English history as well. The novelist's presumptive paternal grandfather, William Dickens (1719–1785), died at age 66, some time before the birth of his presumed, posthumous son, John Dickens (1785–1851), the novelist's well-known father, the latter becoming a model for famously eccentric Dickensian characters such as Wilkins Micawber in *David Copperfield*. Grandfather Dickens, along with his wife Elizabeth (26 years his junior), were both employed as servants in the aristocratic Mayfair household of Baron John Crewe (1742–1829) and Lady Frances Crewe, both noted Whig political supporters, but reportedly not on particularly good terms with each other as man and wife. The Crewes were in turn part of an eminent political circle that included the likes of parliamentary statesman Charles James Fox (1749–1806), MP and playwright Richard Brinsley Sheridan (1751–1816), and Irish-born MP Edmund Burke (1729–1797). All were celebrated, if not notorious, for their radical, comparatively pro–American views, and (with exception of Burke) dissolute lifestyles. In light of these cumulative facts, it has been suggested by more than one biographer that John Dickens believed himself to be, or was in fact, the illegitimate son of English nobility, further evidenced by striking personality differences with his older brother, as well as a unique fondness for high culture (i.e., books), living beyond his means, and an otherwise inexplicable access to political patronage, at least during his younger years. Charles Dickens the novelist was a product of this same paternal line, and if the suggestions are true, then it would explain a lot about his own political attitudes and views.[6] In short, Charles Dickens may have been the illegitimate grandson of a famous 18th-century peer, and was probably aware of this, though publicly silent on the topic. Instead, he expressed his personal views mainly through the art of storytelling, and *Barnaby Rudge*, for all its shortcomings as a novel, gives readers a distinctively Dickensian spin on the ubiquitous historical fiction of Sir Walter Scott, which up until the 1840s overshadowed everything in its wake, including the work of Charles Dickens.

Earlier in his writing career, with *Oliver Twist*, Dickens had learned that he could strike an effective popular chord utilizing non-human characters such as Bullseye, the reformed pet mongrel of villain Bill Sikes. In *Barnaby Rudge*, Dickens introduces Grip, a pet raven belonging to lead character Barnaby Jr., based on Dickens' own real-life pet raven, also named Grip. Unfortunately, the real-life Grip died in 1841 shortly after inspiring the novelist and was unable to enjoy any literary celebrity during its lifetime, although Dickens later owned a series of other pet ravens, all named Grip as well. More unfortunately, the novelist intended Barnaby's pet raven, along with its occasional utterances, to be comical or ironic within the context of the story, when in fact the effect is mostly creepy and disconcerting. Interestingly, and more fortunately, Dickens' eccentric personal fascination with the *corvus corvax* species soon afterwards came to the attention of Edgar Allan Poe (1809–1849) during Dickens' first American tour in 1842, thus inspiring one of the great poetic masterpieces of English literature, Poe's *The Raven*. Poe, however, was the one who got it right. The foreboding subject matter (to Poe, "Nevermore") is far more fitting for Halloween, rather than a Victorian-era semi-comedic novel about forgotten historical events during the late 18th century. As a final bizarre coda to this literary sidebar, the physical remains of Dickens' very own Grip #1 may still be viewed today in the form of taxidermy in the Rare Books Department of the Philadelphia Free Library, of all places.

Apart from strained, misplaced humor, *Barnaby Rudge* the novel, as noted by more than one critic, suffers from other problems which subsequently carried over into later film adaptations, beginning with its daunting length (82 chapters plus preface). As succinctly noted by Claire Tomalin, "the book is far too long for what it does" and too often fills space with "crude melodrama."[7] Using the good-hearted but feeble-minded Barnaby Jr. as a main character focus, rather than the heroic yeoman locksmith Gabriel Varden, was probably a mistake as well. And yet, despite all this, there is also considerable merit to be found in the tale for patient readers. The leisurely yet detailed exploration of mob psychology by Dickens was both groundbreaking for its time and eerily contemporary for the modern era. The dramatization of reactionary counterrevolution ("No

Popery!") against progressive legislation remains contemporary as well. Barnaby, Gabriel, Dolly, and all the main characters move daily through an English society deeply divided by class, wealth, and privilege, while fighting a losing war against the American colonies, barely scraping out a living, and trying (with limited success) to confront their own emotions and personal problems. The novelist somehow, against considerable odds, maintains his familiar sympathies for the proletariat while vividly depicting the irredeemable baseness of individual motivations, whether these be the evil schemes of the manipulative aristocrat Sir John Chester, or his illegitimate, unacknowledged, and depraved son Maypole Hugh.[8] The gradual build-up and volcanic explosion of irrational mass violence, along with all of its demagogic agitators and innocent victims, during the historically accurate Gordon Riots of 1780 are presented within a highly believable dramatic framework, and these episodes certainly mark the most memorable chapters of this far too-often maligned work of so-called fiction. Moreover, the theme of privileged illegitimacy and its evil effects on society introduced by Dickens appears unnecessary until one considers questions surrounding the personal history of his family during that same time and place in British history.

Somewhat surprisingly, the character from *Barnaby Rudge* exerting the most lasting influence on the popular consciousness, however unaware it may be of its source, was Dickens' extroverted and vivacious Dolly Varden, favored daughter of Gabriel Varden and sweetheart of everyman hero Joe Willets. In today's jargon, Dolly would be labeled a sexpot, although a Victorian writer, or one during the late 1770s, would not have used or been familiar with the term. Dolly has also been tagged as insipid by feminist critics, but modern readers must remember that she belonged to a society which considered all women, especially those young and attractive, as being only once removed from the status of chattel. Despite these handicaps, Dickens' Dolly Varden tends to eventually get whatever she wants, after handily surviving various trials and tribulations destroying many seemingly more powerful male characters. A mere two years after publication of the novel, the fictional Dolly was immortalized in a series of paintings by noted British artist William Powell Frith (1819–1909), surpassing in excellence even the original book illustrations by Cattermole and Phiz. Although Dickens' novel itself is today mostly forgotten, his imagined name of Dolly Varden lives on in diverse forms, including distinctive species of Pacific salmon and Caribbean crab, a rural hamlet in Ohio (as well as a Cincinnati chocolate company and nickelodeon), a mountain range in Nevada, a railroad line through northwest Indiana, early American baseball teams, a vaudeville musical, 19th-century women's fashion, and more recently, an indie rock band from Chicago, to name just a few. In rare

20th-century film attempts at the novel, the character of Dolly sometimes becomes the visual focus of the story, if not the center of the story itself, with variable degrees of dramatic success.

Tellingly, the first movies inspired by *Barnaby Rudge* had little or nothing to do directly with the Dickens novel, instead latching on to the irresistible crowd appeal of Dolly Varden herself. In 1906, the French-based Gaumont Film Company produced a silent short, *Dolly Varden*, directed by Alf Collins, who three years earlier (in 1903) had also directed Gaumont's *Dotheboys Hall*, drawn from Dickens' third novel, *Nicholas Nickleby*.[9] Seven years after the Gaumont effort (in 1913), American rival the Edison Company produced a somewhat longer silent short of *Dolly Varden*, directed by Charles Brabin.[10] Both the Gaumont and Edison silent shorts of *Dolly Varden* are now considered irretrievably lost. Based on surviving synopses, both represented free adaptations of a minor episode from the Dickens original text. It is also likely that both the Gaumont and Edison studios were inspired by the short-lived success of an obscure British comic operetta, *Dolly Varden: The Musical Delicacy* (1901) by Julian Edwards (1855–1910) and Stanislaus Stangé (1862–1910), a work likewise related remotely at best to the Dickens novel. Aside from rarely performed sheet music, the most visible artifacts of this early stage production are colorful and campy posters that can still be viewed and purchased from various online purveyors.[11] Even though both films are now lost, it is noteworthy that the Gaumont and Edison shorts attempted to visualize scenes from a popular live music show of the same era, suggesting some attendant dramatic interest (thanks, no doubt, to Dickens) adaptable to even the silent format. The poster images, along with paintings and etchings by British artists, represent the earliest surviving visual legacies for *Barnaby Rudge*, which in turn would later transfer to the big screen for the limited number of film productions based on the same original text.

As if in reaction to the ephemeral frivolity of the vaudeville show, early British megaproducer Cecil M. Hepworth (1874–1953) and his A-Team director Thomas Bentley produced in 1915, as the Great War raged throughout Europe, the legendary but now sadly lost, 5.5-reel silent epic, *Barnaby Rudge*. This was the same year (1915) that in the United States, D.W. Griffith directed his epic masterwork *The Birth of a Nation* (at 12 reels in length). With respect to *Barnaby Rudge*, eminent Dickensian scholar and critic Joss Marsh has written, "In it [the movie], for one of the very first times, the fiction film assumed its paradoxical role of historical record."[12] The Hepworth-Bentley production came one year after the same team had delivered Dickens' *The Old Curiosity Shop* (1914) and *The Chimes* (1914), and two years after their *David Copperfield* (1913). This was also four years after Vitagraph's monumental (for the time), 11-minute *A Tale of Two Cities* (1911) which, along with the recent work of Griffith, no doubt inspired Hepworth and Bentley to do a historical epic on an even grander scale.[13] Reviews at the time were enthusiastic, making it doubly unfortunate that the film is lost.[14] The cast was interesting as well. Kentucky-born stage and film actor Tom Powers played Barnaby Jr. and would later go on to successfully transition his career into the talkies, culminating with a memorable performance in the noir classic *Double Indemnity* (1944).[15] Twenty-year-old Chrissie White, one of the biggest British stars of the silent era, played Dolly Varden.[16] Though lost, stills from this production continue to be widely available online and are fascinating to behold, including Barnaby's notorious pet raven, which appears to have been a real bird. Given that only one filmed attempt at *Barnaby Rudge* has survived into the present day, the unhappy loss of the 1915 silent epic by Hepworth and Bentley clears the competitive field for our comparison purposes.

Fast forward 45 years to the post–World War II era in Great Britain, also the dawn of the Camelot political era in the United States. Nothing on film for *Barnaby Rudge* had been attempted since 1915, either in the U.K. or the U.S. Then in 1960, as the BBC continued to pioneer its prolific TV serializations of Dickens' work, a decision was made to produce a new version of *Barnaby Rudge*, possibly for the historical record. Reportedly made on a shoestring budget, and totally unlike the 1915 silent epic by Hepworth and Bentley, the 1960 BBC production eschewed celebrity star power and expensive sets, opting instead for minimum wage stage actors, with network founding father Morris Barry (1918–2000) stepping in to direct as a labor of love, and a methodical, workmanlike screenplay by staff writer Michael Voysey (1920–1987).[17] Given these limited circumstances, the overall results were predictably flawed, though highly competent in execution. The 13-episode, over six-hour series aired to British audiences late during that same year and still may be found on a two-sided DVD in many American public libraries of the heartland as part of the BBC Video "Classics" series. Hampered by a rather dated production style, fair (at best) black and white video quality, and music limited to instrumental operatic excerpts played over the opening and closing credits, the 1960 *Barnaby Rudge* is nevertheless a faithful representation of the novel's many weaknesses and surprising strengths. It is also still the only video production available to date for general viewership.

Similar to the 1985 BBC production of *The Pickwick Papers*, the 1960 BBC *Barnaby Rudge* gradually builds momentum and dramatic tension after a somewhat tedious and slow beginning. After characters, context, and conflicts are firmly established in the opening episodes, things start to move quickly. Opening scenes set in the year 1775 (immediately before the American Revolution) introduce viewers to the families of Varden,

5. Barnaby Rudge (1840–1841) 55

Willet, Rudge, Chester, and Haresdale. Young Joe Willet joins the British Army after temporary disappointment in love, only to be later crippled in action during the American conflict overseas. Each family represents broad strata from English society leading up to the Gordon Riots of 1780— Protestant, Catholic, working class, aristocratic, or (worst of all) poor. The two big reveals are that Barnaby Sr. (the father of Barnaby Jr.) is a murderer and career criminal, while Maypole Hugh, a spirited but vicious thug, is the illegitimate son of villain-antagonist Sir John Chester. Some of the performances are outstanding, especially that of Dame Joan Hickson as the insufferable but ultimately redeemable Mrs. Varden—Hickson later going on the much greater television fame as Agatha Christie's Miss Marple. Raymond Huntley, a much-underrated performer, gives an effectively understated portrayal of pure evil as the diabolical Sir John Chester. Historical figures such Lord George Gordon and Edmund Burke make brief appearances as well. A glaring weakness in the series is the casting for Dolly Varden, intended by Dickens as a focal point, but colorlessly played by Jennifer Daniel.[18] Taken as a whole, American audiences get a rare glimpse of the ordinary Brit's view of London life during the American War of Independence, as seen through the early Victorian lens of Dickens. It also strongly reflects the intolerant mood of the early Cold War era in Great Britain (and the United States), which then clearly becomes a subtext for the vicious anti–Catholic Gordon Riots of 18th-century London.

Dickens' *Barnaby Rudge*, despite its many shortcomings as a work of historical fiction, still can speak loudly to open-minded modern audiences, especially given all our contemporary political uncertainties and interminable gridlock, often guided by official misinformation and mass gullibility. The weak-minded Barnaby Jr. becomes disturbingly symbolic for all ordinary Anglo-American citizens, both then and now, especially those swept away by violent mob delusions based on conveniently designated scapegoats or deliberately limited access to empirical facts. And yet in the end Barnaby Jr. survives because wiser, cooler, and compassionate heads come to his rescue, whereas an unrepentant and ever-defiant Maypole Hugh goes to the gallows with no intervention whatsoever from his more powerful benefactors.[19] The single surviving video production of this unusual novel from 1960 effectively conveys these ideas and more. Even the remaining stills from the lost 1915 silent epic do the same. This commentator speculates that the time now may be ripe for a new dramatic assay of this deeply underrated work. As the 21st century enters its third turbulent decade, the London Gordon Riots of 1780 look to be more topical and instructive than ever before, at least for those audiences open to entertainment being blended with education.

As for Charles Dickens the novelist, shortly after creating his least popular story, he would go on to publish his deservedly most famous one. In Dickens' *A Christmas Carol*, a little remarked upon interlude in this universally popular tale occurs when the Ghost of Christmas Present reveals to a horrified Scrooge the children of "Ignorance" and "Want."[20] These children are not physically handicapped like Tiny Tim, or for that matter, mentally handicapped like Barnaby Rudge Jr.; on the contrary, they are deprived minors more suggesting Maypole Hugh, who as an adult gleefully participates in the anti–Catholic Gordon Riots, or the Vardens' untrustworthy servant Miggs, who passively supports all the outrages committed. To the novelist, Ignorance and Want may well have represented Hugh and Miggs as children, criminally abused and neglected by society, until as adults they finally turn against it, either openly or secretly. As a work of moralistic historical fiction, *Barnaby Rudge* would many years later be overshadowed by Dickens' *A Tale of Two Cities*, but as dramatized by the novelist, the forces propelling the Gordon Riots were not all that different from those sparking the French Revolution later that same decade. To neglect the children of today through indifference or complacency is to ensure big trouble when these children become adults, and perhaps even sooner than that.

6

A Christmas Carol (1843)

> *"'This boy is Ignorance. This girl is Want. Beware them both, and all of their degree, but most of all beware the boy, for on his brow I see that written which is Doom, unless the writing be erased.'"*[1]

During the worldwide pandemic of 2020 and its isolated Christmas season, the anti-isolationist holiday spirit exhorted in Charles Dickens' *A Christmas Carol* is more relevant than ever.[2] The message never grows old, and in fact only gains more urgency as time passes. And yet the deeper underlying message of Dickens' timeless classic is too often glossed over or missed completely. If *Barnaby Rudge* delved into mob psychology while sternly condemning it, then *A Christmas Carol* suggests the true beginning of a much larger societal disorder—within the indifferent or hostile attitudes of privileged classes towards its less fortunate members, and especially towards underprivileged children. These neglectful attitudes apply not only towards the fictional likes of Oliver Twist, Smike, Tiny Tim Cratchit, and other Dickensian children of lowly or disabled status, but more critically towards the unloved, unwanted, or "wolfish" (to quote Dickens) human offspring cast off by society, left to their own devices, and surrounded by an uncaring, hostile environment.[3] These pitiful yet frightening children are revealed to a horrified Scrooge by the Ghost of Christmas Present in the novella's pivotal scene (see epigraph), in which it is not too subtly implied, they will soon violently turn against the very same society producing them, unless urgently and benevolently attended to. This underlying message of Dickens' *A Christmas Carol* remains shockingly contemporary.

Thankfully, the purpose of this study is not to attempt any comprehensive summary of endlessly insightful commentaries on Dickens' rather concise text—that would easily comprise an entire book by itself—however, a few a brief agreed-upon facts are worth repeating, especially since these have affected nearly all subsequent film adaptations of the work.

These oft-overlooked factoids include Dickens' chance encounter with the Edinburgh tombstone of the non-fictional Ebenezer Scroggie in mid–1841; Dickens' brief but important interaction with Edgar Allan Poe (1809–1849) during his first American tour in early 1842; and, perhaps most significantly, Dickens' personal inspection of the London Field Lane Ragged School for indigent children later in 1842. Ebenezer Scrooge, like most immortal literary creations, is a composite of real-life people, but there can be little doubt that inspiration came partly from the since-vanished tombstone of Ebenezer Scroggie (1792–1836), by coincidence also the grand-nephew of famed Scottish economist Adam Smith.[4] Shortly thereafter, during the first half of 1842, Dickens toured America and there met one of his many literary admirers, the 33-year-old Edgar Allan Poe, who shared with the younger Dickens a love of the supernatural as a storytelling device, as well as a penchant for blurring the supernatural with the psychological. As for Dickens' subsequent tour of the Field Lane Ragged School, it must have brought back memories of *Oliver Twist*, since Dickens set the fictional Fagin's den of thieves near that same location.[5] Although the time period for *A Christmas Carol* is imprecise, and may well be early Victorian, it also harks back to the same late 1830s era of *Oliver Twist*, with vivid flashbacks to the distant past and Scrooge favorably citing the New Poor Law of 1834 while denying charitable obligations beyond his paying taxes in support of designated workhouse institutions.[6]

Michael Caine as Ebenezer Scrooge with Kermit the Frog as Bob Cratchit in *The Muppet Christmas Carol* (1992). Caine opted to play Scrooge completely straight, and as effectively as anyone in a crowded field (AA Film Archive / Alamy Stock Photo).

Above all, Dickens interjected into his synthesis what novelist Jane Smiley has called a "quintessentially

6. A Christmas Carol (1843)   59

modern mode of seeing the world"—"the root source of his greatness," as she put it.[7] Having completed his *American Notes* (based on his recent tour), and laying aside his partially complete, ambiguously received serial novel *Martin Chuzzlewit*, the 31-year-old Dickens returned to his wheelhouse, namely, combining social criticism with popular sentiment, and produced arguably his greatest masterpiece in less than three months. *A Christmas Carol in Prose: Being a Ghost-story of Christmas* "by Charles Dickens" with illustrations by John Leech, was published by Chapman & Hall on December 19, 1843.[8] The title came from the opening chapter (Stave I) in which street children attempt to serenade Scrooge at the office, but are rebuffed and physically driven off by him, thus beginning his long, Christmas night of the soul. It is the pre-conversion, "Bah! Humbug!" Scrooge, however, that everyone remembers—not the reformed crank he later becomes. The novella was an immediate hit, and has never been out of print, but also was, initially at least, a financial disappointment to Dickens since he had lavished high production costs on a work of which he was obviously proud. A century later, *A Christmas Carol*, along with *Oliver Twist*, became a top favorite among adaptors of Dickens for film, which is also to say that these rank among the most popular stories of all time for movie interpretations.[9] As for this survey, it will not attempt to cover or comment upon all the videos made to date, these including not only straight adaptations, but also endless variations on similar themes and plots from the same novella.[10] Instead, we shall focus on selected high points to date, and these alone will prove more than enough to fill an entire chapter.[11]

Fittingly, the earliest surviving fragment of a "feature" length silent film based on a Dickens book is drawn from *A Christmas Carol*. Retitled *Scrooge, or, Marley's Ghost* (1901), the short work was a product of British film pioneer producer Robert W. Paul and director Walter R. Booth, both of whom had earlier worked on now-lost segments from *Oliver Twist*.[12] The portion of *Marley's Ghost* still surviving prominently displays primitive special effects for the supernatural elements of the story, as well as the famous tombstone scene, among other attractions. The script or storyboard was reputedly based on a popular stage play developed by British acting stalwart Seymour Hicks, later going on to star in his own silent film version of the story (1913), and much later the first complete sound film version in 1935.[13] Also of note, and still surviving, is an 10-minute 1910 American silent feature produced by Edison and starring workhorse Irish-Australian performer Marc McDermott as Scrooge and the accomplished American thespian Charles Stanton Ogle as Bob Cratchit.[14] Many other silent adaptations from the same era, however, are considered lost, including notable productions from 1908, 1916, and 1923.[15] Loss of the 1916 version (*The Right to Be Happy*) is especially unfortunate in that it was considerably longer in length and featured the prominent New Zealand-born filmmaker Rupert Julian (1879–1943) both as director and lead actor.

Despite a highly competitive and prolific field, the first sound or talkie versions of *A Christmas Carol*, appearing between 1928 and 1951, have come to define what many audiences visualize for this tale, especially those within the Baby-Boomer age category. The distinction of the first sound excerpt for the novella goes to the UK-produced *Scrooge* (1928), starring Hackney (London)-born comedian Bransby Williams, a true Dickensian specialist working off his own script, and who for many early audiences came to represent the characters themselves. This nine-minute film is now believed to be lost. Williams later reprised his role in BBC live televised versions from 1936 and 1950, the last one when Williams was 80 years old.[16] As early as 1935, however, the venerable Seymour Hicks, who had helped to inspire Robert W. Paul in 1901, entered into the talking-pictures genre with his memorable performance in Twickenham Films' *Scrooge*, a still well-regarded effort demonstrating how much can be achieved with a good script and good acting, notwithstanding otherwise meager resources.[17] In response, Hollywood MGM came back three years later with *A Christmas Carol* (1938) starring Reginald Owen in a caricature of Dickens' protagonist shrewdly designed by producer-writer Joseph Mankiewicz to amuse rather than offend American audiences.[18] More interesting was the portrayal of the Cratchits by members of the Canadian American Lockhart clan (Gene, Kathleen, and June) as a kind of hardscrabble, Depression-era, indestructible family unit. For some, the 1938 MGM film remains definitive, although it does not hold a candle quality-wise to other MGM Dickens films of the period such as *David Copperfield* (1935) or *A Tale of Two Cities* (1935). Part of the problem is a host of changes in the script to the novella text, adding little or nothing dramatically (despite the star power employed) but still leading many viewers to incorrectly believe they are getting an accurate read of Dickens' original. Another problem with this and most pre-war film versions is they omit the disturbing scene of Ignorance and Want presented to a stunned Scrooge by the Ghost of Christmas Present, thus severely diminishing overall shock value to both Scrooge and to most viewing audiences.

Thirteen years later, in 1951, after the disruptions of World War II had somewhat subsided and Anglo-American audiences yearned for a return to normalcy, came *Scrooge*, a British joint venture with United Artists featuring a bravura performance by Scottish stage actor Alastair Sim in the title role, surrounded by a veteran English cast and a 12-year-old Glyn Dearman as Tiny Tim.[19] Distinguished British film composer Richard Addinsell (1904–1977) supplied a simple but effective score, incorporating

English folk melodies into the soundtrack. Dickens' novella was considerably reworked for the script but, crucially, the original revelation of Ignorance and Want was reinstalled for the first time on film. Unsuspecting critics initially reacted with horror, but the otherwise prevailing mood of jollity won the day, and it is now not uncommon to see this production lauded as the *Christmas Carol* to end all *Christmas Carols*, especially for general audiences coming of age after the war. The overall effect of this classic movie is that of a sweet confection leaving a slightly bitter aftertaste—an effect probably near to the original intent of the novelist.

Music has always figured centrally to Dickens' storyline, beginning with the novella text, its title, its singing characters, and even the organization of sections into musical "staves" rather than chapters. Later, almost all film adaptations of *A Christmas Carol* have made generous use of music, mostly composed specially for these productions, from the very moment sound was first incorporated into the medium. By the postwar era of 20th-century television, and most notably in the immediate wake of Alastair Sim's 1951 tour de force, *A Christmas Carol* had become a holiday viewing franchise and was ripe for embellishment.[20] Accordingly, a number of nearly full-blown musicals and, by the 21st century, even some chamber operas, had begun to appear.[21] The most interesting of these earliest musical adaptations oftentimes centered around the person of highly underrated British performer and Dickensian specialist Basil Rathbone. In 1954, Rathbone played Marley to Fredric March's Scrooge in a CBS television broadcast with music and lyrics by the distinguished American team of Bernard Herrmann (1911–1975) and Maxwell Anderson (1888–1959).[22] Soon afterwards, in 1956, Rathbone starred as Scrooge for *The Stingiest Man in Town*, another musical, this time for ABC's *The Alcoa Hour*, with music and words by Austro-American composer Fred Spielman (1906–1997) and Italian-American Janice Torre (1914–1985).[23] Over two decades later, in 1978, Spielman & Torre's musical *The Stingiest Man in Town* was revived by the American producers Arthur Rankin, Jr., and Jules Bass, this time as a Japanese-style animated feature with Walter Matthau voicing over a Scrooge very near to Matthau himself in cartoonish appearance.[24] Both live and animated versions of *Stingiest Man* were well-received and still can be found on DVD.[25]

If *The Stingiest Man in Town* today is fondly remembered by many, then the 1970 musical film extravaganza *Scrooge* continues to divide critics and audiences despite many accolades received during its own day. Following in the immediate aftermath of the 1968 Dickensian blockbuster *Oliver!*, the musical *Scrooge* brought to the table big-budget Panavision and a formidable creative team, beginning with 33-year-old matinee idol Albert Finney in the lead role as Scrooge, one of the youngest actors to ever portray the iconic miser on screen. Director Ronald Neame (1911–2010) had an impressive resume that included working with David Lean on his seminal versions of *Great Expectations* and *Oliver Twist* during the late 1940s. Along similar lines, veteran stalwart Alec Guinness was recruited to play Marley's ghost.[26] For music, British film specialist Leslie Bricusse was brought in after having previously failed to musically translate Dickens for American audiences with his *Pickwick* ("If I Ruled the World") from 1963. This time around, the results were unfortunately similar, despite Bricusse having notable successes at the time with other movie themes associated with James Bond, Willie Wonka, Doctor Doolittle, and Mr. Chips. For *Scrooge*, American critics were particularly savage in their negative reviews. Part of the problem was a big disconnect between the original text and the movie. Dickens' Scrooge, by definition, is simply not a song and dance man until after his conversion late in the story; yet there he is from the beginning of the movie, singing and dancing. Disturbing images of Ignorance and Want are completely omitted and understandably so, given the overall mood of merriment. Audiences just did not buy it. Nevertheless, *Scrooge* the musical was showered with prizes, including Oscars, Golden Globes, and BAFTAs.

While *Scrooge* the musical was getting a decidedly mixed reception, another notable film version of the Dickens novella came unexpectedly from an unlikely direction. *A Christmas Carol* (1971) was produced for BBC/ABC television and directed by maverick Canadian-born animation specialist Richard Williams (1933–2019), later going on to great fame with *Who Framed Roger Rabbit* (1988).[27] The legendary Williams' first Academy Award, however, was for *A Christmas Carol*, for which Shakespearean stage star Michael Redgrave was brought in to narrate, Redgrave's stage colleague Michael Hordern to do Marley's ghost, and last but not least, a 71-year-old Alastair Sim was persuaded to reprise and voiceover the role of Scrooge. Images of Ignorance and Want are not omitted. Williams based his animation on the original 1843 illustrations by John Leech, giving the production an unusually bleak visual style. Serious Australian composer Tristram Cary (1925–2008) was retained to provide a darkly somber soundtrack rather than song-and-dance numbers. The 25-minute result is still considered by many to be the finest animated version of the tale among a very crowded field. Williams' surprising achievement gained immediate recognition from the Oscars (Best Animated Short Film), thus firmly establishing an already considerable reputation, enabling him to successfully assay more ambitious future projects.

The lofty animation standards set by the Richard Williams production of 1971 did not prevent other good or not-so-good ones from following over the next 30 years, if nothing else to fill a steady demand

6. A Christmas Carol (1843)

for celebrity actors wanting to voiceover the same material. A sampling of these animated films extending from the late 1970s to the end of the century included Looney Tunes' *Bugs Bunny's Christmas Carol* (1979), Burbank Films Australia's *A Christmas Carol* (1982), Walt Disney Pictures' *Mickey's Christmas Carol* (1983), Hanna-Barbera's *A Flintstones Christmas Carol* (1994), DIC Production's *A Christmas Carol* (1997), and Illuminated Films' *Christmas Carol: The Movie* (2001).[28] One obvious financial advantage to this repeating template (especially for television) was that one could employ the voice and production credit of a brand name celebrity without having to pay a full celebrity fee for acting. Alternatively, a tried-and-tested animated brand name such as Bugs Bunny or Mickey Mouse could be combined with a tried-and-tested public domain book such as Dickens' novella without having to pay much extra for original material. In effect, no good opportunity for easy profit went unexploited. The inevitable downside was that the market for this prototype became quickly saturated, and hence today, contemporary animated productions of Dickens' indestructible holiday tale are much harder to come by.

During the early 1980s, however, a happy confluence of circumstances converged to result in what is widely regarded the finest movie version of *A Christmas Carol*. In 1982, American Oscar-winner George C. Scott had teamed with British director Clive Donner—another alumnus from the 1951 film *Scrooge*—for a well-received, if somewhat offbeat version of *Oliver Twist*.[29] After this notable success, the same creative partnership was renewed in 1984 for *A Christmas Carol*.[30] Around the same time, British actor Roger Rees was gaining international fame for his lead role in the Royal Shakespeare Company's *Nicholas Nickleby*, and Rees' services were retained to both narrate Donner's *Christmas Carol* and play opposite Scott as Scrooge's irrepressible nephew Fred. A crucial decision was made to stick as closely to the novella text as possible. Scott as Scrooge was at his typically understated best. Filming was done in the well-preserved medieval town of Shrewsbury. Above all, at the height of an age in which greed was considered good, Scrooge's calculated miserliness, along with jolting visual images of Ignorance and Want, hit television holiday audiences like a sledgehammer. This British production has never been surpassed in pure terms of fulfilling Dickens' authorial intentions; moreover, it is still, nearly four decades later, aired on a regular basis, and justifiably so.

Although not a strict retelling of Dickens' novella, and certainly not a faithful adaptation of his work, the mass popularity of Paramount's *Scrooged* (1988), along with its retention of enough specifics from the original text, merits inclusion herein. American comic virtuoso Bill Murray as Scrooge-like TV producer Frances Xavier Cross somehow fits right into the spirit of the proceedings, like a stock character reflecting Dickens' persistent love for *commedia dell'arte*.[31] Featuring star turns by the likes of Robert Mitchum, Alfre Woodard, Karen Allen, Michael J. Pollard, John Forsythe, Carol Kane, and even former New York Dolls lead singer David Johansen, this "apogee of cultural integration" (Joss Marsh) moved the pre–Victorian London setting to New York City of the late 1980s and did not suffer for the change.[32] An appropriate soundtrack was provided by the prolific American composer Danny Elfman (b. 1953). *Scrooged* was not the first film effort to transport Dickens' Victorian tale to New York City, or even to the United States, but it is undoubtably the best remembered among these.[33] The true pioneer in this regard may have been a now-lost 1955 live television broadcast of another modernized *Christmas Carol* from the *Eye on New York* documentary series, written as a labor of love by CBS President Bill Leonard, with highly underrated American character actor and Charles Dickens enthusiast Jonathan Harris as a ruthless corporate executive named Ebenezer Scrooge.[34]

An even greater "apogee of cultural integration" appeared in late 1992 with *The Muppet Christmas Carol*, which easily could have been a trite and forgettable affair, but instead became one of the best-loved films of the novella ever made.[35] This was in no small part due to a tremendous lead performance by Michael Caine, who had been looking for a good Dickensian role to devote his considerable talents to ever since being rejected to play the character of Bill Sikes in the stage musical *Oliver!* back in 1960. Whereas many a gifted actor would have balked at being surrounded by puppetry doing children's song and dance numbers, Caine saw a creative opportunity, and he delivered, playing the role of Scrooge straight, seriously, and with restrained intensity, much like George C. Scott from the previous decade. After a relatively slow start at the box office, *The Muppet Christmas Carol* eventually went on to become a highly profitable venture for Walt Disney Pictures, mainly based on its word-of-mouth reputation among viewers. Its exponential success also began a long process by which the Muppets franchise was later acquired by Disney from its creators, the Jim Henson Company, in 2004.

By the mid–1990s, more innovation was forthcoming. Along these lines, Lifetime cable presented American television viewers with the first female Scrooge to reach a mass audience. *Ebbie* (Ebbie Scrooge), subtitled *Miracle at Christmas: Ebbie's Story*, hit the airwaves in December 1995, starring soap opera icon Susan Lucci (*All My Children*) in the title role as a mean-spirited department store owner. For good measure, Scrooge's long-suffering assistant, "Roberta" Cratchit (played by Wendy Crewson), is also female, while acclaimed Canadian performer Molly Parker, long before she became more famous in various major roles on Netflix, plays

Scrooge's tragic sister Frannie. Marley is portrayed by Jeffrey DeMunn, later becoming associated with the popular films of director Frank Darabont. Ignorance and Want are briefly but effectively reinserted into the plot. Lifetime's experiment in gender-reversal was well received by audiences and critics, and then two years later, in 1997, an edgier version of the same concept appeared with the formidable Cicely Tyson starring in the USA Network television special *Ms. Scrooge*, now widely available on Hallmark, YouTube, and other platforms. With a gritty Providence, Rhode Island, setting (filmed in Toronto, Ontario), *Ms. Scrooge* continued Tyson's longstanding creative partnership with director John Korty (b. 1936), and co-starred the late Katherine Helmond (*Soap*) as a very convincing female version of Marley, playing opposite Tyson's Ebenita Scrooge, an urban banker coming across more like a loan shark. American character actor Michael Beach ably plays Ebenita's likeable nephew, the Reverend Luke, a church minister, whose father (Ebenita's brother) had been killed in Vietnam. Though relatively ignored at the time, *Ms. Scrooge* has held up well over the years as a feature film and still displays an attractive combination of skillful acting, clever writing, and vivid cinematography. It also represents a pronounced forerunner of the contemporary trend for making Dickens adaptations a multiracial, multicultural experience for viewing audiences.

Dramatization of *A Christmas Carol* in the form of a one-man show was an established tradition extending all the way back to Charles Dickens himself, who had read excerpts from this popular work during his last public reading shortly before his death in 1870.[36] As the 20th century concluded, British Shakespearean actor Patrick Stewart, flush with popular success and personal wealth from his lead role in *Star Trek: The Next Generation*, returned to the live stage by reviving this old art form. In the hands of someone talented and skilled like Stewart, acclaim was immediate. By the end of the 1990s, a decision at TNT had been made to surround Stewart with a first-rate cinematic team that included the late director David Jones (1934–2008), the late screenwriter Peter Barnes (1931–2004), and fellow Brit movie and stage performer Richard E. Grant, playing Bob Cratchit opposite Stewart's well-honed Ebenezer Scrooge. Digital special effects were combined with several episodes in the novella not typically dramatized on screen, along with the essential but disturbing images of Ignorance and Want. The finished product was broadcast to American television audiences in December of 1999. Though not possessing the detailed nuance of George C. Scott nor the understated intensity of Michael Caine, Stewart's depiction of the world's most famous fictional miser drew deservedly positive notices, as well as visceral audience response. It was a good way to end the century for Dickens' masterpiece on film, and quite a technological advance from the modest ambitions of *Scrooge: or, Marley's Ghost*, some 98 years earlier in 1901.

Curiously, the 21st century began with yet another serious attempt to convert the tale into a popular musical experience. Hallmark's *A Christmas Carol: The Musical* (2004) featured a celebrity cast, the most interesting of which included the three ghosts of Christmas represented by Jane Krakowski (*30 Rock*), Jesse L. Martin (*Rent*), and Geraldine Chaplin, daughter of Charlie Chaplin. Other recognized names were utilized to depict Scrooge and Marley, played respectively by Kelsey Grammer (*Frasier*) and Jason Alexander (*Seinfeld*), but their performances received mixed reviews. Stage and screen veteran director Arthur Allan Seidelman presided over the collaborative effort. The 2004 production was based on a successful 1994 Madison Square Garden show written by American lyricist Lynn Ahern (b. 1948).[37] Unlike the 1970 musical version, Ignorance and Want were fully dramatized for the 2004 television movie. For music, heavyweight in-house Disney composer Alan Menken (b. 1949) was brought in. Although the music itself proved to be forgettable, the visual results were noteworthy, while the plot provided some unusual aspects and clever embellishments.

Five years later, in 2009, another offbeat venture appeared under the Disney banner. *A Christmas Carol*, directed by American special-effects specialist Robert Zemeckis (b. 1952) was the third time that Disney had adapted the story for the screen and the first time that 3D motion capture technology was used for Dickens, oftentimes to very creepy effect. American celebrity star Jim Carrey was brought in for voicing not only Scrooge, but the three ghosts of Christmas as well. The rest of the voiceover cast was equally impressive, including the likes of Gary Oldman, Colin Firth, Bob Hoskins, Robin Wright Penn, and Lesley Manville.[38] Effective music was provided by American film composer Alan Silvestri (b. 1950). Fittingly, Ignorance and Want were not excluded from the screenplay. Despite critics' professed shock at the prevailing darkness of tone, the innovative production proved to be a huge box office success.

Possibly encouraged by the unlikely profit margins of the 2009 Disney production, the BBC in 2019 launched its own three-part miniseries for *A Christmas Carol*, broadcast in the United States on FX Networks. Written by Steven Knight (*Peaky Blinders*) and starring British-born independent film icon Guy Pearce as a very convincing Ebenezer Scrooge, the latest expansive BBC version had little to do with Dickens' original text, except to follow an approximate outline of events. The tone and look of the series were unrelentingly dark. While nearly everyone liked Pearce's lead performance, the BBC miniseries failed to attract an audience beyond Anglocentric fans of *Peaky Blinders*.[39] Perhaps more than anything, the miniseries demonstrated once again the dangers and pitfalls of taking too much liberty with a classic Charles Dickens storyline. Deceptively simple in appearance and effortless on the surface, the genius behind the creation of the original novella is possibly best demonstrated whenever the smallest details are injudiciously changed.

By contrast, a brand-new feature-length version of Dickens' holiday ghost story (arriving in theaters as this is being written during the 2020 pandemic Christmas season) must be considered a case study in how far the traditional tale can be adapted to modern tastes without violating the spirit of the original text. The latest cinematic version of *A Christmas Carol* is mainly the imaginative product of a British up-and-coming, sister-brother, director-writer team, Jacqui and David Morris.[40] The Morris siblings recently gained international attention with their 2018 documentary titled *Nureyev: Lifting the Curtain*, and their latest work appears to be a natural outgrowth of that earlier, critically acclaimed effort. Combining live action Dickensian drama with ballet, voiceovers, and spectacular visual effects, the Morris' *Christmas Carol* features a highly diverse cast, including Andy Serkis, Daniel Kaluuya, Carey Mulligan, Martin Freeman, Simon Russell Beale, Leslie Caron, and Siân Phillips, to name a few.[41] The unorthodox results are bound to cause a degree of controversy among audiences and critics, only to prove (if nothing else), that the compelling fictional works of Charles Dickens remain as relevant as ever to our unsettled contemporary existence.

For Charles Dickens the novelist, his long journey through popular fiction that began in 1837 with *The Pickwick Papers* (along with its own famous Christmas interlude chapter) seemed to come full circle six years later in 1843 with *A Christmas Carol*. Afterwards, Dickens was occasionally referred to as The Man Who Invented Christmas, although this is surely an overstatement. It would be far more accurate to say that Dickens as a storyteller helped to popularize the modern notion of Christmas celebration in the English-speaking world, especially for those living in or near an urban environment. To place this significant achievement into a wider context, we should remember that, to write *A Christmas Carol*, Dickens temporarily set aside another novel he was then working on— one much longer, complex, and difficult to read—to achieve lasting fame with his immortal holiday parable. Despite their many differences, however, *Martin Chuzzlewit* and *A Christmas Carol* both share an unrelenting hostility towards modern notions of capitalism, particularly in its distinctively cruel American interpretation. Nevertheless, *A Christmas Carol*, though much shorter in length than *Oliver Twist*, *The Old Curiosity Shop*, *David Copperfield*, *A Tale of Two Cities*, and *Great Expectations*, joined the core group of famous works for which Dickens will always be remembered, even among those who do little or no reading, thanks in large part to their easy adaptability for both stage and screen. And yet, before Dickens was finished writing, four additional Christmas novellas, all much lesser known than the original prototype, would be forthcoming.

7

Martin Chuzzlewit (1842–1844)

> "*Martin knew nothing about America, or he would have known perfectly well that if its individual citizens, to a man, are to be believed, it always is depressed, and always is stagnated, and always is at an alarming crisis, and never otherwise; though as a body they are ready to make oath upon the Evangelists at any hour of the day or night, that it is the most thriving and prosperous of all countries on the habitable globe.*"[1]

Following publication of *A Christmas Carol* in December 1843, Dickens resumed work on a much longer novel that had never ceased regular publication in monthly installments during this same period, but by late 1843 taken a new direction following its lukewarm reception (and sales) earlier that same year. By July 1844, *The Life and Adventures of Martin Chuzzlewit* had completed its initial serial run ("Edited by Boz"), and the full novel "by Charles Dickens" was published soon afterwards by Chapman & Hall of London, with illustrations by "Phiz" (aka Hablot Knight Browne), and dedicated to Dickens' fabulously wealthy sponsor of charitable activities, Lady Angela Georgina Burdett-Coutts (1814–1906). The sales of the serialization for *Martin Chuzzlewit* were disappointing (especially compared to what Dickens was otherwise used to), causing the novelist to change publishers—despite many previous successes with Chapman & Hall—and to fiercely defend the artistic quality of this novel ever afterwards. To salvage the project midstream, Dickens temporarily shelved writing it (but not its serialization), took a few months off to write *A Christmas Carol*, then resumed *Martin Chuzzlewit*, after having decided to change the plotline by sending its young namesake hero briefly across the Atlantic Ocean, and to incorporate a rather lengthy and heavy-handed satire of the pre–Civil War United States, having recently toured the eastern part of North America himself only a year earlier.

Even after considerable alteration of its storyline and tone, however, final sales figures for *Martin Chuzzlewit* remained far below the novelist's normal expectations, and the work has continued over the years to draw heavy criticism from readers and reviewers alike, especially because of its pronounced anti–American sentiments. Nevertheless, in the words of biographer Claire Tomalin, *Martin Chuzzlewit* contains many "scatterings of brilliance" as well as valuable insights into Dickens' skeptical attitudes towards Anglo-American commerce and its dogmatic apologists.[2] Like the relatively forgotten *Barnaby Rudge* written before it, *Martin Chuzzlewit* offers surprising rewards to open-minded modern readers, and at least one outstanding film interpretation.[3] Tomalin again on the novel: "The satire on high finance is as good today as it was then."[4] The sharply portrayed, sanctimonious vanity of Seth Pecksniff and criminal brutality of Jonas Chuzzlewit have lost none of their offensiveness over the centuries. In contrast to the morally reformed Ebenezer Scrooge of *A Christmas Carol*, the unrepentant, self-serving behavior of these repulsive villains from *Martin Chuzzlewit* are still perhaps Dickens' most effective representations of anti–Christian behavior from the novelist's point of view. In a similar vein, the less odious, but comically opportunistic machinations of the story's alcoholic nursemaid, Mrs. Sarah Gamp, are vividly depicted to the extent that this celebrated character, in many respects, has within the public imagination outlived the same novel in which she originally appeared.[5]

Critics of the novel have focused on various anomalies, such as its blunt anti–American slant, disjointed narrative flow, and structural unevenness. The true weakness of *Martin Chuzzlewit*, however, is rarely commented upon. In his Preface and Postscript to the novel, both added many years later (circa 1868), Dickens repeatedly referred to the time of its publication—accurately stated as 24–25 years earlier—and hence its approximate time of conceptualization as well. Both references are slightly apologetic in tone for Dickens' biting criticisms of the then 66-year-old United States, noting that his impressions were that of a reliable eyewitness in 1842, but that upon a second visit in 1868–24 years afterwards and post–Civil War—things in the U.S. had noticeably improved. This written correction and update were understandable since, by that time, Dickens was addressing his remarks to American, British, and all English-speaking audiences. These same comments, however, only underscore what is left unspoken by Dickens—namely, that *Martin Chuzzlewit*, in stark contrast to his previous works—is lacking in any personal nostalgia, other than inclusion of critical impressions offered by the novelist less than two years after his experiences. There is a conspicuous absence of personal hindsight within the novel itself—no references to childhood, to the older generations of his parents or grandparents, and certainly no pre–Victorian settings of time or place. On the contrary, to read *Martin Chuzzlewit* today is to be placed squarely within the early Victorian period of English history and its American antebellum counterpart circa 1842–1843. More specifically, the urban environment of the Chuzzlewit family is that of London, then at the apex of English world power and prosperity, contrasted with a turbulent American backwater ranging from ramshackle to barbaric in its comparatively regressive economic and political development.

Despite scathing reviews for his critique, there is no indication that Dickens was being anything less than completely truthful in his descriptions of the American frontier from the early 1840s. To begin with (and to repeat), the novelist was there himself in 1842. Pushing west along the Ohio River Valley from Cincinnati, Ohio, Dickens arrived at Cairo (pronounced Cay-roe), Illinois, at its confluence with the Mississippi River, then he apparently lost interest in going any farther, turned around, and returned East. Dismally portrayed in the novel as the isolated startup river town of "Eden" where young Martin and his faithful companion Mark Tapley disembark, Cairo was at that point in American history little more than a wilderness outpost on the map with a wishful-sounding name. Not until some 20 years later would it begin to significantly grow when a still-obscure Brigadier General Ulysses S. Grant used it as a staging ground for his great Southern Offensive of 1862—a military campaign that would eventually win the war in the West for the federals. In 1842, however, Cairo, Illinois, struggled to attract people, commerce, or development. Before being transformed into a federal arsenal during the

Jean Simmons as Miss Havisham in *Great Expectations* (1989). The 60-year-old Simmons had, as a 17-year-old, played the young Estella in David Lean's *Great Expectations* some 43 years earlier (Moviestore Collection Ltd / Alamy Stock Photo).

war, Cairo consisted of little more than primitive infrastructure interspersed with breeding grounds for disease. Even Native Americans tended to avoid the place. This is what Charles Dickens saw for himself in 1842, describing "Eden" as "The waters of the Deluge might have left it but a week before; so choked with slime and matted growth was the hideous swamp which bore that name."[6]

More offensive to Anglo-American sensibilities than Dickens' repulsive physical description of the western Ohio River Valley was his depiction of the American character, dominated by hucksters and con artists, embodied by the unsavory (and suggestively named) War Correspondent Jefferson Brick.[7] Young Martin encounters these unscrupulous promoters in London, just when a fragile relationship with his powerful grandfather (the older Martin Chuzzlewit) is about to deteriorate, and the restless youth is completely taken in by them. On one hand, while constantly complaining, finding fault, or blaming scapegoats, these skillful salesmen simultaneously laud the U.S., and "Eden" in particular, as a land of unparalleled opportunity and prosperity (see epigraph). Young Martin is conned, suffers for it, later comes to his senses, and eventually repents, but apart from this optimistic scenario, the prevailing images staying with readers are that of American hucksterism and the gullibility of its victims. In a similar manner, the dignified but outspoken frankness of Martin's humble sidekick Mark Tapley is contrasted with the repressed ("grinning assent") silence of an African American slave named Cicero, who is assigned to attend Mark and Martin after the latter has been thoroughly deceived by the slave's American masters.[8]

The topic is worth reflection because it likely helps to explain why film adaptations of *Martin Chuzzlewit* have been so scarce over the last century or more. One can endlessly debate the literary merits of the work—Dickens himself had a high opinion of it—but at the end of the day there can be little denying that the novel simply did not tell audiences things they wanted to hear, and sales have suffered accordingly. As for Dickens' reasons in writing the novel over an extended period (by his otherwise rapid standards, at least), interrupted by *A Christmas Carol* in late 1843, several motivators may be easily surmised. First, there is a likelihood that Dickens' alleged hostility towards the United States was in fact innate and long suppressed, despite its sudden published emergence following his 1842 American tour. Dickens was born in early 1812 at Portsmouth, England, where his father, John Dickens, was on the payroll of the British Navy, then embroiled in the Napoleonic Wars against France. Great Britain was also in the process of gearing up for its three-year conflict against the United States, an indecisive but bitter struggle not likely forgotten by partisans on either side. After that, came an international debate over slavery, legally abolished by Great Britain by 1833, but stubbornly preserved in the United States until the hideous bloodletting of its War Between the States. Dickens, despite an overtly ambivalent personal attitude towards African Americans, repeatedly wrote against slavery as an institution, first in his *American Notes* of 1842, and then in *Martin Chuzzlewit* of 1842–1844. Just as he had been unimpressed with the American western frontier during his recent tour, his brief encounters with American slavery had left him disgusted as well. Lastly, at a time when he was still struggling financially, Dickens came to realize that most Americans had no intention of paying him any royalties for book sales, however robust these sales were, and moreover appeared offended at the very notion of honoring copyrights whenever Dickens brought the matter to their attention. Given these elements, it therefore seems likely that *Martin Chuzzlewit* gave Dickens full opportunity to vent his longstanding objections against the U.S., notwithstanding an otherwise professed admiration, especially given his recent firsthand experiences while on tour.

In 1912, precisely one hundred years after Dickens' birth, came several silent films celebrating his centenary, among these *Martin Chuzzlewit*, a short three-reel adaptation by the American Edison Studios.[9] This film now appears to be lost, but some rumors of existence persist.[10] Co-directors were the prolific Oscar C. Apfel (1878–1938) and James Searle Dawley (1877–1949); starring actors included well-known marquee names from the silent era such as Guy Hedlund (Jonas), Charles Ogle (Pecksniff), and Harold Shaw (the benevolently innocent Tom Pinch, yet another remarkable Dickens character creation).[11] It is unfortunate the film is lost or unavailable for screening because production quality was reportedly high—the creative team assembled was certainly outstanding—and given the unusualness of the novel on film at any point in time, along with ongoing controversy surrounding the book itself, any surviving fragments would be considered valuable for these reasons alone.[12] American reviews of the film at the time were grudgingly respectful while simultaneously circumspect regarding anti–American content. The British press was predictably more enthusiastic.[13] Surprisingly, however, another American adaptation of *Martin Chuzzlewit* was soon forthcoming, just as World War I was beginning in Europe.

In October 1914, Edison's domestic film rival and soon-to-be corporate partner, the American Mutoscope and Biograph Company, released its own two-reel silent version of *Martin Chuzzlewit*.[14] This later work reportedly still exists within the archives of the George Eastman Museum located in Rochester, New York. The Biograph Company had in fact pioneered the depiction of Dickens' novels on film with its benchmark 1897 silent short, *Death of Nancy Sykes*, drawn from *Oliver Twist*. For the 1914 update of *Martin Chuzzlewit*, British director Travers Vale (1865–1927) was brought in to oversee production. An interesting cast included a 22-year-old Alan Hale Sr. (born Rufus Edward Mackhan) as the young namesake hero of the story, long before Hale Sr. became a Hollywood icon during both the silent and talkie eras of filmmaking.[15] The anti–American aspects of the novel were reportedly cut or toned down in this newer version, which probably explains why the film was made so soon after the 1912 Edison production, presumably as a concession to American nickelodeon audiences. Some three years later, in 1917, the United States would officially enter World War I, effectively coming to the rescue of Great Britain and France by breaking an entrenched stalemate on the Western Front. Whether there is any causal connection between the momentous American intervention in the Great War and the Biograph Company's earlier decision to make its British novel adaptation appear less overtly anti–American, is unknown.[16]

After the 1914 Biograph *Martin Chuzzlewit*, literally half a century passed with no known further attempts at filming the novel. It would not be exaggeration to say that Dickens' least popular work was nearly forgotten during the interim, even by students of English literature. Then in early 1964, BBC television produced a sprawling, 13-episode, six-hour-plus miniseries for *Martin Chuzzlewit*, employing a first-rate creative team led by British playwright Constance Cox, who also adapted for the BBC Dickens' *Bleak House* (1959), *Oliver Twist* (1962), *The Old Curiosity Shop* (1962), and *A Tale of Two Cities* (1965) during that same era.[17] Notably (and disappointingly), the BBC 1964 production of *Martin Chuzzlewit* appears to be now lost as well.[18] In addition to the interesting writer-director team of Constance Cox and Joan Craft, this miniseries featured several intriguing cast members. For example, the late and very long-careered Angela Baddeley is listed as portraying Dickens' astringent nurse-for-hire, Mrs. Gamp, an important role apparently more restored to the plot thanks to the longer-length advantages of a miniseries. At the time, Baddeley was coming directly off a minor role in Tony Richardson's Oscar–winning film version of *Tom Jones* (1963), based on the novel by Henry Fielding, a writer known to have been admired by Dickens. Later, Baddeley would go on to greater fame as the family servant-cook Mrs. Bridges in the hit BBC TV series *Upstairs, Downstairs* (1971–1975). Today, not being able to screen her 1964 portrayal of Dickens' Mrs. Gamp must be considered a tragedy for the performing arts. After this, it would be another 30 years before anyone would attempt to film *Martin Chuzzlewit*. It seemed as if the 1844 novel was somehow cursed, or, more alarming still, banished from the cinema given its ongoing anti–American reputation.

By 1994, 72-year-old British Shakespearean actor Paul Scofield had deservedly won for himself just about every accolade possible for someone in that profession. Earlier the same year (in 1994) he had appeared in Robert Redford's critically acclaimed film, *Quiz Show* (as game show host Mark Van Doren), for which he would soon be nominated for an Oscar as Best Supporting Actor. Yet it was well known within the industry that Scofield's true passion was for the stage, not cinema, and by this time he was looking more to fulfill his own personal aspirations. Curiously, at this late point in his career, he had done little related to Charles Dickens.[19] Scofield not only set about changing that, but also (in typical fashion for him) chose a project that most of his colleagues had avoided, namely, the widely disparaged *Martin Chuzzlewit*. The result in late 1994 was a six-episode, nearly seven-hour miniseries jointly produced by the BBC and WGBH Boston.[20] Scofield opted to play not one, but two roles—that of Old Martin Chuzzlewit, plus that of his evil brother, Anthony Chuzzlewit. Given Scofield's legendary skills with makeup, it was not even necessary to pretend these brothers were twins, which in fact they were not supposed to be according to the original text. The British writer-director team of David Lodge (b. 1935) and Pedr James (b. 1940) were brought in, along with British composer Geoffrey Burgon (1941–2010) to provide a musical score. Many of the controversial American scenes from the original text were reinstated, although young Martin's brief, unhappy sojourn to the United States is presented as more the result of his own impulsiveness and gullibility, rather than the relentless hucksterism of American promoters. The fortunate result of this collaborative effort was a worthy and memorable film production—the only one in fact currently available for general viewership.

Casting for the 1994 miniseries contained other delights too numerous to fully list herein. First was an 86-year-old John Mills as Anthony Chuzzlewit's put-upon servant Mr. Chuffey, a more elderly stylistic relation to Dickens' Bob Cratchit from *A Christmas Carol*. Mills had an impressive Dickensian track record, beginning with his game-changing performance nearly half a century earlier as Pip in David Lean's classic *Great Expectations* (1946). Another was the always-excellent Elizabeth Spriggs as Mrs. Gamp.[21] A still relatively unknown Pete Postlethwaite, then beginning to make a name for himself as a recognizable film villain, was recruited to portray the unsavory Montague Tigg, Dickens' small-time London street hustler transforming himself into a high-finance swindler and brains behind the sinister Anglo-Bengalee Disinterested Loan and Life Assurance Company.[22] First-rate British comediennes Julia Sawalha and Emma Chambers portrayed the two scheming and feuding daughters of Seth Pecksniff, ironically named Mercy and Charity. Last, but not least, was the full realization of the odious Pecksniff himself by future British celebrity actor Tom Wilkinson. Although Wilkinson had been gradually coming into prominence since the late 1970s, it was his bravura performance in the 1994 *Martin Chuzzlewit* miniseries that drew widespread attention and rave reviews. Three years later, in 1997, this would lead directly to his casting for a major role in the hit film, *The Full Monty*, and Wilkinson has been visible on the public viewing radar ever since. It is difficult to imagine Pecksniff being depicted any more vividly than in Wilkinson's interpretation, for which he displayed a strong affinity with Dickensian fictional characterization. In this memorable performance, Wilkinson's Pecksniff from *Martin Chuzzlewit* becomes a clear forerunner to more famous Dickensian villains such as Uriah Heep (*David Copperfield*) and John Jasper (*The Mystery of Edwin Drood*).[23]

The close literary relationship between *Martin Chuzzlewit* and *A Christmas Carol*, intertwining both chronologically and thematically, has long been overshadowed by the former's perceived political incorrectness and lack of popularity. The bad behavior of the villains, whether these be the false piety of Pecksniff, the murderous instincts of Jonas, the scheming deceptions of Tigg, the self-serving scams of American con men—all of these are viewed as morally much, much worse by the novelist than say, the reformed miserliness of Ebenezer Scrooge or even the tardy repentance of Jacob Marley. Perhaps fully aware that the tough lessons of *Martin Chuzzlewit* were not being accepted by the Victorian reading public, Dickens turned to writing more Christmas-themed novellas, in fact, four more after *A Christmas Carol*, obviously trying to take advantage of that concurrent work's near-universal popularity. It was also likely a way for him to develop similar themes in a less heavy-handed manner than in the longer novel form. Despite his firm opinion that *Martin Chuzzlewit* was a work of high quality, Dickens may have come to the sad realization, perhaps for the first time in his professional writing career, that high quality was sometimes, if not oftentimes, at odds with popular and critical demand. Dickens' disappointment in the lackluster commercial appeal of *Martin Chuzzelwit* was later punctuated by several stark realities: that only four meaningful attempts have been made to dramatize it on film, that it took until 1994 (150 years after publication of the novel) to achieve sustained cinematic availability, and that it was *the very last* major work by Dickens to become generally available on video. And even this was mainly thanks to the eccentric, yet highly bankable, acting talents of Paul Scofield.

8

Other Christmas Novellas (1844–1848)

> *"'The voice of Time,' said the Phantom, 'cries to man, Advance! Time is for his achievement and improvement; for his greater worth, his greater happiness, his better life; his progress onward to that goal within its knowledge and its view, and set there, in the period when Time and He began.'"*[1]

When the financially disappointing *Martin Chuzzlewit* completed its serialization in mid-1844, Dickens turned his fuller attention to earning a living, more specifically, to writing more "Christmas" novellas. Although the high production costs of *A Christmas Carol* in late 1843 had prevented it from being a monetary windfall for its author, gross sales were robust and critical praise lavish. Four more similar works were to follow over the next four years (1844–1848), though none would achieve a fraction of the fame or long-term popularity of their prototype. To begin this process, during the summer of 1844, Dickens, with his entire family in tow, traveled rapidly from London via Paris to the arch-Catholic, pre-unification, former maritime republic of Genoa, Italy, hometown of Christopher Columbus. It was his first trip to Italy, and Dickens' first Grand Tour as an Englishman through southern Europe. Two years later in 1846, Dickens published his second major travelogue, *Pictures from Italy*, a relatively unknown work containing valuable insights into the novelist's impressions and mindset during this same period. Within three months after his arrival in Genoa, Dickens was ensconced in the magnificent, centrally located Renaissance-era Villa delle Peschiere (built 1560), dreaming dreams of Shakespeare, meeting some of his own personal demons in these dreams, and finding inspiration from his Italian surroundings. He immediately began writing a short story with a recognizably London setting seen through the filter of his immediate northern Italian environment.

The Cricket on the Hearth (1909) by D.W. Griffith, a notable Dickens afficionado and film pioneer, made several years before the director became world famous. From left: Charles Inslee, Dorothy Bernard, Owen Moore, Violet Mersereau, Herbert Prior, and Linda Arvidson.

Before the end of 1844, *The Chimes: A Goblin Story of Some Bells That Rang an Old Year Out and a New Year In* was published by Chapman & Hall, with engravings by four different artists, including Daniel Maclise, who had painted Dickens' portrait five years earlier, and John Leech, illustrator of *A Christmas Carol*.[2] Before publication, Dickens found time to race back to London and give a private reading of *The Chimes* for some of the most illustrious English literati of time, the scene famously sketched by Maclise depicting Dickens with a halo over his head. This private reading, in which distinguished guests fawned over Dickens the storyteller, appears to have been the first time he engaged in this kind of promotional effort, eventually becoming a regular activity bringing the novelist great fame and fortune. The title of the work is an allusion to Shakespeare's Falstaff from *Henry IV, Part II*, with a direct refence to the loud church bells of London or Genoa.[3] The story itself is divided into four "Quarter" chapters, another timekeeping reference to ringing church bells. In his *Pictures from Italy*, Dickens vividly recalls these bells, as well as the villa in which he stayed while writing the work. Strictly speaking, *The Chimes* is not a "Christmas" story, but rather a New Year's Eve or New Year's Day tale, during which its events transpire. It is a fine work of fiction, and did well commercially in its own day, but as biographer Claire Tomalin has pointed out, is "hardly read today."[4] *The Chimes*, like Dickens' other "Christmas" novellas, has also been overshadowed by its earlier prototype, *A Christmas Carol*. The same holds true regarding a dearth of modern film adaptations for *The Chimes*.

As a work of fiction, *The Chimes* makes an interesting, astringent comparison to *A Christmas Carol*. Both are ghost stories as much as holiday morality tales, but beyond this, overt similarities end. *The Chimes* concerns a dark night of the soul, not for Ebenezer Scrooge, but rather for Toby "Trotty" Veck, an elderly, impoverished, half-crazed porter, whose daughter (his only child) is to be married to an unemployed but kind-hearted blacksmith on New Year's Day. Toby's arrogant, itinerant, well-to-do employers are alternatively disapproving or threatening. Then in his dreams that night, Toby meets the spirits and gargoyles inhabiting local church bells, revealing to him a dark, Malthusian future of deprivation, death, and prostitution for his immediate family in accordance with the recent criticisms from his unsympathetic patrons. Then Toby wakes, and all seems well with reality after the nightmare; however, no one is reformed, and no future is guaranteed. In effect, rich elites are condemned while poor commoners are glorified, all in a somewhat heavy-handed manner. This quality may help explain why the book's popularity was short-lived—it may have been a bit too harsh for privileged defenders of the status quo, then or now—although any open-minded reader is likely to be impressed by its uncompromising fervor.

Unfortunately, this high literary quality has not translated into numerous video interpretations during the modern era, although initially at least, that did not seem to be the case. In 1914, as World War I began, not one but two silent short film versions of *The Chimes* were made. Both, however, are now considered lost, with only photographic stills reportedly existing. First from Great Britain came a two-and-a-half-reel production from the famous director-producer team of Thomas Bentley and Cecil Hepworth.[5] Hepworth and Bentley during this same period created a series of silent Dickens adaptations, and the loss of their *Chimes* must be considered especially unfortunate.[6] Hard on the heels of this British production came an American version of *The Chimes*, double the length (at five reels), co-directed by British-born Herbert Blaché (1882–1953) and British Dickensian veteran Tom Terriss (1872–1964), the latter also starring in the lead role of Trotty Veck.[7] That same year (1914), Blaché and Terriss had also collaborated on one of the earliest movie versions of Dickens' *The Mystery of*

Edwin Drood, now lost as well. After this flurry of Anglo-American film activity in 1914, incredibly, nothing more of *The Chimes* for the big screen would be heard for the next 86 years. The reasons for this shortage may be the same as those previously stated, namely, that the work on film has been overshadowed by Dickens' *A Christmas Carol*, and that Dickens' fierce attack against unrestrained capitalism in *The Chimes* may have been considered too unfashionable or too un-bankable, especially during the post–World War I and World War II eras of the 20th century.

Then in 2000, just as the old century and an older way of life were about to pass, a 23-minute clay-animated film adaptation of Dickens' *The Chimes* came out of left field, produced by the relatively obscure Xyzoo Animation working out of Cape Town, South Africa, commissioned by New York City–based Billy Budd Films, Inc. Normally it would be reasonable to dismiss such an effort as trite, but viewers taking time to screen this work will be pleasantly surprised on at least three counts. First is the state-of-the-art animation, one of only a handful all-clay movies created by Xyzoo founder Lindsay van Blerk, later winning a Special Jury award for excellence from CINE (Council on Non-Theatrical Events), before seemingly disappearing from general circulation. The second surprise is a straightforward but compelling story narration by British Dickensian stalwart Derek Jacobi. The third is a sympathetic adherence to the original spirit of the tale, namely, that a truly legitimate goal in life is to make us into better persons (see epigraph). Post-Apartheid South Africa was apparently less shocked by Dickens' polemic against the privileged of society than were many Anglo-Americans. Some 20 years later, we are fortunate indeed to have any video productions of *The Chimes* still available for viewing, as is this one on YouTube or VHS format. We are doubly fortunate in that this unusual production is serious-minded, beautifully executed, and relatively faithful to Dickens' original 1844 novella.

Buoyed by a favorable reception for *The Chimes*, Dickens wrote his third "Christmas" novella, *The Cricket on the Hearth: A Fairy Tale of Home*, in late 1845, although the story has nothing to do with Christmas beyond the seasonal timing of its creation, publication, and marketing.[8] For *Cricket*, Dickens toned down the political polemic in favor of a more pronounced sentimentality. Reviews were hostile, sales massive. An astounding 17 different stage adaptations were produced soon afterwards.[9] Dickens was later paid to do readings.[10] Published by Bradbury & Evans of London, with illustrations by a team of engravers led by Maclise, *The Cricket on the Hearth* was dedicated to Lord Francis Jeffrey (1773–1850), a literary-inclined jurist and family friend, and recent godfather to Dickens' son Frank (1844–1886). Divided into three sections rather than chapters ("Chirp the First," "Chirp the Second," and "Chirp the Third"), the story features an antagonist (Tackleton) reminiscent of Scrooge in that he begins as miserly but becomes generous by the end. The chirping cricket itself is repeatedly referred to as a protective "Fairy Voice" for the poor but sympathetic households of Peerybingle, Plummer, and Fielding—thus more akin to pagan myth than any Christian holiday symbol or tradition.[11] This overt de-emphasis of Christianity in *Cricket* was most likely due to Dickens' desire for widening the story's appeal to non–Christians, an objective in which he succeeded without qualification, and somewhat to the jealous dismay of his more orthodox British literary colleagues.

Dickens' ultimate foray into populist sentimentality is also noteworthy in that it was adapted into a silent short for the Biograph Company as early as 1909 by legendary American director D.W. Griffith (1875–1948), himself a professed Dickens enthusiast and most certainly a great connoisseur of sentimentality.[12] Six years later, in 1915, Griffith would cement an important place in filmmaking history with his silent epic *Birth of a Nation*. In addition to displaying Griffith's technical prowess as a filmmaker, his *Cricket on the Hearth* reveals the dramatic crosscutting of plotlines distinctive to both the novelist and movie director. Clocking in at approximately 10 minutes, Griffith's interpretation is reduced to the tale of a husband made jealous of his wife, then happily proven to be mistaken. There are no subtitles, no Christmas, no Christianity, and no Cricket. Griffith's film starred Irish-born Owen Moore in the lead romantic role of Edward Plummer, future "King of Comedy" director Mack Sennett (1880–1960) in a specially created jester part, and possibly future star Mary Pickford in a brief, uncredited appearance.[13] Names later becoming famous in association with Griffith and *Birth of a Nation*, such as screenwriter Frank Woods (1860–1939) and cinematographer Bill Blitzer (1872–1944), were also involved with the 1909 *Cricket* project.

Curiously, five years later, in 1914, Biograph followed with yet another silent version of *Cricket on the Hearth*, this time at twice the length (two reels), suggesting that the shorter Biograph production by Griffith had created more demand. The 1914 film was directed by Lawrence Marston (1857–1939) and starred Alan Hale Sr. as Edward.[14] This was the same year (1914) that Hale starred in Biograph's *Martin Chuzzlewit* which, like Biograph's *Cricket*, is reportedly preserved in the archives at the George Eastman Museum in Rochester, New York.[15] Also in 1914 came another silent version of *The Cricket on the Hearth* directed by Lorimer Johnston (1858–1941), now considered lost.[16] Then in 1923, another longer (82 minutes) silent version of the same title by the same director was released, with Johnston also playing the role of Tackleton, now considered (mostly) lost as well.[17] All that is left of these obscure productions by Johnston are scattered photographic stills or partial reels. Their comparative rarity suggests that

Griffith, despite all the limitations of his early 1909 effort, still surpassed all rivals in directorial skill and panache. Not until the post–World War II era of television would producers and directors again show an interest in this popular work by Dickens as a vehicle to display artistry while generating profits.

The first such example of renewed interest came on July 8, 1949, when NBC broadcast a very loose, 30-minute adaptation of *The Cricket on the Hearth* as part of its historically significant *Your Show Time* television series.[18] Like other installments in the series, NBC's *Cricket* was filmed prior to broadcast, co-produced by Marshall Grant (1910–1957) and Stanley Rubin (1917–2014), and was the second-to-last episode aired (out of 26 episodes total). The film reportedly still survives in the UCLA Film & Television Archive.[19] Three years later, on June 11, 1952, NBC's Kraft Television Theatre broadcast a one-hour adaptation of *The Cricket on the Hearth* (Season 5, Episode 40) starring 22-year-old Grace Kelly as May Fielding, playing opposite Russell Hardie as Edward Plummer.[20] This was immediately prior to Kelly's breakout film role in *High Noon* (1952), co-starring Gary Cooper. That NBC would do two separate television adaptations of the same literary work within three years is likely an indication of high ratings, especially with the second one utilizing a soon-to-be-celebrity name like Grace Kelly. Disappointingly, the Library of Congress catalogue does not list this episode among its extensive holdings for Kraft Television Theatre, and it is unknown whether it still survives as a film or kinescope.

Another 15 years passed before Dickens' third "Christmas" novella made it to prime time, but then did so in conspicuous, even garish fashion. In 1967, three years after its blockbuster success with *Rudolph the Red-Nosed Reindeer* (1964), Rankin/Bass Productions unleased its animated version of *The Cricket on the Hearth*, clocking in at under 50 minutes.[21] Dickens' original text was rewritten for a teleplay that placed the Christmas holiday front and center, with British character actor Roddy McDowall brought in for voicing over "Crocket" the Cricket with a pronounced English accent, the cricket also given an emphasis in the teleplay that would have startled Dickens the novelist. One year later, MacDowell would be donning ape costume and makeup for a major role in *Planet of the Apes* (1968). Of more interest was the father-daughter team of Danny and Marlo Thomas recruited to voice-over the father-daughter characters of Caleb and Bertha Plummer, with Danny Thomas (born Amos Muzyad Yaqoob Kairouz) also doing an in-person introduction, epilogue, and co-producing.[22] The production eliminated the subplot of wrongly suspected infidelity between Peerybingle and Dot, and for good measure, songs provided by the ad hoc musical team of Maury Laws and Jules Bass.[23] This free adaptation of the Dickens original is still widely available

8. Other Christmas Novellas (1844–1848)

for viewing in a number of platforms.[24] The Christian-Christmas emphasis of the Bass/Rankin interpretation is apparent from the outset, in which opening credits are sung in carol-like fashion, then immediately segue into a cartoon rendition of "Deck the Halls." If nothing else, it may be confidently asserted that the 1967 animated film forcefully transposed the holidays into its source material.

As for Charles Dickens the storyteller, he had two more "Christmas" novellas to write, motivated by both financial profits and (no doubt) a desire to work out some persisting artistic needs or personal demons. *The Battle of Life: A Love Story* appeared in late 1846, and then in late 1848, *The Haunted Man and the Ghost's Bargain*, both published by Bradbury & Evans, and both again illustrated by a team of engravers led by Maclise and Leech, although the latter work also included drawings John Tenniel (1820–1914), better known as the original illustrator for Lewis Carroll. *The Battle of Life* tells the story of two sisters in a rural English setting, one of whom chooses to go into prolonged hiding so that her sister can be married by the best local suitor. The title refers both to the plot and to an unspecified ancient battlefield located near the rural village setting. Christmas allusions within the tale are remote at best. *The Haunted Man* relates the tale of a Professor Redlaw, reminiscent in some respects to both Scrooge and Goethe's Faust, who bargains with a supernatural spirit to first forget a troubling personal past, next cause those around him to do the same, and then finally reverse his and others' forgetfulness. The benevolent sentiments of Christmastime are invoked throughout, thus expressly returning the story setting to a holiday season, as in *A Christmas Carol*. Given that the quality of Dickens' own marriage and family life are now known to have been deteriorating during the mid and late 1840s, the plotlines of these two later novellas today seem to take on a troubling personal significance for their author.

To date, no known commercial film adaptations have been made for either *The Battle of Life* or *The Haunted Man*. None. This unusual situation partially reflects these novellas being overshadowed by an oversupply of video productions for *A Christmas Carol*. While it is true that neither *Battle of Life* nor *Haunted Man* are among Dickens' strongest works, they are far from being without merit, and both enjoyed successful stage productions during Dickens' own time.[25] Ultimately, both novellas have suffered neglect during the era of cinema because it is financially less risky to figuratively produce the 100th video version of *A Christmas Carol*, than to try something new with which the viewing public is unfamiliar. That is a shame since these stories, like many of Dickens' other minor creations, are still much better than the drivel typically available on television or at the cineplex. Furthermore, it is striking that the only videos generally available to date for *The Chimes* and *The Cricket on the Hearth* are animated productions, in the latter case, one whose screenplay strays considerably from the original text. The reasons for this scarcity are the same as those for Dickens' last two Christmas novellas. Perhaps given a growing emphasis in the 21st century on presenting a more honest biography of the novelist—rather than the jovial image that he and his publicists wished to project at the time—interest may also revive doing film adaptations of his more obscure works, particularly those shedding light on the novelist's true biography. Quite apart from interest in literary biography, however, these obscure tales are entertaining in and of themselves, fully deserving to be dramatized for the viewing public more often, or at least once in some instances.

One recent sign that interest in Dickens' biography might be becoming more marketable was a relatively well-received 2017 film, *The Man Who Invented Christmas*, based on the somewhat fanciful, semi-historical 2008 book of the same title by Floridian author Les Standiford. Directed by British-Indian auteur Bharat Nalluri (b. 1965), with a screenplay adaptation by Canadian dramaturg Susan Coyne, *The Man Who Invented Christmas* boasts an outstanding cast led by the talented Dan Stevens (*Downton Abbey*) in the lead role as Charles Dickens, supported by Christopher Plummer as an imaginary Scrooge, Jonathan Pryce as Charles' very real father John, and Simon Callow as illustrator John Leech. The main problem with this movie is that it offers little insight into Dickens' creative process, no matter how hard it may have tried to do so. No mention is made whatsoever of the events in Dickens' life leading up to his writing *A Christmas Carol* and four subsequent Christmas novellas over the next four years. There is no mention of Dickens encountering the Edinburgh tombstone of Ebenezer Scroggie, his meeting with Edgar Allan Poe in America, his recent touring the Field Lane Ragged School in London, and certainly no indication that his carefully constructed marriage and family life were all on the verge of collapse. Instead, more of the old Dickens image—that of a beneficent, high-spirited, and self-made Victorian ideal—is pushed to the extreme, and hardly credible in dramatic terms, notwithstanding the effort. Ultimately, the film must be viewed as a missed opportunity, although it may have pointed the way towards a new genre focusing upon how great works of art are oftentimes the product of an unhappy personal environment for their creators.

While Dickens preoccupied himself in 1843–1848 with producing Christmas novellas (and earning substantial royalties), his novel-writing efforts with respect to longer works suffered for it. The long-gestating *Martin Chuzzlewit*, often cited as Dickens' least successful and least satisfying novel, was finally completed in 1844. Then came a nearly two-year

8. Other Christmas Novellas (1844–1848)

storytelling hiatus (except for the novellas), during which he tried, with varying degrees of success, to branch out into other activities such as journalism, acting, travelogue, and philanthropy. For example, what began in 1845 as an abortive idea to establish a home journal periodical (*The Cricket*) soon transformed Dickens into Editor in Chief for the newly founded liberal newspaper *Daily News*, a position from which he sought to escape almost from the moment he was employed. By early 1846, he was headed for Switzerland on holiday, leaving his wayward father John Dickens to help with the *Daily News* in any capacity possible (and proving himself surprisingly adept at doing so), as well as his close friend and future biographer John Forster.[26] Then around late 1846, Dickens seems to have remembered his true calling in life, and once again began writing a longer novel, eventually published in 1848 as *Dombey and Son*. It would represent for him a return to form, as well as a rousing financial success. After this, there would be no further need for holiday season novellas aimed at turning a quick profit.

9

Dombey and Son (1846–1848)

> "But what was a girl to Dombey and Son! In the capital of the House's name and dignity, such a child was merely a piece of base coin that couldn't be invested—a bad Boy— nothing more."[1]

In late 1844, as Dickens was encountering both huge sales figures and savage reviews for *The Cricket on the Hearth*, he also entered a two-year period of writer's block with respect to the longer novels for which he is now better known.[2] Dickens' then most recent two longer works, *Martin Chuzzlewit* and *Barnaby Rudge*, had both been less than rousing successes with readers and reviewers. Thus began the novelist's "crisis" (Claire Tomalin) of 1844–1846, in which he attempted several other livelihoods, with varying degrees of success or failure, including more Christmas novellas, travelogues, journalism, acting, and philanthropy.[3] Then in late 1846 appeared the first serial installment of *Dealings with the Firm of Dombey and Son: Wholesale, Retail and for Exportation*, published by Bradbury & Evans of London, with illustrations by "Phiz" (Hablot Knight Browne) and the completed novel later published in early 1848. Dickens began writing *Dombey and Son* while on holiday in Switzerland, continued working on it in Paris, and then completed the serial in London.[4] Seemingly oblivious to noteworthy political crises of the time, such as the Irish Famine of 1847 or Chartist Uprising of 1848, *Dombey and Son* instead returns Dickens to what he was known best for doing, namely, harking back to the tumultuous days of his own childhood and a bygone England of the 1820s and 1830s. Critics have since often correctly noticed that *Dombey and Son* is in fact two combined novels in the chronological sense, a short story leading up to the death of Paul Dombey Jr. (Chapters 1–16) and another lengthier work taking place following that traumatic event (Chapters 17–62).

9. Dombey and Son (1846–1848)

Dombey offers to readers a wide array of memorable characters, in true Dickensian fashion, well suited for vivid dramatic portrayal on stage or screen. The title characters, Paul Dombey Sr. and Paul Dombey Jr., share little in common besides their names, blood, and tragic fates. Paul Jr. obviously represents the novelist reminiscing back to his own childhood, although Dombey's sternly capitalist, chauvinistic father bears little resemblance to Dickens' own father John. In fact, the real-life inspiration for Paul Dombey Sr. remains as mysterious as those for Paul Jr. are obvious. Florence, the beloved older sister of Paul Jr., is a bit colorless as befits her role within the storyline, but she is also a paragon of virtue, strength, and patience. In a true stroke of genius, Dickens introduces another cast of sympathetic characters from the quaint (and a bit forlorn) Wooden Midshipman waterfront retail outlet inhabited by Florence's sweetheart Walter, Walter's devoted Uncle Sol, and their steadfast friend, Captain Cuttle, a handicapped but unresentful English naval veteran of the Napoleonic Wars. Also sympathetic is the kindhearted, hired nurse of Paul Jr., Mrs. Polly Toodle, presumptuously renamed Richards by Paul Sr. simply because he finds her real name to be absurd. In dark contrast to Richards is the insufferable, destructive Mrs. Pipchin and her nursery for children, by Dickens' own admission based on a real person and place from his own difficult childhood.[5] Lastly is the villainous assistant to Paul Sr., James Carker, who elopes with Dombey's mercenary and unhappy second wife Edith, only to later meet his own violent demise at the hands of the fledgling British Railway system, used to effective symbolic effect throughout both halves of the novel.

Catalysts for Dickens' outburst of invention in *Dombey and Son* were plentiful at the time of its creation. The novelist's second youngest and only successful son as an adult, Henry Fielding Dickens (1849–1933), would not be born until the following year and, until after the writing of *Dombey*, all of Dickens' hopes for a competent male heir had been seemingly disappointed. Leading up to *Dombey*, Dickens' favorite child was his youngest daughter, Catherine "Kate" Dickens Perugini (1839–1929), who in 1847 was about the same age (eight) as Florence "Floy" Dombey at the beginning of the novel. More tellingly, the novelist's musically talented and esteemed older sister Frances "Fanny" Elizabeth Dickens (1810–1848) was by 1847 terminally ill with consumption, and her slow demise may well have triggered childhood memories finding their way into his characterizations of both Florence Dombey and the doomed first wife of Paul Dombey Sr., also named Fanny.[6] Dickens' bitterly ironic comment regarding the second-class stature of daughters within English family hierarchies (see epigraph), likely represented his own personal tributes to both his favorite daughter and admired but soon-to-be deceased elder sister. By

Early silent film special effects in *Scrooge, or Marley's Ghost* (1901). Scrooge was played by Daniel Smith (right). The actor in the role of Marley's ghost is unidentified.

the end of the story, Dombey and Son has literally become Dombey and Daughter, with little apparent loss of family prestige or prospects, notwithstanding the tragic illness and death of Paul Jr., as well as the failure of Dombey's business thanks in large part to managerial neglect and dishonesty.

Dombey and Son proved to be yet another breakthrough work for its author, successful on every level both artistically and commercially. Despite numerous structural and stylistic limitations, many of which were recognized by critics even at the time, the novel was widely praised for its powerful dramatizations and, more importantly for its author, sold extremely well. Royalties were substantial enough that Dickens was able to reinvest his earnings, and from all accounts, he was never again in financial straits. By his late 30s, he had fully arrived both in terms of literary fame and fortune. Nevertheless, today the title of this important work is less than widely known, and less fully comprehended, even among modern fans of Dickens, and it certainly does not belong to the core group of some six books forming the basis of the novelist's long-term reputation. On the other hand, it is not unusual among true afficionados of Charles

Dickens to hear *Dombey and Son* cited as their favorite novel among all those he wrote. The storyline is a highly personal one, and quite unusual in that Dickens makes the hero, or rather heroine of the story, a woman. This was the first time that the preeminent Victorian male novelist attempted such a device, and in some respects *Dombey and Son* must be considered his most compelling effort in this respect.

The underlying reasons for a dichotomy of opinion on *Dombey and Son* are no doubt complex and beyond the scope of this study; however, insofar as these reasons relate to the subsequent film history of the work, they may be speculated upon herein. Despite frequent moments of poignancy and pathos, the main character of *Dombey*, Paul Sr., is profoundly unsympathetic. He is cold towards his family, deeply chauvinistic, and obsessed with money. British Victorian readers of the turbulent late 1840s responded to his limitations, but subsequent generations less so. It may well be that many character aspects of Paul Dombey Sr. were reflections of Dickens the man, being a novelist already known as not overly flattering towards himself. Moreover, this negative image went strongly against the concocted, benign portrayal of the novelist later presented to the public, as modern biographers later discovered, oftentimes to their chagrin. When the first film versions based on *Dombey* appeared between 1917 and 1931, two of Dickens' younger children (Kate and Henry) were still alive, and it would not be until their frank, unvarnished revelations about their father went public, and these revelations somewhat grudgingly accepted, that a better appreciation of the novel both on film and the written page became more manifest.

Dickens was about 34 years old when he broke out of writer's block to create *Dombey and Son*, but the title character of Paul Sr. is portrayed to be in his late 40s when the story begins with the birth of Paul Jr. and subsequent death of Dombey's first wife.[7] The novelist was likely projecting an older, fictional version of himself, one which he hoped sincerely never to become. During this period in Dickens' own life, his biological sons thus far, though still rather young, were all proving to be disappointments to him—none were going to be as talented or self-reliant as he—and the birth of his successful second youngest son Henry still lay in the future. Among his daughters, pre-teenaged Kate was the professed favorite, affectionately nicknamed "Lucifer Box" by Dickens because of her explosive temper.[8] With the simultaneous, rapid decline in health of his beloved sister Fanny, Dickens was likely inclined to produce a new literary work debunking the chauvinistic myths of Victorian society, or at least to the extent he was capable of debunking these as a writer. Dickens never aspired to become like Paul Sr., and yet, in a sense, he did, because 12 years later at age 46 he would cast off his wife (and the mother his children) in favor of a much younger actress, not unlike the widower Dombey Sr. marrying the younger Edith in the novel while neglecting his son and daughter. Many, many years later Dickens' daughter Kate alleged (with probable accuracy) that her father did not understand women, and Dickens may have been quite aware of his own shortcoming in this regard.[9] If this surmise is correct, then *Dombey and Son* likely represents the novelist's attempt to come to grips with personal deficiencies. It is therefore no wonder that most modern film adaptations, at least until that of 1983, had such a difficult time fitting this unusual story into a pre-existing template for Dickensian movie adaptations. *David Copperfield* it simply was not.

Oddly, the first two adaptations of *Dombey and Son* on film saw fit to contemporize the setting of the novel and to tamper in varying degrees with Dickens' storyline. After having missed the initial wave of enthusiasm for Dickens-based silent movies during the late 1800s and early 1900s, a British production of *Dombey and Son* appeared in 1917, at the height of the Great War, directed by the prolific Maurice Elvey (1887–1967), and featuring English silent stars Norman McKinnel as Paul Dombey Sr. and Lilian Braithwaite as his second wife, Edith.[10] The story was set in the year 1917. Not surprisingly, this film bombed in England, understandable given surrounding wartime circumstances. Then a truncated version was given an American postwar release in 1919, where it also met with commercial failure and hostile reviews, being criticized for both poor technical standards as well as its melodramatic treatment of a very serious work by Charles Dickens.[11] By the late silent film era, Dickens was still perceived by the general public as a Victorian icon of cheerful respectability, and the more modern view of the novelist as a complicated and tortured personality would take another half century to reach a wider audience—thanks to the revelations of Dickens' surviving children to 20th-century biographers—and still is oftentimes met with strong resistance. Thus fared the first tentative attempt at making *Dombey and Son* accessible to modern moviegoers. This rare film work is reportedly still preserved within the archives of the George Eastman Museum in Rochester, New York, but has otherwise completely disappeared from the modern moviegoing consciousness.[12]

Then, 14 years later, in 1931, apparently believing that the problem could be remedied simply by changing titles and names, Hollywood's Paramount Studios released *Rich Man's Folly*, a pre-code sound picture "suggested by" Dickens' *Dombey and Son*.[13] Set in the early Depression-era United States, the film was directed by the experienced and respected American auteur John Cromwell (1886–1979), who brought into the mix a distinguished cast often associated with the classic work of Austro-American director Josef von Sternberg, including heavyweight lead star George Bancroft as Brock Trumbull (= Paul

9. Dombey and Son (1846–1848)

Dombey Sr.), Frances Dee as Anne (= Florence), and Juliette Compton as Paula (= Edith). This "near-Dickens talkie" (Michael Pointer) is comparable to the near-contemporary 1933 Monogram *Oliver Twist* in its misguided badness.[14] Improved technical standards are nonetheless betrayed by heavy-handed melodrama; anyone who had not read the book could never have guessed that this movie had anything to do with Charles Dickens. Like its 1917 British silent predecessor, *Rich Man's Folly* proved to be a critical and commercial flop, with even director Cromwell later having deep reservations about the effort. Nevertheless, *Rich Man's Folly* holds the unusual distinction of being the very first full-length feature with sound based on a story by Charles Dickens (as well as the first sound version for *Dombey and Son*) and is today reportedly preserved within the extensive holdings of the UCLA Film and Television Archive. This was followed by 38 years of silence from the film industry for *Dombey*, but also in the interim came a major revisionist view of the novelist's perceived biography, one firmly attested to by those still alive who once knew Dickens personally as a man quite apart from his work. These included Irish playwright George Bernard Shaw (1856–1950), who publicly and emphatically verified the disturbing picture of Dickens the novelist presented by daughter Kate to biographer Gladys Storey, later published as *Dickens and Daughter* in 1939.[15]

By the late 1960s, much had changed from the 1930s. The medium of television and postwar BBC serialization of Charles Dickens novels had demonstrated the many advantages, both financial and aesthetic, of presenting Dickens' stories to the public in this format. After the six best-known of Dickens' works had been serialized by the BBC during this period, as well as lesser-known works such as *Barnaby Rudge* (1960) and *Martin Chuzzlewit* (1964), came a 13-episode, six-hour BBC miniseries for *Dombey and Son* in 1969.[16] This rare production reunited the experienced team of director Joan Craft, Irish screenwriter Hugh Leonard, and producer Campbell Logan (1910–1978), the latter in his last major Dickens project for the BBC. The previous year, in 1968, the same trio had produced its influential miniseries of *Nicholas Nickleby* for the BBC, and its *Dombey and Son* was a similarly noteworthy effort. Featuring British horror film and bad-guy character specialist John Carson as Paul Dombey Sr., the 1969 BBC *Dombey* also memorably cast Gary Raymond to play the villainous James Carker—the British-born Raymond then coming off a recurring and highly visible role in the American hit TV series *The Rat Patrol*. Apparently, by this point in time, it was believed by the BBC that the viewing public might finally be ready for one of Dickens' darkest self-portraits in fiction (in the person of Paul Dombey Sr.). The 1969 BBC *Dombey* is today nearly impossible to find in the U.S. but is still available as a British import DVD for those whose disc players have specialized capacity for that restrictive format.

As bold as the 1969 television series was, however, the BBC was not yet finished with *Dombey and Son*. Fourteen years later, in 1983, it offered yet another new, 10-episode miniseries version, clocking in at five hours, colorized with a bigger budget and more star power, led by the versatile, unclassifiable Julian Glover as Paul Dombey Sr. Glover was then about 48 years old—the same age as his character in the text.[17] The British acting virtuoso presents Dombey Sr. as a nightmare *doppelganger* vision of the novelist himself—cold, venal, mercenary, older and none the wiser for it until finally (and somewhat unrealistically) softened by his daughter's unshakable devotion. In hindsight, the storyline hit closer to home than likely was ever intended, with Dickens himself likely realizing near the end of his life that his favorite daughter Kate was as deserving of esteem as much as anyone in his family. As for Glover, viewers had seen him as early as 1963 in Tony Richardson's *Tom Jones*, and more recently in *The Empire Strikes Back* (1980) and *For Your Eyes Only* (1981), but his 1983 performance for the BBC in *Dombey and Son* reminded audiences yet again that Glover was in fact a seriously trained stage actor capable bringing tremendous nuance and subtlety to his parts. Oversight of the newer BBC project was led by two *Doctor Who* alumni, director Rodney Bennett (1935–2017) and producer Barry Letts (1925–2009), with a major assist from screenwriter James Andrew Hall (b. 1939). Hall had recently scripted a very convincing *Great Expectations* for the BBC in 1981, and *Dombey* would firmly establish his reputation as a top-notch Dickens screen adaptor.

The 1983 BBC *Dombey and Son* also featured an outstanding supporting cast of British acting talent. Then-newcomer Lysette Anthony played the role of vindicated but long-suffering daughter Florence with unaffected sincerity and conviction. Two years later, in 1985, she would go on to effectively portray Oliver's Aunt Rose in the BBC miniseries for *Oliver Twist*, and then on to a long, diverse career in film, television, and stage. As the horrible Mrs. Pipchin, the late, prolific, and always-excellent Barbara Hicks gave one of her more memorable performances as a harmful woman always seemingly in the wrong place at the worst possible moment. Other notable castings in this production included veteran British character actors such as the Welsh Shakespearean-trained Emrys James (as Captain Cuttle) and familiar RADA alumnus James Cossins (as Major Bagstock). Another RADA graduate, the late Paul Darrow, played the villainous James Carker with appropriate menace and panache. Still another RADA alumna, Sharon Maughan, portrayed Edith, the manipulative and gold-digging second Mrs. Dombey.[18] All in all, the 1983 *Dombey and Son* miniseries is a worthy, representative effort, in no small part because of

9. Dombey and Son (1846–1848)

Glover's tremendous lead performance, plus a brilliant supporting cast, skilled ensemble acting, and judicious screenwriting. We are doubly fortunate to have such a fine video production for one of Dickens' more difficult and least understood masterpieces. It remains widely available for viewing in various platforms, though still no doubt a bit puzzling for uncomprehending American audiences more used to *Oliver!* the musical as being representative of the novelist.[19]

Dombey and Son the novel proved to be an unequivocal success for its author, both financially and critically, at least during its own day. Subsequent generations of readers have been more ambiguous or qualified in their praise. Nevertheless, looking back, even the novel's alleged faults—its lopsided structure, one-dimensional characterizations that seem to come and go abruptly, a hard-to-believe plotline—seem to all work in its favor. Like the reality of life itself, *Dombey and Son* as a literary creation is unapologetically asymmetrical and impossible to pigeonhole or to water down. While subsequent books such as *David Copperfield* continue to chart the novelist's semi-autobiographical path from childhood to manhood, *Dombey* cuts off childhood with the tragic death of Paul Jr., then resumes a difficult spiritual journey for Paul Sr., leading to his final reconciliation with, and recognition of, the true worth of his surviving daughter Florence. It was as if Dickens was trying to kill off his own haunting childhood, then take a good, hard look at his own unflattering adult image in a literary looking glass. The problem was, and continues to be, that Dickens' nostalgic literary examination of his troubling past within pre–Victorian English surroundings is exactly what his readers have always responded to the most, and precisely what gives his fiction such intensely powerful focus. For his next major novel, Dickens would attempt to better reconcile himself with his somewhat disadvantaged personal history, while in the process creating what is still perhaps his best known and most beloved work.

10

David Copperfield (1849–1850)

> "But, sometimes, when I took her up, and felt that she was lighter in my arms, a dead blank feeling came upon me, as if I were approaching to some frozen region yet unseen, that numbed my life. I avoided the recognition of this feeling by any name, or by any communing with myself; until one night, when it was very strong upon me, and my aunt had left her with a parting cry of 'Good night, Little Blossom,' I sat down at my desk alone, and cried to think, Oh what a fatal name it was, and how the blossom withered in its bloom upon the tree!"[1]

My first serious encounter with Charles Dickens as a writer came during my early teen years, not from one of his novels or movies derived from his novels, but rather indirectly from (of all things), the 1966 British film *Fahrenheit 451*, based on the 1953 science fiction work by Ray Bradbury.[2] In the 1966 movie version, unlike the 1953 novel, Bradbury's hero Montag, living and working within a totalitarian society that classifies all novels, indeed most books, as contraband, discovers his own love of reading by encountering a forbidden copy of Dickens' *David Copperfield*. He begins reading and is hooked for life. Later in the film, Montag reads out loud, in Dickensian fashion, to an unwilling home audience a passage from the same novel poetically describing the physical decline of David's first wife Dora, and underscoring the relative briefness, fragility, and pathos of life in general (see epigraph), reducing his audience to both anger and tears in the process. Towards the end of the movie, one of Montag's fellow "book people" expresses enthusiasm for Dickens' *The Pickwick Papers* to the point where he has memorized the entire text.[3] Following this youthful movie experience, I then read the novel *David Copperfield* and had a similar enthusiastic reaction. My admiration for the storytelling skills of Charles Dickens has since remained unchanged for over half a century.

10. David Copperfield (1849–1850)

The Personal History, Adventures, Experience and Observation of David Copperfield the Younger of Blunderstone Rookery (Which He Never Meant to Publish on Any Account) was published in monthly serial form between May 1849 and November 1850, then immediately appeared as a complete novel thereafter, published by Bradbury & Evans of London, lavishly illustrated by "Phiz" (Hablot Knight Browne). It proved to be another rousing success, both critically and commercially. Dickens later cited *David Copperfield* as his favorite creation, and fans of his work have often shared that same high opinion.[4] The work continues to stand as one of Dickens' half-dozen or so bedrock achievements, and in the modern age of video has consistently been one of the novelist's most frequently adapted books for film.[5] Strikingly, within the text, Dickens utilized an unprecedented (for him, at least) first-person narrative ("Chapter 1. I Am Born"), leading readers then and now to conclude that *David Copperfield* is his most autobiographical work—as was likely intended by the novelist. Designed as a coming-of-age *bildungsroman*, the text of *David Copperfield* contains many of the novelist's trademark devices, including a nostalgic, bittersweet view of the past, a perilous childhood odyssey, flashes of professional brilliance combined with personal folly, slow and gradual discovery of true love, a kaleidoscopic range of unforgettable characters, plus much, much more.[6] Over 170 years after its original conception, Dickens' allegedly most intimate "fictional" story continues to fascinate readers and filmmakers alike and is likely to continue doing so well into the foreseeable future.

Another facet of the novel making *David Copperfield* such a creation of great genius is that it accomplishes what very few other literary works in the English language manage to accomplish, namely, it effectively blurs the line between myth and reality, even for those audiences trained to distinguish between the two. Again, this effect is no doubt what the novelist intended, and very much like what William Shakespeare had achieved with his "History" plays in replacing documented English history with Tudor-biased propaganda. At age 38, Dickens had finally reached the height of his literary ambitions, both in terms of fame and fortune, and now was obviously seeking to make better sense of the tangled path in life leading him to achieve such fantastic success. It is now known that many of David Copperfield's fictional life experiences corresponded with those of Charles Dickens himself, though many (if not most) others do not. Instead, Dickens has presented audiences with a mostly attractive, mythologized version of his own autobiography, and this distinctive quality was widely recognized even at the time of publication. *David Copperfield* was how the novelist wanted to view himself in 1850—and how he wanted readers to view him—as he approached midlife, before a severe midlife crisis would completely upend this illusion, leading to *Great Expectations* (another landmark novel) about a decade later. By the end of *David Copperfield*, on the other hand, Dickens clearly sees himself as "the hero of my own life," as he phrases it in the very first sentence of the first chapter.[7]

As engaging as the storyline is of *David Copperfield*, the expansive cast of secondary characters delineated by the novelist is even more memorable. This cast has transferred to film exceedingly well over the last century or more and has attracted some of the finest character actors of the last four generations.

W.C. Fields (left) as Wilkins Micawber and Freddie Bartholomew as Davey in MGM's *David Copperfield* (1935) (Masheter Movie Archive / Alamy Stock Photo).

Foremost among these secondary characters is David's surrogate father, the loquacious and grandiloquent Wilkins Micawber, surely one of the outstanding literary creations in all English language fiction and closely based on Dickens' own biological father John.[8] Nearly following Micawber in memorability is David's great aunt, Betsey Trotwood, perhaps the strongest female character in all of Dickens' output and Exhibit A against those contending the novelist could not create strong female characters.[9] One compelling theory is that Aunt Betsey was partially based on a real-life spinster, Miss Mary Pearson Strong (1771?-1855) of Broadstairs, Kent (northeast of Dover), a friendly and respected seaside neighbor of Dickens in her late 70s at the time of writing, and like Aunt Betsey, notoriously adverse to donkeys crossing her property lines. David's preposterously silly first wife, Dora Spenlow, surely drew inspiration from Dickens' first serious romantic interest, Maria Beadnell, while his highly competent and admirably virtuous second wife, Agnes Wickfield, is partially based on Dickens' sister-in-law (and housekeeper) Georgina "Georgy" Hogarth.

10. David Copperfield (1849–1850)

The tragic figure of James Steerforth is likely not based on a real person, but rather represents Dickens' unique take on the iconic Byronic hero literary type, Lord Byron (1788–1824) himself having died young at age 36 when Dickens was only 12 years old—suggestively, the same approximate age as the fictional David when he first meets Steerforth at boarding school. Steerforth's bitter cousin, the combative, formidable Rose Dartle, also convincingly refutes any critical claims that the novelist did not know how to present strong female characterizations.[10]

Given these many dramatic qualities, it therefore came as no surprise when the best filmmakers of the pre–World War I golden age for silent movies applied their talents adapting *David Copperfield* to the big screen. The American Edison company came first out of the pack with its now-lost 1910 short, *Love and the Law*, a reference to David's gradual falling in love with Agnes Wickfield while thwarting similar aspirations from her father's law clerk and later unwilling partner, the villainous Uriah Heep.[11] Also now lost is Britannia's silent short *Little Emily* from 1912, focusing on the young David's childhood friendship with his extended, adoptive family.[12] Fortunately preserved (at least in part) from that same era, however, are longer works by the eminent filmmaking teams of American director Theodore Marston and producer Edwin Thanhouser, along with British director Thomas Bentley and producer Cecil Hepworth. Marston-Thanhouser produced three memorable (and consecutive) silent shorts from 1911 based on the novel, including *The Early Life of David Copperfield*, *Little Em'ly and David Copperfield*, and *The Loves of David Copperfield*.[13] Later, in 1913, Bentley-Hepworth released a sprawling (for that era) eight-reel silent movie, *David Copperfield*, while ably condensing the entire storyline into an approximate 10-minute feature film.[14] The silent movie era of interpretation for Dickens' classic novel then culminated in 1922 with *David Copperfield* by the acclaimed Danish director Anders Wilhelm Sandberg (1887–1938) which, despite its foreign subtitles, was still the arguably the highest quality film version of the novel made up to that early date.[15]

With the advent of sound in the motion picture industry during the late 1920s and early 1930s, American Hollywood stepped up to produce the first serious efforts at adapting Dickens novels for big screen talkies. First out of the box in early 1935 for successful big-budget forays of this type came MGM's *David Copperfield*, produced as a personal labor of love by none other than David O. Selznick (1902–1965), son-in-law of studio co-namesake Louis B. Mayer.[16] Top-flight director George Cukor (1899–1983) oversaw the proceedings, but stealing the show was W.C. Fields (aka William Claude Dukenfield) as Micawber, after Charles Laughton, originally slated for the role, bowed out. Fields, an avid Dickens fan whose own father was from Yorkshire, England, jumped at the chance and turned in a fabulous performance notwithstanding his American accent. Fields was surrounded by an excellent Anglo-American cast drawn from MGM's regular payroll, including Frank Lawton as the adult David, child star Freddie Bartholomew as young David, Lionel Barrymore as Daniel Peggotty, Maureen O'Sullivan as Dora Spenlow, Basil Rathbone as Murdstone, and Edna May Oliver as Aunt Betsey, among many others. Also appearing in a cameo role was the English novelist Hugh Walpole (1884–1941), who shared co-screenwriting credits. The 1935 *David Copperfield* was well received and profitable for the studio, helping to encourage an entire portfolio of similar high-quality Dickens-based film productions during the mid and late 1930s. It is still worth screening based on Fields' performance alone.

After World War II, the quality bar for Dickens film adaptations was raised considerably, thanks to David Lean's *Great Expectations* (1946) and *Oliver Twist* (1948). As the age of television became dominant during the 1950s, video producers began looking at Charles Dickens novels with a much more ambitious, expansive viewpoint. Leading the vanguard in this respect was the BBC; however, American television was surprisingly competitive, thanks in part to the tremendous popularity of Dickens' work with American movie decision-makers. For example, in 1954, American actor-turned-producer Robert Montgomery (1904–1981) used his own TV show on NBC, *Robert Montgomery Presents*, as a platform for a modest two-episode, two-hour miniseries of *David Copperfield*, with help from noted American director Norman Felton (1913–2012) and staff screenwriter Doria Folliott (1906–1974).[17] The same team had produced a well-received version of *Great Expectations* earlier that same year in 1954. Now came *David Copperfield*. Though unpretentious by modern standards, and certainly not as entertaining as the 1935 MGM effort, the 1954 NBC production for prime-time television certainly raised some eyebrows, particularly in Great Britain where the BBC was itself then in the process of reinventing popular Charles Dickens video adaptations into a more up-to-date, full-blown TV miniseries format.[18]

Two years later, in 1956, the pioneering BBC Sunday-Night Theatre offered its own 13-episode, six-hour *David Copperfield*, starring a 31-year-old and still-unknown Robert Hardy as the adult David.[19] The successful miniseries then reran in 1957. Director Stuart Burge (1918–2002), producer Douglas Allen (1903–1984), and screenwriter Vincent Tilsley (1932–2013) at the time were all, like Hardy, comparative unknowns, although 10 years later, in 1966, Tilsley would rework this same script for yet another 13-part BBC production of *David Copperfield*, this time starring the (then) relatively unknown Ian McKellen as David.[20] Veteran director Joan Craft and producer Campbell Logan oversaw the 1966

10. David Copperfield (1849–1850)

miniseries. This same duo, along with screenwriter Constance Cox, had recently turned out, in 1965, a similar BBC miniseries version for *A Tale of Two Cities*. Earlier, in 1959, the ABC-UK network released a series of half-hour vignettes for *Fredric March Presents Tales from Dickens*, half a dozen of which focused on subplots from *David Copperfield*. Future *Doctor Who* regular William Russell starred as the adult David.[21] Suffice it to say that, by the mid–1960s, the BBC had re-established its ascendancy as a premier television producer of Dickens' classic novels, and that no single work better demonstrates this dominance than *David Copperfield*. The same novel, however, also shows how American television producers were often catalysts or competitors for similar film adaptations.

After this flurry of activity from the BBC, 20th Century–Fox decided to make its own movie version of *David Copperfield* (1969), clocking in around two hours, and filmed in the UK as a joint production, directed by Delbert Mann (1920–2007).[22] Subsequently, in 1970, the film had its U.S. release on NBC television. With a big budget came big names and talent. For screenwriting duties, the late, great Jack Pulman (1925–1979), future BBC adaptor of *I, Claudius* (1976), was brought in, along with distinguished British composer Malcolm Arnold (1921–2006) to provide a soundtrack. The all-star, mostly British cast included Robin Phillips (as the adult David), Edith Evans (Aunt Betsey), Cyril Cusack (who had also starred in Truffaut's *Fahrenheit 451* from 1966) as Barkis, Susan Hampshire (Agnes), Pamela Franklin (Dora), Ralph Richardson (Micawber), Michael Redgrave (Daniel Peggotty), and a very bankable Ron Moody (also Fagin from *Oliver!* in 1968) as Uriah Heep. Cyril Cusack's daughter Sinéad (Emily) and Redgrave's son Corin (Steerforth) were also brought in for major parts. Portraying perhaps the most diabolical Creakle and Tungay ever dramatized on screen, respectively, were Laurence Olivier and Richard Attenborough. Notwithstanding this star power, however, the result received mixed reviews, and in hindsight, the most charitable thing that can be said is that the whole did not equal the sum of some excellent individual parts. Pulman's script valiantly attempted to condense a long, complex story with multiple subplots into two hours of video entertainment, becoming a series of flashbacks for the adult David, sometimes coherent, sometimes disjointed. The movie is still worth viewing, but also demonstrates the shortcomings and pitfalls of trimming Dickens, especially in comparison to the episodic advantages of the miniseries format.

More successful as an overall viewing experience was the 1974 joint BBC and Time-Life miniseries *David Copperfield*, presented in six one-hour installments.[23] For this 1974 production, Joan Craft reprised her 1966 directorial effort, this time in tandem with the considerable screenwriting skills of late British playwright Hugh Whitemore (1936–2018).

Unlike the 1969 20th Century–Fox feature film, no celebrity performers were utilized, but rather an experienced ensemble of British character actors. Some of these included a young (27 years old) and still unknown David Yelland as the adult David Copperfield, Arthur Lowe as a sympathetically inept Micawber, and Martin Jarvis as an effectively repulsive Uriah Heep. Also, unlike the 1969 big-budget affair by 20th Century–Fox, this relatively modest production received nearly unanimously favorable notices at the time and is still available as a two-DVD set. It proved yet again that Dickens' novels could be effectively dramatized with a more expansive format and without big-name actors, combined with skillful writing and sensitive direction.

By the early 1980s, both the film industry and film technology were changing, and video presentations of Dickens' novels changed along with these. The first fully animated *David Copperfield* of note came in 1983, once again led by Burbank Films Australia, who had scored successes the previous year in 1982 with *Oliver Twist* and *A Christmas Carol*.[24] These were immediately followed in 1983 with animated versions of *Great Expectations* and *David Copperfield*, both stories having conspicuous subplots of Australian immigration for marginalized members of English society. This was a theme that obviously resonated with Australian film animators and is given appropriate emphasis in the Burbank productions. The Aussies clearly felt personal connections to characters such as the Micawbers and Peggottys, not to mention the intimidating Magwitch from *Great Expectations*. Burbank would animate four more Dickens novels over the next two years. A decade later, in 1993, another animated *David Copperfield* would air on American NBC television, this time with an anthropomorphic twist, featuring celebrity voiceovers. Taking its cue from Disney's audacious and hugely popular *Oliver & Company* (1988), the 1993 NBC *David Copperfield* in fact has little to do with Dickens' original text, the Copperfields becoming an extended family of talking cats, with the additional bonus of children's song and dance routines added to a much-altered storyline.[25] Some of the voiceover castings, however, were quite interesting. The adult David was voiced and sung by Julian Lennon (eldest son of John Lennon), and Agnes Wickfield by former Prince protégé Sheena Easton. The always excellent Michael York took on the much-expanded, villainous role of Murdstone, conflated with that of Uriah Heep (eliminated as a separate character) and turned into a humanized lion, representing probably the best thing about the movie. This production can still be easily found on DVD or YouTube.

In the middle of all this animation activity the BBC unveiled yet another television miniseries for *David Copperfield* (1986), this one assembling a first-rate creative team, though none of whom possessed big-box office appeal.[26] This highly competent group was led by director Barry Letts (1925–2009) and producer Terrance Dicks (1935–2019), both *Doctor Who* alumni, along with talented screenwriter James Andrew Hall (b. 1939).[27] This trio brought a wealth of experience and good taste to the venture, and is reflected in the high overall quality of the finished product. Clocking in at roughly five hours, the series had originally been broken into 10 half-hour episodes for British audiences, but then sensibly reduced to five one-hour episodes for its American premiere on *Masterpiece Theatre* in early 1988. Although featuring mostly a then-unknown cast, the 1986 production boasted an outstanding Micawber in the person of Dickensian specialist Simon Callow, plus a memorable Ham Peggotty from future *Game of Thrones* star Owen Teale. Above all, the 1986 *David Copperfield*, like its 1974 BBC predecessor, once again demonstrated that the lengthy novel typically benefited from a more expansive miniseries format in filming, as opposed to condensing it into two hours or less for a feature film.

The BBC was not quite finished, however, giving Dickens' quintessential *bildungsroman* its trademark miniseries treatment. On Christmas Day and St. Stephen's Day 1999, a two-part, three-hour, joint production by the BBC and WGBH Boston aired, then again in early 2000 as part of the 29th season for *Masterpiece Theatre*. It was the fifth miniseries of *David Copperfield* by the BBC in 43 years (since 1956). Directed by Simon Curtis (b. 1960) and scripted by Adrian Hodges (b. 1957), the 1999–2000 BBC *David Copperfield* starred a 10-year-old Daniel Radcliffe as the young David, a role that would lead directly to him being cast as Harry Potter the following year for the beginning of that auspicious book-film franchise.[28] Irish actor-novelist Ciarán McMenamin was cast as the adult David, along with a star-studded supporting cast which included Bob Hoskins as Micawber and Maggie Smith as Aunt Betsey, the latter two performances possibly being definitive in a crowded, highly competitive field. Other notable performers included Ian McKellen (who had played the lead role of David in 1966), this time as David's nemesis Creakle, the ever-reliable Alun Armstrong as Daniel Peggotty, a delightfully repulsive Zoë Wanamaker as Jane Murdstone, a comical but sympathetic Imelda Staunton as Mrs. Micawber, and Nicholas Lyndhurst as a compellingly devious Uriah Heep, among others. As a bonus, Tom Wilkinson, fresh off stardom from *The Full Monty* (1997), provided contextualizing, first-person, offscreen narration in the true spirit of Dickensian storytelling. Overall, the 1999 BBC production effectively combined and balanced the advantages of miniseries expansiveness with feature film brevity, while also avoiding the disadvantages of both. It deservedly won a Peabody Award in 2000 and is widely available for screening on Amazon Prime but remains curiously obscure among the general viewing public. This is possibly because the story has become so popular onscreen that few people nowadays have read the nearly 900-page novel.

Following almost immediately after the definitive 1999 miniseries, Hallmark-TNT released its own three-hour (three episode) version of *David Copperfield* in 2000. Perhaps noting that the BBC production did not achieve the viewer ratings that it deserved, Hallmark-TNT set about rectifying this by bringing in better name recognition for the performers and avoiding the many subtleties of the novel itself. It succeeded in both respects. The 2000 *David Copperfield*, directed by Peter Medak (b. 1937), was gorgeously filmed in Ireland, but in all other respects comes across as deficient and inferior to the benchmark 1999 BBC version. An eclectic Anglo-American cast introduced a 25-year-old Hugh Dancy as the adult David and more improbably, Michael Richards (better known as Kramer from *Seinfeld*) as Micawber, Marvel film star Paul Bettany as Steerforth, and the unmistakable Sally Field as Aunt Betsey, filling in at the last moment for an indisposed Angela Lansbury, who had been originally slated for the role. Wickfield was competently portrayed by the excellent Edward Hardwicke, while Nigel Davenport did likewise for the character of Daniel Peggotty. For that matter, the performances seemed to become more skilled for the less prominent characters; for example, English stage veterans Eileen Atkins and Anthony Andrews delivered exceptional portrayals of the evil Murdstone siblings. All in all, the 2000 *David Copperfield* was favorably received by the public at the time of its release, and remains available for viewing, but today has become a rather forgettable affair in comparison to several other miniseries and feature film versions.

After so many successful or not-so-successful attempts at filming Dickens' novel over the last century or more, one might expect there is little left to for moviemakers say on the subject, but this has proven not to be the case. In late 2019, *The Personal History of David Copperfield* was distributed by Lionsgate UK-Searchlight Pictures, then given a late 2020 release in the United States during the height of the ongoing pandemic. Directed by British-Italian auteur Armando Iannucci (b. 1963) and co-written by Simon Blackwell (b. 1966), the film is barely two hours long but grabbed widespread attention by highlighting a single aspect of Dickens' novel previously overlooked—its biting satire—a strength for which Iannucci has been widely noted.[29] Recent works by Iannucci in a similar vein have included *The Death of Stalin* (2017) and the HBO sci-fi series *Avenue 5*, helping to his establish his reputation as a modern-day Jonathan Swift for the big screen. Partially filmed at London's historic Ealing Studios, the 2019 *David Copperfield* stars British-Indian star Dev Patel in the lead role, surrounded by a cast of surprising ethnic diversity.[30] That such diversity

10. David Copperfield (1849–1850)

is so successfully carried off by Iannucci's creative team is even more surprising as applied to a novelist sometimes lumped together with the likes of Rudyard Kipling for being allegedly tone-deaf regarding race relations. Rounding out an exciting Anglo-Irish-Scots-Welsh-African-Asian supporting cast is Tilda Swinton (Aunt Betsey), Hugh Laurie (Mr. Dick), Peter Capaldi (Micawber), Ben Whishaw (Uriah Heep), Rosalind Eleazar (Agnes), Nikki Amuka-Bird (Mrs. Steerforth), and Benedict Wong, the latter as a very alcoholic and helpless Mr. Wickfield. Iannucci's startling contemporary masterpiece provides clear evidence that both *David Copperfield* and Charles Dickens remain highly relevant to our troubled modern times while simultaneously providing delightful entertainment both at home and in the theater.[31]

By the conclusion of the mid–19th century in 1850, Charles Dickens found himself at the top of his world and profession, with the novel *David Copperfield* epitomizing his celebrity. Only two decades earlier, he had been an unknown teenaged freelance journalist, hopelessly smitten with a young woman, Maria Beadnell, who would nonetheless be soon forgotten, trying to find his way through life with little meaningful assistance from his biological family. By 1850, Dickens was a pillar of Victorian respectability and artistic admiration wherever the English language was read, and sometimes even beyond that in translation. Publicly, on the surface of this projected image, he was happily married with a large family of children, along with plenty of friends, charitable connections, and wealthy business associates. Like David Copperfield, he had become the hero of his own life, at least to those who did not know him well. The reality, however, was that this image was on the verge of collapse, as the next 20 years would grotesquely demonstrate. Meanwhile, his legendary, mythical reputation continued, and surprisingly continues into the present day.[32] Dickens the novelist, on the other hand, would change directions after 1850, beginning with a series of "social novels" that would seemingly attack the very foundations of capitalist society, while simultaneously earning even greater amounts of wealth for him both as an author and public reader for hire. The public may have been fooled about his personal life, but the novels continued to speak for themselves, and to tell quite a different story from his perceived autobiography.

11

Bleak House
(1852–1853)

> *"Dead, your Majesty. Dead, my lords and gentlemen. Dead, right reverends and wrong reverends of every order. Dead, men and women, born with heavenly compassion in your hearts. And dying thus around us every day."*[1]

During the late 1970s when I was a struggling law student, one of the few bright spots of that trying experience was a stimulating course in Wills and Trusts in which our esteemed instructor earnestly warned the entire class of many potential corrosive and destructive effects stemming from all contested estates. Cited as a prime example was the famous (though fictional) case of *Jarndyce v. Jarndyce* from the English Court of Chancery in which the fortunes and hopes of all contestants are wiped out (while only attorneys are enriched) long before any final resolution of the estate occurs.[2] No one in my class objected that the cited case was fictional—the product of a novelist's imagination, drawn from *Bleak House* by Charles Dickens—even though many of us were perfectly aware of the fact.[3] So effectively did Dickens' imagined legal deadlock represent reality for those of us familiar with the book, that there was no question whether a true-life court case would make a better exemplar. For most of the law students in that class, fiction had effectively become reality, even though we well knew better, all thanks to the prodigious storytelling skills of Charles Dickens. When the novelist furiously summarizes the unnecessary and pointless death of Poor Jo the Crossing Sweeper (see epigraph), he speaks to his reading public in the same dramatic manner as a legal advocate would address a judge and jury, not dissimilar to the drawn out, slow decline of Dora Spenlow in *David Copperfield*—in the former instance, however, more like a legal witness testifying before a court of judgment.

Bleak House by Charles Dickens first appeared in monthly installments between 1852 and 1853, then immediately as a complete novel, with

11. Bleak House (1852–1853)

illustrations by "Phiz" (Hablot Knight Browne), published by Bradbury & Evans of London. By this time, Dickens was no longer using the pseudonym "Boz" and in fact had not done so in nearly a decade. There were no more Christmas novellas forthcoming.[4] By 1852, Dickens was 40 years old and beginning to move into new, more serious directions, both as a man and as a writer. Almost simultaneously with *Bleak House*, Dickens wrote perhaps his most obscure work, *A Child's History of England* (1852–1854), his only attempt at young adult non-fiction, written mostly by dictation to his sister-in-law Georgy Hogarth, and by his own admission a book written to steer his own growing children towards more liberal political views. By contrast, *Bleak House* was the first in Dickens' consecutive trio of towering "social" novels during the mid–1850s—the other two being *Hard Times* and *Little Dorrit*—reflecting his intensified interest in the contemporary social and economic problems of Great Britain, as well as a heightened awareness of his own power as a novelist to influence political change by telling an effective story. Despite a significantly increased seriousness and darkness of tone, *Bleak House* proved to be, like its immediate predecessors *David Copperfield* and *Dombey and Son*, an unqualified commercial and critical success, although it has fallen a bit into neglect during the 20th and 21st centuries. In the words of biographer Claire Tomalin, "Dickens spoke to the people, and the people responded, and saw that *Bleak House* is among the greatest of his books."[5]

An 1868 portrait of Anglo-Scottish philosopher Thomas Carlyle by George Frederick Watts. Carlyle was a friend of Dickens and the dedicatee of *Hard Times* (1854). This was the first Dickens novel to completely forego illustrations, and modern film adaptations have been scarce (© Victoria & Albert Museum, London).

Although the novelist was pushing into new artistic territory with *Bleak House*, he did not forget the qualities always giving his work a distinctive appeal, beginning with a nostalgically sentimental, pre-Victorian setting in the 1820s and 1830s. The dominant, older characters in the novel represent the same generation that lived through, fought, and won the Napoleonic wars for Great Britain. And what a cast of characters they are. The doomed Captain Hawdon, alias Nemo ("Nobody"), a Waterloo combat veteran consigned to poverty, neglect, and obscurity, along with his devoted but more fortunate former comrade-in-arms Mr. George, become almost patriarchal figures within the storyline, despite their limited appearances.[6] Hawdon, along with his lover Honoria (later transforming herself into the aristocratic Lady Dedlock), are gradually revealed to be the biological parents of Esther Summerson, first-person narrator of *Bleak House*, and Dickens' only female narrator, herself partially based on the real-life Esther Elton, an orphaned young woman known personally to Dickens and helped by him through his many charitable activities.[7] The fictional Esther Summerson from the novel is illegitimately born and socially handicapped because of this lowly status, despite her genteel origins, and possibly like Dickens' own biological father John, who is now suspected of having been the illegitimate child of English nobility, thus making Dickens himself possibly the illegitimate grandchild of English nobility.

Inequities within the English class system, however, are only a starting point for the many social criticisms of Dickens in the novel, and these inequities, as epitomized by a large, eccentric cast of characters, have transferred exceedingly well to film during the era of cinema. The previously mentioned Court of Chancery and interminable disputes of *Jarndyce v. Jarndyce* magnify the futility of achieving legal justice or recompense no matter how just the claim, leading the Dickens-like surrogate paternal figure and proprietor of Bleak House, John Jarndyce, to advise (in vain) his wards Richard Carstone and Ada to forgo any such claims for the sake of physical health, if nothing else. Far more disturbing is Jarndyce's close associate Harold Skimpole, an amoral ascetic, useless in both business and friendship, based on Dickens' own acquaintance with Leigh Hunt, who, along with his family, were deeply troubled by his unflattering portrayal within the novel.[8] In contrast to Skimpole, the law clerk William Guppy makes horrible first impressions, but by the end of the story proves himself to be both an effective helper and magnanimous in motive. Guppy's underlying benevolence is initially recognized only by the incredibly vicious and opportunistic moneylender Joshua Smallweed, a type of very real personage that apologists for unrestrained capitalism seem to never acknowledge, but who was obviously quite familiar to the novelist. Smallweed is deformed both morally and physically ("Shake me up, Judy!") and is most adept at taking advantage of other people's weakness, even those of disreputable associates such as Hawdon's landlord Krook, who dies grotesquely of alleged spontaneous combustion, a malaise long since discredited by

11. Bleak House (1852–1853)

science but given credence by many of Dickens' less educated readers. Last but far from least comes Poor Jo the Crossing Sweeper, a young street child befriended by Hawdon and later, after Hawdon's demise, dying his own pointless and tragic death from neglect and disease.[9] So poignant was Jo's death to many readers, that it served for inspiration for some of the earliest film dramatizations of Dickens' work during the silent era.

One other character creation from *Bleak House* deserves special mention, in that it eventually became an early prototype for countless other books and movies following in its wake. Inspector Bucket of Scotland Yard was not the first literary detective in the English language—that signal distinction goes to C. Auguste Dupin from *The Murders in the Rue Morgue* (1841) by Edgar Allan Poe (1809–1849)—although Bucket certainly represents a significant milestone in the genre and, as Claire Tomalin observed, "*Bleak House* is one of the first detective stories in the language."[10] Dickens had briefly met Poe during his first American tour a decade earlier, and based alone on Dickens' subsequent output, Poe and his groundbreaking work clearly made an impression on the English novelist. As for Dickens' memorable character of Inspector Bucket, he appears, like so many other characters in *Bleak House*, based on actual prototypes drawn from the early days of Scotland Yard in London. Subsequent film adaptations, beginning in the silent era, would not fail to portray Bucket nor to dramatize his objective, professional view of repulsive criminal behavior in the novel.

While *Bleak House* has received neither the most numerous nor the most famous film treatments among Dickens novels, almost all attempts have been noteworthy and, in their own peculiar ways, unique or, in some cases, indispensable. For example, as recently as 2012, a one-minute silent short titled *The Death of Poor Joe*, originally made in March 1901 and reportedly not seen since 1954, presumably since lost, was rediscovered in Great Britain. It is the oldest known surviving film featuring a Charles Dickens character, Jo from *Bleak House*. More precisely, it is currently the oldest known surviving feature using a scenario suggested by a Dickens novel, with "Joe" (not Jo, as in the text) dying outdoors on the street from exposure and exhaustion in the arms of a watchman. This is unlike the silent short *Marley's Ghost* from later that same year in 1901, which is significantly longer in length and follows more closely the storyline from *A Christmas Carol*. Almost half a century after publication of Dickens' novel, the pathetic death of Poor Jo the Crossing Sweeper had become synonymous with the unnecessary, underaged street casualties of urban London, as well as with the famous Victorian author and his novels which brought this phenomenon more to the center of public consciousness. *The Death of Poor Joe* was filmed by the British jack-of-all-trades and experimental director George Albert Smith (1864–1959), with the director's wife, Laura Bayley, portraying the adolescent Joe in the great British stage tradition of cross-gender roles.[11] Another effective storytelling device, one often employed by Dickens, was the tragic, premature deaths of older children or underaged minors, such as those found in *Nicholas Nickleby* (Smike), *The Old Curiosity Shop* (Little Nell), and *Dombey and Son* (Paul, Jr.)—all massive best-sellers. For the novelist, Poor Jo of *Bleak House* was the latest in a long line of this noteworthy character type apparently found fascinating by Victorian readers.

After this came two British silent movies dramatizing a subplot from *Bleak House* in which the evil lawyer Tulkinghorn attempts to blackmail Lady Dedlock on her former relationship with Hawdon, presumably using information from Hawdon's friend Jo. Both works were titled *Jo the Crossing Sweeper*, the first from 1910, and then a more expanded version of the same story in 1918.[12] Both films are now considered lost—a shame because we can now only guess at how this story was developed for movie audiences during this decade. Lady Dedlock is another one of Dickens' more complex female characters, a beautiful and intelligent woman achieving respectability by concealing her past, even while her illegitimate daughter Esther lives and narrates the tale. Dedlock's role in film has attracted high caliber actors from the start, beginning with silent star Dora de Winton in 1918, while the cast from 1910 version remains unknown. For the 1918 British expanded remake, noted director Alexander Butler was brought in (1869–1959) both to direct the movie and to play the villainous lawyer Tulkinghorn, along with screenwriter Irene Miller (1880–1964), and another female actor (Unity More) playing the adolescent male role of Jo, as well as noted character actor Rolf Leslie to portray Inspector Bucket.

With the early 1920s came two attempts in the U.K. to develop *Bleak House* as a more serious cinematic experience. First in 1920 came a production by the Ideal Film Company, followed up by a shorter segment in 1922 directed by British film pioneer Henry Boughton Parkinson (1884–1970) as part of his series, *Tense Moments from Great Plays*.[13] Both prints reportedly still survive.[14] The 1920 film featured stage and screen icon Constance Collier (Laura Constance Hardy) as Lady Dedlock, while the same role in the 1922 *Bleak House* went to the famed thespian Sybil Thorndyke. The earlier 1920 production was directed by the highly visible Maurice Elvey, who had recently directed an early silent version of *Dombey and Son* under wartime conditions in 1917. By the late 1920s, however, all silent films had become obsolete, thanks to sound technology. Then rather improbably, in 1928, a nine-minute short feature titled *Grandfather Smallweed* (based on the minor character from *Bleak House*) was produced in Great Britain utilizing a primitive recorded accompaniment, starring

11. Bleak House (1852–1853)

the professional Dickensian character actor Bransby Williams in the title role.[15] Thus *Grandfather Smallweed*, along with its lost 1928 short counterpart *Scrooge* (also by Williams) holds the unusual distinction of being the first surviving talking film based on a Dickens novel, although Paramount's *Rich Man's Folly* (1931), coming three years later and loosely based on *Dombey and Son*, was the first full-length feature in that respect. Then after *Grandfather Smallweed* of 1928, came three decades of cinematic silence for *Bleak House*.

Finally, in 1959, the BBC began to apply its game-changing miniseries television format to Dickens' underappreciated masterwork, some three years after its successful similar production for *David Copperfield* (1956). The first BBC production for *Bleak House* consisted of 11 half-hour episodes (about five hours total), as well as being the first such effort from British screenwriter Constance Cox, who would then go on to adapt a series of similar Dickensian efforts during the late 1950s and early 1960s.[16] The 1959 BBC miniseries featured an experienced and capable, but relatively unknown cast of stage actors led by the late Australian-born Diana Fairfax as Esther Summerson. The patriarchal role of John Jarndyce was portrayed by British TV favorite Andrew Cruickshank who, curiously enough, was two years later cast for a minor role in the epic Hollywood film *El Cid* (1961), for which he is probably best remembered by American audiences. This rare but significant video is still available as a British import DVD for viewers with compatible hardware. Another quarter century would then lapse before *Bleak House* was again seen on Anglo-American television.[17]

The second BBC miniseries for *Bleak House* appeared in 1985, part of a bumper crop of similar Thatcher-era productions during the mid–1980s immediately following the spectacular stage success of *Nicholas Nickleby* for the Royal Shakespeare Company.[18] The 1985 *Bleak House* (re-running in 1991) starred the late great Diana Rigg as Lady Dedlock in a very long eight-episode, eight-hour presentation.[19] In addition to its extraordinary length, however, the 1985 miniseries suffered from Diana Rigg's valuable screen time being used too sparingly, as well as from a somewhat long-winded script and dated style of cinematography. On the positive side, the supporting cast featured some of Great Britain's then best character actors, including Denholm Elliott as John Jarndyce, Peter Vaughan as Tulkinghorn, Ann Reid as Mrs. Bagnet, and Irish-born T.P. McKenna as a wonderfully repulsive and manipulative Harold Skimpole. The 1985 BBC *Bleak House* also holds the unusual distinction of being the first Dickens novel fully dramatized for American TV audiences on the popular *Masterpiece Theatre* series, that franchise having by then run over 14 successful seasons on PBS. It can still be easily viewed by viewers having access to Amazon Prime.

Twenty years later, in 2005, the BBC produced its third miniseries for *Bleak House* in 15 episodes—like its 1985 predecessor, clocking in at a total of eight hours. Again, like the 1985 production, the 2005 *Bleak House* was featured on PBS *Masterpiece Theatre* that same year in a revised format of six long episodes.[20] Starring as Lady Dedlock was the 38-year-old American-born celebrity actor Gillian Anderson, by that time well-established as a household name, thanks in large part to her decade-long appearances on the hit TV show *The X-Files* (1993–2002). Anderson's transition to more serious roles such as this one reflected her undeniable talent as a performer. Sensibly co-directed by Susanna White (b. 1960) and Justin Chadwick (b. 1968), the miniseries also benefited enormously from sharp, sympathetic screenwriting by British virtuoso literary adaptor Andrew Davies (1936) and striking on-site locations for filming. A powerful supporting cast included (among many others) Timothy West as Sir Leicester Dedlock, Anna Maxwell Martin as Esther, Burn Gorman as William Guppy, Denis Lawson as John Jarndyce, Charles Dance as Tulkinghorn, Alun Armstrong as Inspector Bucket, and notably, a 20-year-old Carey Mulligan as Ada. The 2005 *Bleak House* deservedly won a Peabody Award for excellence that same year, and remains, without question, the best film adaptation of this complex but rewarding Dickens novel.

Viewers are especially fortunate to have the superb quality *Bleak House* of 2005 from the BBC, because there does not appear to have been any big financial payoff for its production. The novel has never belonged to the "big six" of Dickens' total output, despite its high reputation among critics and connoisseurs, and the market niche for its appeal has always been limited, not unlike the limited market niche for *Masterpiece Theatre* itself as a television entertainment outlet. We suspect that a big reason for this storyline lacking mass appeal is the tough nature of Dickens' subject matter. In short, *Bleak House* is too bleak. The endless futility of Chancery court dominates the plot, destroying the physical and mental health of anyone overly invested in the process. For many unwilling participants—even in modern times, as I learned long ago in school—the story setting is a harsh reality from which most readers or viewers would rather escape than have to confront during their leisure hours.[21] Add to this unpleasantness the recurring theme of respectable society discarding or trying to discard its combat veterans like Captain Hawdon or Mr. George, a much more unflattering reflection than the unlimited cheerfulness of Dickens' Captain Cuttle from his earlier *Dombey and Son*. The same men who beat Napoleon were later disowned by those for whom they fought—in Hawdon's case, he is literally discarded by his lover and the mother of his daughter—and the problem seems to be as perpetual as it is vividly modern. Lastly, Dickens' scathing indictment of a supposedly respectable

11. Bleak House (1852–1853)

society allowing disadvantaged children like Poor Jo to die neglected in poverty is timeless and contemporary as well.[22] Given these tough innovations, it is a wonder that the book sold as well as it did during its own day. For that matter, perhaps even Victorian readers were not fully prepared for what was delivered to them by the novelist.

The one bright spot in the tale is Dickens' narrator Esther Summerson, who ends the story relatively happy despite her disadvantaged birth, a near-death encounter with smallpox, and the sufferings or demise of all those surrounding her. Esther becomes, like David Copperfield, the heroine of her own life, but at a higher personal cost and with a much rougher journey through life. In fact, Esther's happiness pales somewhat in comparison to the unhappiness of her doomed parents, the wretchedness of Poor Jo, the forlornness of Ada, the loneliness of Jarndyce and Guppy, the madness of Richard Carstone and Miss Flite, the depravities of Skimpole and Smallweed, the evil motivations of Tulkinghorn, and so forth. Even the character of Esther has been criticized by some readers for her relentless positive attitude while constantly surrounded by unrepentant wickedness. If Dickens the novelist was trying to educate Victorian readers on the many shortcomings of their society, he certainly pulled no punches while doing so. Just as he simultaneously tried to educate his own children with a more liberal political outlook and less blinkered view of turbulent English history, Dickens also attempted to educate his devoted reading public on the squalid, secretive urban England existing beyond the protective bubbles of the privileged class. Accordingly, *Bleak House* marked a new beginning for its creator in which the boundaries of hard truth-telling within the framework of storytelling mass entertainment would be pushed and tested to the limits. The forthcoming second of Dickens' "social novels" would be even more uncompromising in this same respect.

12

Hard Times (1854)

> "'Some persons hold,' he pursued, still hesitating, 'that there is a wisdom of the Head, and that there is a wisdom of the Heart. I have not supposed so; but, as I have said, I mistrust myself now. I have supposed the head to be all-sufficient. It may not be all-sufficient...'"[1]

One plausible explanation for the tremendous success of Charles Dickens as a combined novelist and social critic was that he typically attacked what he perceived as bad ideas or bad institutions, rather than the actual people who endorsed them. His villains, like his heroes, tend to be drawn imprecisely enough so as not to have been readily identified with living persons. There are, of course, notable near-exceptions; for example, Dickens' scathing portrayal of his social acquaintance Leigh Hunt as Harold Skimpole in *Bleak House*—a portrayal which caused the novelist considerable embarrassment. While modern literary scholarship has done a respectable job of identifying real-life models or composites for Dickens' unforgettable characterizations, many remain to this day mysterious, abstract, or appropriately obscure so as not to cause an undue or overly distracting backlash. On the other hand, no reader can ever forget Oliver Twist asking for more (and being rebuffed), or Scrooge barking "Bah! Humbug!" at anyone's suggestion of charity, although it is unknown if the inspirations for these characters and situations are real or purely imagined. We suspect most are based on reality, but in Dickens' world, one remembers the sin more than the sinner. For his next major work, the novelist would turn his focus on the surprisingly interrelated worlds of formal education and popular entertainment, while remaining true to a creative genius which condemned harmful actions rather than the actors themselves.

Hard Times: For These Times first appeared during mid–1854 as a serial in *Household Words*, a weekly journal founded and edited by Dickens himself, but within that same year was published as a finished novel

12. Hard Times (1854)

by Bradbury & Evans of London. The completed work was dedicated to the Anglo-Scottish historian and philosopher Thomas Carlyle (1795–1881), a prominent Victorian establishment figure who befriended and praised Dickens, perhaps recognizing the novelist's unique ability to influence public opinion through his art. *Hard Times* was (and is) in many respects unique as a Dickens work of fiction. The second in his towering consecutive trio of "social" novels, it had no illustrations in the original editions, and was less than a third in overall length of what Dickens' reading public normally expected. Immediately after the serialization of *Hard Times* in *Household Words* circa late 1854, another social protest novel of considerable note, *North and South* by Elizabeth Gaskell (1810–1865), a near-contemporary author mutually befriended by both Dickens and Carlyle, appeared in the same journal.[2] Dickens had inserted his latest release, as well as the novel by Gaskell, to boost periodical sales. The move succeeded impressively for Dickens (less so for Gaskell), despite mixed critical

"Attorney and Client, Fortitude and Impatience": 1853 illustration from the first edition of *Bleak House* by Hablot Knight Browne (aka "Phiz"). After the rousing success of *David Copperfield*, Dickens would embark upon his trilogy of darker "social" novels, beginning with *Bleak House*.

reception for Dickens' work and his uncompromising stance on controversial issues such as labor relations, public education, and popular entertainment. *Hard Times* today remains one of Dickens' more challenging and least popular novels for the same reasons, although at the time of its release it served its intended commercial purpose magnificently, as well as to solidify Dickens' reputation as a champion of Victorian English society's more weak and exploited elements.

The favorable reception of *Hard Times* among Dickens' core audience was also a bit surprising in that the plot dispenses with several of the novelist's favorite storyline devices. The fictional setting of Coketown is likely based on the northern English mill town of Preston, Lancashire, which he had visited earlier that same year to observe growing labor unrest.[3] Except for a few storyline interludes, gone is the urban London town nearly synonymous with this author, in favor of a northern provincial setting, one located, with a fair amount of precision, at the cradle of the modern Industrial Revolution.[4] The presumed timeframe is firmly contemporary (circa 1854), with limited sentimentality of outlook and no nostalgia whatsoever for the distant past, both qualities otherwise found in abundance within the more typical Dickens novel. For example, among the characters, absent are discarded war veterans, street hustlers, fallen women, or any other reminders of common folk not typically acknowledged by polite society, except for the hapless mill worker Stephen Blackpool, trapped between his mistrustful, exploitive employer, a stridently demanding labor union, and an abusive, alcoholic wife. Stephen only wants to work, but instead finds himself first locked out of the mill and later fired by the mill owner because he is unwilling to be a strikebreaker, then unjustly accused of theft, and finally dying a pointless death from unsafe working conditions while in exile. He ranks as one of Dickens' most pathetic tragic figures, and yet Victorian readers responded to him. It is less likely these readers responded with similar enthusiasm to the novelist's laser-like focus on the necessary overlap between good education and good entertainment, notwithstanding protestations from an unsympathetic Thomas Gradgrind that he had modified his personal views on this question (see epigraph). Ultimately, as critics such as Claire Tomalin have noted, *Hard Times* is difficult for most modern readers to approach as entertainment because the novel "fails to take note of its own message that people must be amused."[5]

One thing that Dickens did not alter in *Hard Times* was his prodigious gift for characterization, a quality that would serve later generations well for film adaptations of all his novels, including this one. Central to the grim plot is Thomas Gradgrind, a successful merchant-educator turned elected M.P., and a professed Utilitarian disciple of John Stuart Mill (1806–1873), another Victorian philosopher famed during his own lifetime for his emphases on facts, figures, and immediate usefulness as legitimate activity.[6] Readers meet Gradgrind as he browbeats his reluctant students on the importance of memorization, in particular the circus castaway child, Sissy Jupe, who wins our sympathy through her wisdom and constancy despite being relentlessly criticized and looked down upon by her presumed social betters. Two of Gradgrind's sons are named after the revered philosophers Adam Smith and Malthus—neither one esteemed by Dickens—while his two eldest children, daughter Louisa and son Thomas Jr., then become central to the plot.[7] Both Louisa and Thomas Jr. are reared and educated based on strict Utilitarian principles but come to grief despite this. Tom dies young as a thief, liar, and fugitive, while Louisa marries strictly to please her father, then has an unhappy affair with her father's opportunistic colleague James Harthouse, all the while lamenting her strict and joyless upbringing. Thus, Dickens attacked John Stuart Mill not by name, but rather through the character of Gradgrind. The main antagonist of the storyline is the selfish mill owner Josiah Bounderby, who marries a much younger Louisa while wreaking havoc on any other innocent lives he happens to encounter, including that of Stephen Blackpool. Other than the much put upon Sissy Jupe, the only other character in *Hard Times* to engage considerable reader sympathy is Sleary, the speech-impaired ringmaster of a traveling circus, who nonetheless oftentimes speaks with the wisdom of a Greek Chorus while always acting to the benefit of others, whether it be Sissy, Thomas Jr., and anyone else crossing his path, deserving or not.

Twentieth-century film adaptations of *Hard Times* have been scarce but high in quality and of considerable interest whenever undertaken. First, in 1915, just as the Great War was making its terrible impact felt on a worldwide scale, came a silent feature from Great Britain, written and directed by the respected adaptor Thomas Bentley, and starring Dickensian specialist Bransby Williams as Thomas Gradgrind.[8] Like many other important works by Bentley from this same era, the 1915 *Hard Times* is now considered lost.[9] The additional loss of Bransby Williams' portrayal of Gradgrind must also be considered particularly frustrating, given that actor's famed legacy among Dickens enthusiasts. All that is left today are printed reviews of the work upon its initial release, some noting that the biting realism and social critiques of the printed novel had been toned down considerably for the film version, a not surprising feature as British industry was then gearing up in the middle of a wartime effort and likely not to tolerate any work of art questioning its activities.[10] Then again, this was only some six decades after the novel's original publication, less than five decades after the novelist's death, and it marked the very first time anyone had attempted a film adaptation. Arguably Dickens' main appeal as a writer, and his work's biggest appeal as a basis for movies, lay in his sentimentalized characterizations, a device through which he proceeded to amplify some of the most poignant and effectively influential social commentary ever committed to the so-called fictional format of the English novel.

Following the 1915 silent effort there would pass another six decades before filmmakers would again approach one of Dickens' most uncompromising works. During this long interim, two world wars, an economic depression, and postwar boom would all come and go, until the mid–1970s when economic turbulence would again be seriously felt by western civilization, especially in Great Britain. Significantly, during this same period, a major re-evaluation of Dickens' literary biography would be grudgingly initiated and slowly accepted by serious readers of his work. As a result, the radicalism inherent in all of Dickens' novels, especially his "social" novels, would come to be far more appreciated, spurring a much broader examination of his output and spinoffs, including those on film. Another major cultural development between 1915 and the 1970s was the ascendency of television as popular video entertainment. While Dickens' contemporaries stole away to enjoy the traveling circus, modern audiences became glued to their TV sets. One important outgrowth of this newer trend was the invention of the TV miniseries, pioneered by the BBC during the 1950s and early 1960s, leading directly to the long-term establishment of *Masterpiece Theatre* on prime time for English-speaking audiences, specifically, for American viewers, meaning Sunday nights on public broadcasting networks. The highly episodic structure of all Dickens' novels proved to be naturally and ideally suited for this newfangled dramatic format.

When *Hard Times* finally received a full-blown miniseries treatment in 1977, however, it was neither the BBC nor *Masterpiece Theatre* which sponsored it, but rather the BBC's UK rival Granada ITV, in conjunction with the American PBS *Great Performances* series, in existence since 1972, and by 1977 in its fourth successful season. *Hard Times* proved to be its first Dickens adaptation, and indeed the first time that American mass audiences had seen a British-produced miniseries from a Dickens novel. For four, one-hour episodes, Granada brought in an experienced crew to oversee the project, including director John Irvin (b. 1940), screenwriter Arthur Hopcraft (1932–2004), and composer Malcolm Arnold (1921–2006).[11] Shot on location in northern England by a northern English director (Irvin), the production was reportedly the most expensive television drama then made to date in England.[12] Reviews were favorable, including from the *New York Times*, although in hindsight it appears odd that one of Dickens' most uncompromising novels became one of the first that American audiences were widely exposed to as a miniseries.[13] Given the economic turbulence of the late 1970s, both in the United States and in Great

Britain, it is perhaps understandable why this book was chosen, but like the novelist himself in 1854, the producers of the 1977 *Hard Times* seem to have temporarily forgotten that during actual economic hard times, viewing audiences tend to seek escape from such difficult circumstances rather than be grimly and toughly reminded of these during their leisurely entertainment.

Granada ITV brought together an interesting cast for its dark-hued production, fitting for a novel with so many memorable characterizations. Leading the pack was a quartet of British male actors bringing both wide experience and considerable name recognition to the table, including Patrick Allen as Thomas Gradgrind, Timothy West as Josiah Bounderby, Edward Fox as James Harthouse, and Alan Dobie as Stephen Blackpool. Fox especially, by the late 1970s, had become a household name through the movies, beginning with his chilling lead role in *The Day of the Jackal* (1973). Allen, West, and Dobie were also by that time all well established as character actors both on stage and screen. Interestingly cast as Gradgrind's adult daughter Louisa was Jacqueline Tong, then fresh off her recurring role of the much put-upon housemaid Daisy in the recent hit BBC-PBS television series *Upstairs, Downstairs* (1973–1975). Another innovative choice in casting was the late Rosalie Crutchley, a formally trained and prolific actor, as Mrs. Sparsit, Bounderby's nosey, ill-treated, and yet devoted housekeeper, bringing an added dimension of interest to this oft-overlooked secondary role. Despite good casting and careful attention to detail, however, American TV audiences of 1977 had many other, less high-minded viewing options, and this benchmark production of *Hard Times* never received the widespread attention that it deserved, despite being arguably the best and most faithful adaptation of this difficult Dickens novel made to date thus far.

The purpose of this survey does not include delving into the many foreign film adaptations influenced by Dickens either directly or indirectly, with perhaps a few exceptions, especially those which appear to have impacted English-speaking markets. One of these occurred rather unexpectedly in 1988 when the 39-year-old Portuguese auteur João Botelho presented *Hard Times* as an uncompromisingly abstract expressionist art film (*Tempos Difíceis*), shot in black and white, and modernizing the setting to urban Portugal of the late 1980s.[14] By this point in history, Botelho had become Portugal's most famous filmmaker, having won prizes for his more recent work and receiving worldwide distribution to populous Portuguese-speaking markets, including that of Brazil in South America. The movie then hit Anglo markets with English subtitles a year later in mid-1989.[15] Although many American viewers find any film with subtitles tedious, and Botelho's meditative, pseudo-documentary style struck some being as too slow-paced, the fact remained that Dickens' shortest novel had been effectively compressed into a two-hour cinematic experience.[16] Also frequently overlooked is the traditional close cultural connection between Portugal and England, as well as that between Brazil and the United States.[17] By 1988–1989, the undesirable long-term economic effects of the Reagan administration in the U.S. and Thatcherism in the U.K. were becoming more widely apparent and intensely criticized. As a result, Botelho's politically critical film, drawing its inspiration directly from the British Victorian era, seems to have found significant resonance among a segment of Anglo-American audiences, while its technical achievements certainly drew attention within the world of cinema. Accordingly, it was not long after this that a comparable English-language (and much shorter) film version of *Hard Times* was produced.

Five years later, in 1994, a new miniseries version of *Hard Times* appeared, this one half the running length of the 1977 miniseries, jointly produced by the BBC and WGBH of Boston.[18] The 1994 production also ran as part of the 24th Season for the consistently popular *Masterpiece Theatre* series on American PBS television. In an effort no doubt to boost ratings over the 1977 miniseries for the same novel, several interesting choices were made. For starters, the distinguished British playwright Peter Barnes (1931–2004) was brought in to both direct and write the screenplay. Barnes had recently scored an important success as a screenwriter for the acclaimed 1991 film adaptation of *Enchanted April*, based on the best-selling 1922 novel by Elizabeth von Arnim (1866–1941). Later that same decade Barnes would go on to write a teleplay adaptation of Dickens' *A Christmas Carol* for Patrick Stewart's notable 1999 film. For the 1994 BBC *Hard Times*, however, Barnes would face the daunting task of distilling Dickens' most condensed novel, and one of his least popular. The end-result, though certainly worthwhile, proved not quite as compelling as the longer 1977 version. By necessity, the 1994 production was more streamlined but less detailed and nuanced than either the novel or the earlier miniseries—streamlining always being tricky business for Dickens' storylines in which every single detail is usually of consequence. For example, Sleary's speaking role in 1994 is greatly reduced from 1977, a problem because his voice is the primary voice of conscience (for the novelist) within the plot.

Nevertheless, the 1994 casting was too intriguing to be overlooked. In the crucial role of Thomas Gradgrind was the late British journeyman actor Bob Peck, then having recently received unaccustomed public visibility for his part in Steven Spielberg's blockbuster film *Jurassic Park* (1993). Even more fascinating was the choice of 60-year-old Alan Bates as Josiah Bounderby, Bates having been a well-known international film presence since the early 1960s. Bates' performance may be the most interesting aspect of the production, although seeing this talented actor playing a one-dimensional, unsympathetic character can be a problem for many viewers, including this one. By contrast, the classically trained comedienne Dilys Laye brought a memorable depiction of Mrs. Sparsit to the screen, one likely inspired by the earlier 1977 performance of Rosalie Crutchley in the same role. Versatile Scottish actor Bill Paterson instilled a suitable pathos into his portrayal of Stephen Blackpool, while the highly accomplished Dame Harriet Walter did the same for Stephen's unrequited companion, Rachael. Other cast members were brought in from recent cinematic successes, including Richard E. Grant as James Harthouse, having appeared in Martin Scorsese's adaptation of Edith Wharton's *The Age of Innocence* (1993), and more notably, a rare but effective performance by Emma Lewis as Dickens' understated heroine Sissy Jupe. Lewis, though not a prolific actor, had gained notice from her minor role in Merchant and Ivory's acclaimed film version for *Remains of the Day* (1993).[19] To repeat, although the 1994 *Hard Times* must ultimately be considered inferior to the longer 1977 BBC miniseries, it is still well worth screening based on its own considerable merits.

Other than several recent stage adaptations of note, there have been no new attempts to film *Hard Times* since 1994.[20] Given the growing socioeconomic instability of our contemporary era, this dearth of interest in Dickens' most polemical socioeconomic novel may soon change; however, for the time being, cinematic focus remains on the novelist's core repertoire, to which *Hard Times* most decidedly does not belong. The problems causing this scarcity of interpretation, unfortunately, are traceable to weaknesses in source material. At the time of writing, Dickens appears to have been mainly struggling at being a good parent—a role that he was never comfortable with, as revealed by modern biographers—and deeply concerned that his children might be educated by Utilitarian merchants-turned-politicians like Thomas Gradgrind. There is no nostalgia for the author's own childhood, no sentimentality, and no London town to speak of. Instead, readers are presented with a provincial industrialized setting dismally torn apart by labor strife and inadequate public education. Despite modest commercial success for this novel, Dickens appears to have been aware of these problems, for he never wrote a preface for the complete work, an anomaly for him.[21] Instead, for his next major project, he would revert to his most distinctive qualities as a novelist, while retaining other a trademark social critique, thus producing one of his most memorable, and yet simultaneously disturbing storylines.

13

Little Dorrit (1855–1857)

> "'But I bear those monotonous walls no ill-will now,' said Mr. Meagles. 'One always begins to forgive a place as soon as it's left behind; I dare say a prisoner begins to relent towards his prison, after he is let out.'"[1]

A strong argument can be made that the defining event in the life of Charles Dickens occurred in May of 1824, when he was 12 years old. It was then that his 38-year-old father John Dickens was incarcerated in a London debtors' prison for failing to pay a running tab at a local bakery. Although John would be freed from debtors' prison and the outstanding debt discharged within less than a year, and while most of his family seems to have chalked up this setback as just another disruptive episode in John's long, roller-coaster life, the psychological effect on his young son Charles, the future famed novelist, appears to have been nothing less than traumatic in the extreme. After his father was imprisoned, Charles' mother encouraged her son to work in the harsh environment of a London shoe blacking factory, another personal experience that was never forgotten by Dickens, and for which he never forgave his mother. This humiliating employment proved to be temporary as well, but little thanks to his mother, who wanted him to stay on. Within a year, the 13-year-old Charles, with his freed father's encouragement, would be back in school and permanently removed from the status of child industrial laborer. Nevertheless, many years later, as an adult storyteller, Dickens would return in his imagination repeatedly to the unhappy period in which his father was imprisoned for debt while Charles, as a preteen boy, would be forced into the drudgery of physical toil for wages. For that matter, anytime he tried to fictionally escape from this miserable chapter of his childhood (such as he attempted to in *Hard Times*), the overall power of his storytelling seemed to suffer for it.

13. Little Dorrit (1855–1857)

Dickens' *Little Dorrit*, the third in his consecutive trilogy of "social" novels, was published as a monthly serial between late 1855 and mid-1857, then as a completed novel shortly thereafter by Bradbury & Evans of London, and lavishly illustrated by Dickens' longtime collaborator Phiz (Hablot Knight Browne). The novel sold well at the time and continues to be held in high esteem by critics, although during the modern era, like *Bleak House*, it has fallen outside the bounds of Dickens' core output

Illustration from the first edition of Dickens' *The Pickwick Papers* by Robert Seymour (1837). Plates from Dickens' novels would exert tremendous visual influence on future film adaptations of his works, beginning with *Pickwick*.

amongst the general reading public. The novelist began writing with the ironic working title of *Nobody's Fault*, angered at British bureaucratic mismanagement of the Crimean War, and no doubt inspiring a scathing fictional depiction of the government Circumlocution Office, an entrenched bureaucracy thwarting every good faith inquiry passing through its doors.[2] This led to a much broader "dark vision of England" (Claire Tomalin) centered around an overarching theme of imprisonment, beginning with the infamous Marshalsea of London, housing first William Dorrit and later the novel's hero, Arthur Clennam, just as debtors' prison had temporarily confined their literary predecessors Samuel Pickwick and Wilkins Micawber.[3] Dickens precisely dates the beginning of the story to the year 1826, only two years after his own father had been an inmate at the same institution.[4] Thus, the master storyteller immediately plunges his readers back into the pre–Victorian British past and the sinister environs of London town, alerting them that *Little Dorrit* was a return to his famous semi-autobiographical style.[5] Although the Marshalsea known to the Dickens family (as well as the fictional Dorrits) had been closed since 1842, portions of the complex were still standing in 1857 when Dickens completed the novel and wrote a Preface reminiscing about his personal impressions after visiting the site.[6]

Memories or suggestions of physical confinement dominate the text of the novel. In addition to the Dorrit family and Arthur Clennam at the Marshalsea, the story begins with the arch-villain Rigaud incarcerated for murder at a Marseilles criminal prison while Arthur and his traveling companions, the Meagles, are quarantined in the same city after returning from the Far East. Mr. Meagles keenly observes that such unpleasant experiences are viewed more dispassionately in hindsight (see epigraph). Other characters, though not legally incarcerated, are unhappily constrained, either by choice or social convention. The Meagles' misnamed servant Tattycoram hates being on the lower rung of the English class system, a system extending even to the confines of the Marshalsea, while Arthur's adoptive mother opts to stay in the same room in a wheelchair in a decaying house, despite being wealthy and iron-willed. Dickens' obsession with involuntary constraint is disturbingly suggestive of his own 20-year marriage at the time, which was about to publicly disintegrate. As for Amy "Little" Dorrit, the youngest, favorite child of William Dorrit, born and reared in the Marshalsea but free to earn a living in the outside world as a seamstress, more than one commentator has noticed her similarity to Shakespeare's Cordelia from *King Lear*, a work well known to the novelist.[7] For that matter, Shakespearean overtones abound in *Little Dorrit*, beginning with the Marshalsea itself, an institution that existed during Elizabethan times and was situated in the Southwark district of London, also home to many Elizabethan playhouses, including the Globe Theatre. During this same period (in 1856), Dickens had realized a lifelong ambition by purchasing the mansion at Gad's Hill in Kent, a location forever associated with Shakespeare's Falstaff from *Henry IV, Part I*.[8] In Dickens' novel, Arthur's troubled relationship with his presumed biological mother is Shakespearean in tone as well.[9] All in all, it may be safely observed that he seems to have had Shakespeare on his mind when writing this great but unsettling tale.

Like all of Dickens' novels, the characterizations in *Little Dorrit* are superb, leaving the firm impression that this collection of eccentrics were personally known by the author in real-life. Subsequent filmmakers, actors, and moviegoers have in turn benefited enormously. The hero Arthur Clennam is about 40 years old, slightly younger than Dickens (43–45) at the time of writing, while his gradually growing love-interest Amy Dorrit is half his age, young enough to be his own daughter, and raising more disturbing questions with respect to Dickens' biography, given that at the time he was about to embark on an extra-marital affair with an actress 27 years his junior. Arthur, like Amy's father William, are men born during the 18th century, while Amy's birth can be squarely dated to around 1806, since she was born in a prison in which her father has been an inmate for 20 years. In fact, William has been in the Marshalsea so long that no one can any longer reckon what his debts were or who his creditors are, but this does not prevent him from easily lording it over the entire establishment due to his high-ranking birthright. Meanwhile, Arthur's "ferociously pious" (Claire Tomalin) adoptive mother calls to mind the novelist's own strained maternal relations, although the flighty and foolish Mrs. Nickleby from Dickens' earlier novel might be more representative.[10] Only slightly less formidable than Mrs. Clennam is Mrs. Merdle, the manipulative and scheming wife of a corrupt investment banker, whose pet parrot makes disruptive utterances that call to mind the pet raven of Barnaby Rudge, but used with far more effective dramatic impact in the later novel. Dickens' youthful romantic obsession Maria Beadell is doubly lampooned, first as the young Pet Meagle, who jilts Arthur in favor of an unworthy suitor, then later in life as the widow Flora Finching, who seeks Arthur's attentions in vain long after her looks are gone and her manifest silliness apparent to everyone.[11] These represent only a small sampling of a large cast later proving a figurative goldmine for both filmmakers and character actors.

And then there is the social commentary aspect of the novel. Apart from the manifest uselessness of debtors' prison, the text of *Little Dorrit* seems to dwell upon the nature of wealth itself, and more importantly, its effect on people, for better and for worse. William Dorrit appears at his most noble and generous when imprisoned and under adversity, while becoming haughty and arrogant only after he inherits a fortune, allowing him to leave prison and travel the continent. Mrs. Clennam, on the other hand, only gains reader sympathy at the end of the story when she leaves the voluntary confinement of her decaying house as she attempts to financially help her adoptive son Arthur. Arthur himself, who clearly represents the voice of the novelist, vacillates between freedom and confinement within the story, and is freed from debtors' prison only with help from Amy Dorrit, Mrs. Clennam, and (of all people) Flora Finching. For that matter, the only characters in the novel who appear uncorrupted by money and wealth are Arthur and Amy, although both must still devote a good part of their energies to earning a living. *Little Dorrit* as a novel sends a message that most people, both good and bad, are in fact corrupted by money to varying degrees, with rare exceptions.

The initial cinematic foray into this wealth of Dickensian characterization came from the notable American producer Edwin Thanhouser, whose silent short adaptation of *Little Dorrit* from 1913 is now unfortunately considered lost.[12] The loss is doubly unfortunate in that *Little Dorrit* was the last Dickens film made by Thanhouser after producing a very high-quality trilogy for *David Copperfield* two years earlier, in 1911, as well as *The Old Curiosity Shop* and a surviving version of *Nicholas Nickleby* from that same period. Thanhouser's 1913 *Little Dorrit* was reportedly directed by D.W. Griffith protégé James Kirkwood Sr. (1876–1963), scripted by studio regular Lloyd Lonergan (1870–1937), and featured an interesting, experienced cast led by the early film star Maude Fealy as Amy Dorrit, among several others. A striking promotional poster, production still, and contemporary reviews may all be viewed, however, along with miscellaneous remnants for the *David Copperfield* trilogy, *Nicholas Nickleby*, and *The Old Curiosity Shop*, at the excellent website for Thanhouser's complete known filmography.[13] Seven years later, in 1920 (post–World War I), another, longer, 20-minute silent version of *Little Dorrit* came out of Great Britain, written and directed by Sidney Morgan (1874–1946), and starring the director's then 14-year-old daughter Joan Morgan, herself a future actor of note and novelist of some repute, in the lead role of Amy Dorrit.[14] A fragment of this 1920 film reportedly exists at the British University of Brighton School of Media (Screen Archive South East), a portion of which may be currently viewed online at their website.[15]

After 1920, the English-speaking film industry went silent on *Little Dorrit*, indeed for all three of Dickens' social novels, over the next six decades or more. The only exceptions came from foreign-language silents or early talkies, most notably *Lille Dorrit* (1924), a Danish-language production from the famed Nordisk Film company out of Copenhagen,

13. Little Dorrit (1855–1857)

directed by Anders Wilhelm Sandberg (1887–1938).[16] Sandberg directed a series of four remarkable Dickens novels adapted for the silent screen during the early 1920s, and *Lille Dorrit* represented his only effort for the Dickens social novels.[17] A print reportedly survives at the British Film Institute.[18] The high quality of Sandberg's work was likely in part attributable to his retaining British Dickensian specialist B.W. Matz (1865–1925) as a consultant.[19] Sandberg, however, was an exception. Only in Germany, curiously enough, would *Kleine Dorrit* (1934) be made into an early talkie by the anti–Nazi Czech director Karel Lamač, starring Anny Ondra, whose loyalty to the Third Reich was questionable at best but never seriously challenged thanks to her marriage to boxing champion and Aryan poster boy Max Schmeling.[20] By contrast, the many upheavals of the 20th century, especially in America—Prohibition, Depression, World War, Civil Rights—caused most viewing audiences, at least those stateside, not to question a basic need for change, as was the intent of the novelist for his British Victorian readers. Not until the late 1970s and early 1980s, when Anglo-American socioeconomic values seemed to undergo a big political shift, did the underlying message of Dickens' most radical statements seem once again to resonate. It was only then that English-language cinematic adaptions of the social novels began to reappear.

Hard Times was produced as a miniseries in 1977 by Granada ITV, *Bleak House* in 1985 by the BCC. Then in 1987 came one of the most unusual film adaptations for a Dickens novel, if not for all literary film adaptations, this one for *Little Dorrit*. German-Polish-British costume designer extraordinaire, former La Scala assistant for Franco Zeffirelli, and maverick director-screenwriter Christine Edzard (b. 1945), along with her husband, the prominent English producer Richard B. Goodwin (b. 1934), decided that the time was right to try something different with the period costume drama genre, and with Charles Dickens in particular.[21] Accordingly, on a shoestring budget, Edzard created a six-hour, two-part version of *Little Dorrit* that seemed to defy all defined categories, as if intentionally making it difficult for audiences to view the film either on television or in the theaters.[22] Each of the two parts told the same story, but from different gendered perspectives, those of Arthur and Amy, respectively. Other than a sweeping ambition likely influenced by the Royal Shakespeare Company's acclaimed all-day stage version of *Nicholas Nickleby* in 1980, Edzard nearly rewrote the book on how Dickens should be presented on screen. With over 240 speaking parts for trained stage actors (plus non-speaking extras), the 1987 *Little Dorrit* had an unprecedentedly stylish look, thanks to custom-sewn costumes, 89 built-from-scratch sets, and a depth of period research previously unknown within the industry.[23] Predictably, relatively few saw the film at the time, but those who did never forgot it, especially other movie makers and reviewers. Edzard's "Dickensathon" represented, wrote Joss Marsh, "the ultimate example of the Dickens film in its aspect of historical reconstruction and virtual tourism as a conceptual turning point."[24] No doubt to save money, operatic music was used as a soundtrack, not surprising given Edzard's working background at La Scala in Milan.

For characterization, Dickensian film innovator Alec Guinness, by then 73 years old, was shrewdly brought in to play the patriarchal role of William Dorrit. Freed late in life from financial necessity thanks to a percentage share for his part in *Star Wars* (1977), Guinness was predictably magnificent as the elder Dorrit, who instantly goes from poor imprisoned nobility to rich nobility touring the continent in style. In the case of Guinness, art imitated life. Michael Pointer justifiably wrote that the famous actor delivered "undoubtably one of his finest film performances"—probably while working for scale wages or less, it should be added.[25] Playing opposite Guinness as Arthur Clennam was Derek Jacobi, well known to art house audiences since the previous decade from his lead performance in the hit PBS *Masterpiece Theatre* series, *I Claudius* (1976). In contrast to these big names, an unknown but youthfully appropriate Sarah Pickering was cast as Amy Dorrit in Pickering's only major film appearance, highlighting the troubling age difference between Arthur and Amy inherent within the text. Supporting cast featured several definitive performances, including Max Wall as an inscrutable Flintwich, Joan Greenwood as a terrifying Mrs. Clennam, and a hilariously effective Miriam Margolyes as Flora Finching. Many other actors, later to become well known in the movies, got some of their earliest casting breaks in minor roles for this production, such as David Thewlis and Paul Rhys, both 24 years old at the time. Between its unmistakable visual style and passionate characterizations, the 1987 *Little Dorrit* of Christine Edzard remains a landmark film production in several respects, 34 years after the fact. For patient audiences, it still may be screened in several platforms.

The only limitation with Edzard's cinematic masterpiece continues to be its challenging six-hour format, which discourages many from watching it. That problem, however, was fully rectified with a new production some two decades later. In 2007–2008, the BBC and WGBH Boston continued its fruitful partnership with a new co-production of *Little Dorrit*, airing during late 2008 in the U.K. and then on PBS *Masterpiece Classics* in early 2009 as part of that franchise's 39th season.[26] Originally aired as 14 episodes over seven and a half hours, then compressed into five 90-minute episodes for American TV, the 2008 *Little Dorrit* is still the longest running version of that novel made to date, but this time spread out into the easily-digestible segments of a television miniseries format. A team of four directors were hired for the project, which gives an interesting variety to the style, but all episodes were scripted by veteran British screenwriter and literary virtuoso Andrew Davies (b. 1936), who two years earlier, in 2005, had written a superb adaptation of *Bleak House* for the same producers. For the 2008 *Little Dorrit*, the results were (once again) stunningly effective, beginning with Davies' impressive telescoping of Dickens' multiple subplots and huge character cast into a manageable, unified entertainment experience. Although Christine Edzard's earlier 1987 *Little Dorrit* remains essential viewing for fans of the Dickensian genre or for film specialists interested in unusually high production values, the 2008 BBC-WGBH reboot of the same title must, in the final analysis, still be considered the overall best video option for the novel made to date, and certainly the most accessible for general audiences. The newer production received an astounding 11 Emmy nominations and seven wins, including a well-deserved adaptation award for Andrew Davies.

Taken as a whole, and rather surprisingly, the overall casting for the 2008 BBC *Little Dorrit* is stronger than that of the 1987 production—no small feat, to be sure, especially given the earlier participation of Alec Guinness and Derek Jacobi. The impressive casting of 2008 began with a then unknown, 24-year-old Claire Foy as Amy Dorrit, long before she became a big star thanks to widely watched series such *Wolf Hall* (2015) and *The Crown* (2016). Although Foy had extensive training and experience for her chosen profession, American viewing audiences had not seen much of her prior to 2008. Within a decade, she would become a household name. Playing opposite her Amy Dorrit was Matthew Macfadyen as Arthur Clennam, coming off his role as Mr. Darcy from the hugely successful 2005 feature production of Jane Austen's *Pride & Prejudice*. Macfadyen was about 34 years old at the time, thus closing the actual age gap by half between Arthur and Amy from what is in the text, and in the process likely making the relationship less troubling and more palatable for general audiences. As family patriarch, RADA alumnus Tom Courtenay portrayed William Dorrit, having recently provided excellent support as Newman Noggs in the popular 2002 film version of *Nicholas Nickleby*. Courtenay made no pretenses at surpassing the great Alec Guinness in that same role, but ably played his part while shifting focus back onto the two romantic leads of Arthur and Amy. Judy Parfitt, another RADA graduate, did the same as Mrs. Clennam, just as she had in earlier miniseries for *David Copperfield* (1966) and *A Tale of Two Cities* (1980), and just as she would later do it the BBC hit television series *Call the Midwife* (2012). Other actors drawing praise for their performances in minor roles in the 2008 series included Andy Serkis (Rigaud), Maxine Peake (Mrs. Wade), and Freema Agyeman (Tattycoram).[27] Special mention should also go to yeoman character specialist Alun Armstrong in his demanding double role as the twin brothers Jeremiah and Ephraim Flintwich.[28] Overall, it may well be said that one of the main attractions of the 2008 production was its reincorporation of subplots and sub-characters important to the original text, thanks to excellent casting and screenwriting.

The original publication of the completed *Little Dorrit* in 1857 marked both the end of Dickens' extraordinary social novel trilogy and the beginning of a controversial new chapter in his personal life, one that has only seen the light of day during the modern era thanks to sustained efforts from objective literary biography. In addition to upending his personal life, Dickens also changed directions in his novel writing. No doubt looking back at certain older projects with dissatisfaction, he decided to revisit the genre of historical fiction, a genre not attempted by him since *Barnaby Rudge* in 1840, over 17 years earlier. Dickens may have been unpleasantly reminded of this project, not only by its tepid commercial and critical reception, but also by his injudicious use of the pet raven for Barnaby, quite unlike a skillful use of the pet parrot for Mrs. Merdle in *Little Dorrit*. Perhaps the novelist simply needed a break from reminiscing about his own difficult childhood. In any event, Dickens now looked back, once again, at the generation of his grandparents (the generation of William Dorrit) and the momentous political events of the French Revolution. The triumphant result was *A Tale of Two Cities*, a work far superior in every respect to *Barnaby Rudge*. The recent trilogy of social novels had likely given him even more confidence in his prodigious and growing powers as a storyteller, not that artistic confidence had ever been much a problem for Dickens. With the conclusion of his brilliant but dark and strange tale of *Little Dorrit*, he now figuratively turned a page in his own writing development, resulting in a work that would inspire future filmmakers no less than his previous novels had.

14

A Tale of Two Cities (1859)

> *"'You might, from your appearance, be the wife of Lucifer,' said Miss Pross, in her breathing. 'Nevertheless, you shall not get the better of me. I am an Englishwoman.'"*[1]

During the summer of 1857, soon after Dickens had completed *Little Dorrit*, the novelist at age 45 entered a full-blown midlife crisis that biographers only began to comprehend about a century later. It was then that he resolved to divorce his wife of 21 years and begin an affair, platonic at first, with an undistinguished actress 27 years his junior. As Dickens' favorite child Kate put it many decades later, "My father was like a madman ... the affair brought out all that was worst—all that was weakest in him."[2] As one would expect, there was little novel writing over the next year as the domestic tragedy ran its course. By the time he wrote his next novel circa 1859, Dickens was a changed man and a changed artist, as vividly reflected by a portrait of him from that era painted by William Powell Frith.[3] The next novel, *A Tale of Two Cities*, undoubtably belongs to Dickens' core group of works for its continuing popularity, arguably *the* most popular of his full-length books, with unique appeal to Anglo-American readers and its surface condemnation of the French Revolution. *A Tale of Two Cities* may also be Dickens' most melodramatic work, well described by biographer Claire Tomalin as "Dickens the showman, amusing his people and drawing their tears."[4] A modern-day psychoanalyst would also no doubt have a field day with *A Tale* and its fictional portrayal of a dissolute, self-sacrificing hero hopelessly fixated on the unattainable object of his adoration. Dickens' personal life may have been in shambles by the late 1850s, but his artistic genius could still channel those unhappy experiences and personal disappointments into a great storytelling vehicle.

Dickens first met the 18-year-old Ellen "Nelly" Ternan, along with her two older sisters and mother, in August of 1857 when the family was hired on short notice to perform for a provincial, twin-bill stage production in which Dickens was himself acting, the melodrama *The Frozen Deep*, co-written by Dickens' close bohemian friend Wilkie Collins (1824–1889), along with the farce *Uncle John* written by London impresario and comedian J.B. Buckstone (1802–1879).[5] Pure restlessness appears to have driven Dickens onstage—certainly not financial necessity—in addition to a lifelong fascination with live theater and increasing dissatisfaction with his domestic life. As stage drama, *The Frozen Deep* is poor stuff but squarely within a long Anglo tradition of popular agitprop, rewriting history as it never was, a quality which undoubtably caught Dickens' attention, the novelist himself co-scripting with Collins and assuming the tragic lead role of symbolic, make-believe hero Richard Wardour.[6] The play reimagines the doomed and sordid British Franklin Expedition to the Arctic Circle of 1845 in a manner appealing to current public sentiment, in which it succeeded to a startling degree, largely because of Dickens' involvement in the production.[7] More importantly, as Dickens readily admitted, the self-sacrificing character of Wardour would later serve as a literary model for Sydney Carton in *A Tale of Two Cities*. Thus, every time modern viewers see a video production of *A Tale* they are witnessing, among many things, dramatic remnants of a Victorian hit play now long forgotten. Dickens' other major source material was Thomas Carlyle's landmark *The French Revolution: A History* (1837, revised 1857), Carlyle having earlier been the dedicatee of Dickens' novel *Hard Times*.[8] Otherwise, Dickens' exact storyline for *A Tale* seems to have come out of the blue, or, more precisely, out of his own vivid imagination and personal experiences.

A Tale of Two Cities was first published as a rapid-fire weekly serial in 1859 to help successfully launch Dickens' new journal, *All the Year Around*, a successor periodical to his earlier *Household Words*. The complete novel was then published that same year by Chapman & Hall of London, with illustrations by Phiz (Hablot Knight Browne), and dedicated to Lord John Russell (1792–1878), a liberal two-time Prime Minister admired and befriended by Dickens as the novelist began moving more frequently within English high society. Chapman & Hall came back into Dickens' professional life after a 15-year hiatus because his more recent publisher Bradbury & Evans declined to publicly take Dickens' side during his ongoing marital separation, as this announcement and the novelist's scandalous liaison with Ellen Ternan became an open secret.[9] Soon many other longtime, distinguished personal and professional associations were severed by Dickens on the same account, including those with illustrator Hablot Knight Browne, literary colleague William Makepeace Thackeray, and charitable patroness Lady Angela Burdett-Coutts.[10] In hindsight, it is in fact quite remarkable that Dickens was able to preserve so many of his professional relationships despite a bitter divorce from Catherine, including his continuing employment as a housekeeper and house manager

14. A Tale of Two Cities (1859)

A Parisian mob looking for revenge: A scene from an early silent film version of Dickens' *A Tale of Two Cities* (1911). The actors are unidentified.

of Catherine's younger sister, Georgy Hogarth, an arrangement soon prompting unfounded rumors that the novelist's extramarital infatuation was with Georgy rather than Ellen Ternan.

Some critics of Dickens' sentimentality have labeled this novel "A Tale of One City—London," but the joke is really a mischaracterization. Dickens, by this stage in life, had come to know and fully appreciate both Paris and French culture, even to the point of vigorously defending the French against the biased attacks of his English associates. That the city of Paris in the novel lacks Dickens' trademark topographical detail, as always given to London, was probably to spare his English readers' more typical unfamiliarity with France. His attitude towards the French Revolution of 1789 and subsequent Reign of Terror seems to have been not unlike that of his mentor Carlyle's—in sympathy with the motivations behind the Revolution, but not the violence itself, or more specifically, the mob violence. As in *Barnaby Rudge*, Dickens offers a subtle analysis of mob mentality and mob violence, this time contrasting France to England. Whereas the violent anti–Catholic Gordon Riots of 1780 were easily suppressed by the English government and English popular opinion, and justice of sorts still dispensed by the English courts (unlike their French counterparts, the revolutionary tribunals), the storming of the Bastille led inevitably to a complete overthrow of the old order, or *Ancien Régime*, and eventually, in Dickens' view, to Napoleonic despotism and war. Madame

Defarge is among the novelist's more memorable, strong female characters and a quite villainous one besides. She is the personification of fanatic malevolence, with overtones from Greek mythology.[11] Her sudden demise near the end of the novel at the hands of a very loyal, very stout, and very English Miss Pross (see epigraph), represents the initial, symbolic climax within the storyline, prefiguring the Battle of Waterloo itself, fought some 26 years later. *A Tale of Two Cities* also provides unique cinematic opportunities for portraying the violent street mobs of the Revolution (or the legal courts in France and England) within a broad historical canvas, which may in fact be the main reason why the novel was so popular with 20th-century filmmakers.

By contrast, Sydney Carton presents himself as one of Dickens' most ambivalent and difficult to decipher heroes. As such, he has attracted a steady stream of well-known leading actors over the years to portray him on screen. A talented but dissolute (read: alcoholic) wastrel, Carton longs hopelessly for an unattainable woman (Lucie Manette), and can do good only by repeatedly saving her husband and in the end, sacrificing himself to the mob. He stands in contrast to the rather boring but steady Charles Darnay (Lucie's husband and a near lookalike for Carton) or Jarvis Lorry, the latter a confirmed bachelor Englishman of commercial business who repeatedly proves his moral worth throughout the story. Carton's being paired with the innocent young Seamstress on the guillotine scaffold is symbolic as well. Like Richard Wardour from *The Frozen Deep*, Sydney Carton can only find love, contentment, and freedom in a dramatically sacrificial death. The novelist may have felt the same way about himself at the time of writing. As in Dickens' previous novels, *A Tale of Two Cities* also dwells at length on the theme of personal imprisonment—incarceration at the Bastille or *La Force* in Paris, or within a London criminal jail cell, for that matter.[12]

The first attempt at filming *A Tale of Two Cities* came in 1908 from the Chicago-based Selig Polyscope Company.[13] Although this effort is now considered lost, it reportedly attempted portrayal of large-scale mob scenes, thus immediately identifying one of the story's primary visual attractions.[14] Three years later, in 1911, this was fully realized by the Brooklyn-based Vitagraph Studios, whose 11-minute *A Tale of Two Cities* found both critical and popular acclaim, in addition to being an astoundingly effective compression of a long and complex novel into a short, silent visual entertainment based mainly on spectacle and melodrama.[15] Not to be outdone, American pioneer auteur Frank Lloyd in 1917, just as the U.S. was entering the Great War in Europe, directed his own much longer version of *A Tale of Two Cities*.[16] In addition to large-scale mob scenes, Lloyd cleverly cast actor William Farnum in the dual lookalike roles of Sydney

Carton and Charles Darnay, giving the director an opportunity to display his mastery with special effects quite impressive for their time. The Lloyd cinematic version of the novel was celebrated and proved influential as well; along with the earlier Vitagraph production, both can typically be found on YouTube in prints of variable quality.[17] Three years later, in 1922, Lloyd would go on to a direct an equally famous version of Dickens' *Oliver Twist*. This silent film craze for *A Tale of Two Cities* continued into 1922 when British film producer H.B. Parkinson included it as part his *Tense Moments with Great Authors* series, now unfortunately lost as well.[18] This was quickly followed, however (in 1925), by *The Only Way*, a lengthy British adaptation of the latest stage version of the novel, directed by Herbert Wilcox and starring John Martin Harvey, perhaps the most famous Sydney Carton of his day.[19] In many respects, this film, which reportedly still exists in the archives of the British Film Institute, represented the culmination of the silent era's consistent fascination with *A Tale of Two Cities*.[20]

With the advent of the sound era, Hollywood immediately produced a formidably cinematic version of the novel at two hours in total length. Rapidly following up acclaim (and profits) for its 1935 *David Copperfield*, MGM released *A Tale of Two Cities* for the Christmas holidays that same year, prominently featuring the 43 year old, British-born Ronald Colman as Sydney Carton.[21] The Shakespearean-trained Colman was destined to play the role and had indeed aspired to do so ever since first reading Dickens' novel.[22] As later noted by critic Joss Marsh, "a romantic role like Sydney Carton offered obvious possibilities for a handsome matinee-idol."[23] Furthermore, producer David O. Selznick (1902–1965) turned the film into a personal pet project and wisely created a separate, specialized unit to film a spectacular Bastille-storming scene.[24] Accomplished studio actors also playing parts in MGM's other Dickens adaptations ably filled supporting roles, including Elizabeth Allan as Lucie, Reginald Owen as attorney Stryver, Basil Rathbone as the unbeatably evil Marquise St. Evremonde, and Edna May Oliver as a sturdy, indomitable Miss Pross. Broadway stage character actor supreme Blanche Yurka was brought in for her first film role to play a ferocious Madame Defarge. Veteran studio composer Herbert Stothart (1885–1949), later earning fame for his musical arrangements in *The Wizard of Oz*, provided an appropriately melodramatic score. *A Tale of Two Cities* was widely seen and generated enormous profits for MGM in the middle of the Great Depression.[25] An amazingly effective job was done at compressing a long novel into two hours of dramatic entertainment, taking many liberties but somehow not doing violence to the text. The film was deservedly nominated for Best Picture of 1935 and, some felt, the rightful winner of that year's Oscar though the award went to another movie.[26] Moreover, a strong argument can be made that the 1935 MGM production is still the best overall video version ever made for *A Tale of Two Cities*, and this despite many notable subsequent efforts.

In truth, the novel appears to have been held in much higher esteem by our parent's generation, than by the Baby Boomers, especially during the post–World War II, Cold War era and high tide of McCarthyism. It is possible that a heavy-handed message of personal and patriotic self-sacrifice was being pushed hard by media at that time, and Dickens' Sydney Carton made a good poster boy to that purpose. Following a BBC revival of *The Only Way* in 1948, the American ABC television network in 1953 responded with a two-part, one-hour miniseries whose grand ambitions far exceeded its primitive technique, other than an interesting soundtrack provided by prolific Hollywood composer Dimitri Tiomkin (1894–1979).[27] Then, during the late 1950s, the floodgates opened. In 1957 the BBC delivered an eight-part, four-hour miniseries, rebroadcast in 1959.[28] Almost concurrent with this was a 1958 British movie version, clocking in at nearly two hours, and though containing many missteps (including a conscious decision to unnecessarily film in black-and-white), featured an interesting cast led by Dirk Bogarde as Sydney Carton, as well as music by the distinguished British composer Richard Addinsell (1904–1977).[29] Not to be outdone, American CBS network, in 1958 under the auspices of producer David Susskind, corporate sponsor DuPont, and director Robert Mulligan (1925–2008), televised a 90-minute version of *A Tale of Two Cities* featuring a stellar cast.[30] Some of the big names included Agnes Moorehead as Madame Defarge, Max Adrian as St. Evremonde, a young George C. Scott as the revolutionary fanatic Jacques, and as Sydney Carton, Scottish-born James Donald, who had recently delivered a notable film performance in David Lean's *The Bridge on the River Kwai* (1957). Although not able to compete commercially with the British film starring Dirk Bogarde, the DuPont *Tale* is reportedly preserved in the UCLA Film and Television Archive.[31] Then seven years later, in 1965, at beginning of the Vietnam era, the BBC televised a 10-part, nearly-five-hour miniseries, led by the ever-reliable creative team of screenwriter Constance Cox, director Joan Craft, and producer Campbell Logan, along with actor John Wood as Sydney Carton, Wood having earlier played Barnaby Rudge in the 1960 BBC production.[32] Thus concluded the initial post–World War II frenzy of presenting Dickens' *A Tale of Two Cities* in various forms and formats to an oversaturated Anglo-American viewing public.

Fifteen years later, during the Reagan-Thatcher era of 1980–1989, came another flurry of productions for *A Tale of Two Cities*. First (in 1980) was yet another BBC miniseries in 13 parts and over six hours, rebroadcast in 1982, produced by *Doctor Who* impresario Barry Letts.[33] For the latest BBC rollout, RADA graduate Paul Shelley was employed to play the dual lookalike roles of Carton and Darnay—the first to do so since William Farnum in 1917—and gave an excellent account of his talent. Other well-known actors cast by the BBC included Judy Parfitt (Madame Defarge), Vivian Merchant (Miss Pross), and the always excellent Nigel Stock (Jarvis Lorry).[34] Then a mere two weeks later, in late 1980, ABC network televised its own two-hour version of the same title, directed by British-born Jim Goddard (1936–2013), and starring Chris Sarandon, also convincingly playing dual lookalike roles as Carton and Darnay.[35] Though stodgy and flawed, the ABC *Tale of Two Cities* from 1980 also featured interesting actors, was the first real attempt to condense the novel into a two-hour viewing experience since the 1958 British film version, and is today still widely available for viewing in a variety of platforms. Idiosyncratic casting included the venerable Flora Robson as Miss Pross, Samuel Beckett muse Billie Whitelaw as an outstanding Madame Defarge, Nigel Hawthorne as Stryver, David Suchet as Barsad, and future horror-sci-fi specialist Alice Krige as Lucie Manette. Chris Sarandon, then recently divorced from Susan Sarandon, and not long removed from his Oscar and Golden Globe-nominated supporting role in *Dog Day Afternoon* (1975), played Sydney Carton. Sarandon's performance as an iconic Dickensian character is compelling. Comparing the two major 1980 productions of *A Tale of Two Cities* from ABC and the BBC again suggests that Dickens' ultimate melodrama among his novels may be uniquely and better suited to feature film format rather than miniseries.

Such was not the case with animated TV versions, however, and in 1984 one such animated version appeared, produced by the irrepressible Burbank Studios of Sydney, Australia.[36] Hyper-compression of Dickens' long novel into a one-hour viewing format did not serve the storytelling aspect well; for example, one of many selected cuts included the crucial, epic confrontation between Madame Defarge and Miss Pross. Nevertheless, this compression did not prevent insertion of a strong and recurring anti-aristocratic bias into the plot—not a surprising feature for the Aussies—to the point where some viewers feel almost a kind of sympathy for violent French revolutionaries. This animated *Tale* is reduced to a simple story of personal sacrifice by Sydney Carton for a greater good. Also of note is a surprisingly grandiose and serious musical score by noted Australian composer Mark Isaacs (b. 1958), somehow all very fitting to the theme. The 1984 Burbank *A Tale of Two Cities* was the sixth in their memorable series of eight animated films of novels by Charles Dickens, including all six of his core novels, and remains the only known animated film version of this novel to date.

In 1989, the bicentenary year of the French Revolution, came what was intended as the apotheosis of film adaptations, but in hindsight now appears to have been merely a last gasp. In that year, British Granada ITV co-produced a two-part, three-hour, big-budget miniseries for *A Tale of Two Cities* with an Anglo-French cast and crew, eventually airing on PBS *Masterpiece Theatre* in the U.S.[37] The screenwriter was the highly experienced and literate Arthur Hopcraft (1932–2004), who earlier in his career had adapted Dickens' *Hard Times* (1977) for Granada and *Bleak House* (1985) for the BBC. Now Hopcraft tackled Dickensian melodrama, rather than Dickensian social criticism. Casting choices were sometimes odd, sometimes effective. Wisely, an Englishman (James Wilby) was chosen to play Carton and a Frenchman (Xavier Deluc) to play Darnay, both as near-lookalikes (rather than the same actor), probably as the novelist originally intended. Future Bond girl Serena Gordon was brought in to provide love interest as Lucie Manette and, more interestingly, French national icon Jean-Pierre Aumont was convincingly cast as Lucie's father, the long-suffering Dr. Alexandre Manette. Most pleasing of all, however, was an 81-year-old John Mills cast as the transcontinental intermediary Jarvis Lorry, Mills having 43 years earlier portrayed Pip in David Lean's landmark *Great Expectations* (1946). The elderly Mills' effectiveness probably led him to being later cast in the one-and-only miniseries of *Martin Chuzzlewit* (1994). Despite these many highlights, however, and despite somewhat strained rave reviews from critics at the time, the 1989 Granada *A Tale of Two Cities* was met mostly with yawns from the general viewing public, and unfortunately, is usually still met that way by those who see it.

In addition to the gold standard of the 1935 MGM production, the 1989 *A Tale of Two Cities* had to contend with another, even more insurmountable problem. Four years earlier, in 1985, the English-language version of the hit French musical *Les Misérables* appeared on London's West End and has been going strong there ever since, 36 years after the fact. Based on the 1862 novel by Victor Hugo (1802–1885), a French writer personally known to and esteemed by Dickens, the book appeared merely three years after *A Tale of Two Cities*, and had known many subsequent stage and film adaptations, but it was not until the 1980 musical by Claude-Michel Schönberg (b. 1944) and 1985 English-lyric translation by Alain Boublil (b. 1941), that "Les Miz" began to dominate the Anglo-American performing arts.[38] The commercial ascendency of *Les Misérables* has allowed for no other competition in the realm of French historical melodrama, not even from the likes of Charles Dickens. The very fact that *Les Miz* is set within the quickly suppressed Paris Uprising of 1832, rather than the more controversial and historically significant French Revolution of 1789, seems to work in its favor, especially for modern English-speaking generally audiences viewing the gradual rise of Bonaparte in France with never-ending suspicion. Moreover, since the 1980s, there can be little doubt that most viewing audiences prefer to identify with Victor Hugo's tortured but triumphant hero Jean Valjean, rather than the dissipated and self-sacrificing Sydney Carton of Dickens' imagination. One stark factoid is indisputable: since the 1989 production of *A Tale*, some 32 years ago and before which the market had been saturated, there have been no more commercial adaptations for *A Tale of Two Cities*, either as feature films or as miniseries.

There is nothing inherently wrong with *A Tale of Two Cities* being surpassed in popularity by *Les Misérables*; in fact, Dickens himself may have agreed the latter is a better novel. Both works, however, are still widely read and admired. One might suggest that Dickens' *Tale* needs a good English-language musical to regain its old dominance—to try and replicate the isolated acclaim of *Oliver!* in 1968—but this has in fact been repeatedly attempted since 1950 when the Australian composer Arthur Benjamin (1893–1960) wrote a serious opera.[39] More recently, in 2007, a full musical staging (but not a movie) with words and music by American composer Jill Santoriello was viably produced on Broadway. Critics have praised such ongoing efforts, but general audiences continue flocking to London's West End to see and hear the franchise that has become *Les Miz*. The true, underlying reasons for the recent scarcity of the novel from the big screen may be more complex and relate to audience attitudes, particularly Anglo-American audience attitudes. The earth-shaking French Revolution of 1789 and subsequent Napoleonic Wars, unlike the American Revolution of 1776 which proceeded it, remains a controversial topic among anyone conscious of distant history. There is good evidence that Charles Dickens himself had a very nuanced attitude towards the event, including his scathing portrayal of the French *Ancien Régime* which sparked the backlash, along with his glimpses of compassion and empathy among even the most hardened revolutionaries. Perhaps more importantly, Anglo-American audience opinions on the duties of individuals towards larger society have certainly shifted since the 1980s. The willing self-sacrifice of a Sydney Carton today seems much more alien that it would have in 1859 or, for that matter, in 1979. Today, Carton instead would have likely gotten the girl, either by stealing Lucie back from Darnay, or possibly by escaping with the innocent Seamstress from execution. Viable commercial theater (or film) must, by definition, appeal to audience prejudices and preconceptions, and no one would have understood that basic principle better than Charles Dickens.

In the final analysis, however, it must be conceded that *A Tale of Two Cities*, despite its longstanding commercial appeal and continuing popularity, does not rank as one of Dickens' best works. Putting aside all contemporary cultural prejudices, the same qualities that made the novel such a blockbuster for over a century also hinder it from being considered an unassailable work of genius such as *Bleak House*, *David Copperfield*, or for that matter, the next semi-autobiographical novel that Dickens would turn to within a few short years. Ultimately, as a melodramatic fiction, *A Tale* has far more in common with the now forgotten *The Frozen Deep* and Dickens' skillful, determined efforts to play upon the sentiments of his audience. That he succeeded so thoroughly is a testament to his unrivaled abilities as a commercial storyteller and must attract our admiration on that basis alone. In the immediate aftermath of this accomplishment, the novelist once again turned to travelogue, another genre in which he excelled, although is often underrated as well, especially by modern readers. The very same writer who well knew not to unnecessarily tax his English-language readership with French topographical detail with which they were not familiar, also, if the occasion called for it, could have a keen and critical eye for tourist settings, either foreign or domestic. Nor was the youngish, pre–Civil War United States of America spared sharp Dickensian criticism in this regard. Whether it be the best of times (for the rich), or the worst of times (for the poor), readers could and can always count on Charles Dickens to honestly report on what he saw and heard. By doing so, in a very real sense, Dickens was reverting to the young journalist that he had been long before becoming the world's greatest novelist and storyteller.

15

Travelogues (1842–1863)

> "*Eight hundred what? 'Geese, villain?'* EIGHT HUNDRED MORMONS. *I, Uncommercial Traveller for the firm of Human Interest Brothers, had come aboard this Emigrant Ship to see what Eight hundred Latter-day Saints were like, and I found them (to the rout and overthrow of all my expectations) like what I now describe with scrupulous exactness.*"[1]

With enduring success achieved by *A Tale of Two Cities*, Dickens fulfilled an old ambition to write historical fiction in the popular style of his predecessor Walter Scott, while maintaining his own trademark style, this time distinguished by heightened sentimentality, subtle political commentary, and probing criticism of the substantial ill effects befalling any society beholden to mob mentality. His primary, commercial objective was to entertain readers, but beyond this, there was always for Charles Dickens more to seek as a writer, usually involving his readers experiencing things they otherwise would not, and in the process, gaining new degrees of empathy or understanding for previously stigmatized and often avoided phenomena. One must always keep in mind that Dickens, before becoming the greatest novelist of his age, had as a young man been a journalist of some repute. In this respect, he was like another influential novelist of a future generation, Ernest Hemingway (1899–1961), who also began professional life as a reporter on the beat, then brought those vivid journalistic experiences to his storytelling. Dickens, however, to a much greater extent than Hemingway, earnestly believed he could help change the world for the better through storytelling. Also, like Hemingway, Dickens continued to dabble with non-fiction writing, specifically travelogue, throughout a long career, oftentimes with striking effect, although this remains a relatively unknown side of the novelist.

Strictly speaking, Dickens' experimentation with travelogue began with early efforts at journalism, and then carried over into his first forays of fiction such as *Sketches by Boz* (1836) and *The Pickwick Papers* (1837). Indeed, it was his genuine talent at making picturesque descriptions humorously entertaining that contributed significantly to Dickens' early acclaim as a novelist. Nevertheless, and despite the rousing commercial reception for his fictional works, Dickens continued to dabble in writing travelogue after he became famous as a storyteller, and many of these shorter pieces continued to be published long after his death in 1870. It is therefore remarkable that, except for a smattering of video allusions to Dickens' two American tours, this aspect of his output has been for the most part ignored by film producers over the last century or more. The reason for this neglect may be that film audiences are simply not interested or (more likely) that film producers believe they would not be interested. As a result, only Dickens' American excursions have been addressed in film adaptations, and sparsely at that, while his many other documented travels to other parts of Great Britain, France, Italy, and the European continent have been mostly or entirely ignored. This dearth of modern film adaptations on real-life Dickensian adventures strongly suggests the subject matter is ripe for further video exploration, especially given the popularity of these literary works in Dickens' own day, along with their intrinsic literary quality.

Travelogue must begin with travel, and for Charles Dickens, personal travel beyond his native English haunts began in 1842, when at age 30 he, along with wife Catherine (but without their children), crossed the Atlantic Ocean for his first American tour, lasting six months. By this early point in his career, Dickens' literary celebrity had been well established in the United States; however, American adulation was quickly blunted by the English novelist's just and frequent complaints that international copyrights were then non-existent, and hence saw no American royalties for his enormously popular books. In short, many Americans, even fans, deeply resented suggestions

Hugh Laurie (Mr. Dick, left), Dev Patel (Davey), and Tilda Swinton (Aunt Betsy) in *The Personal History of David Copperfield* (2019), directed by satirist filmmaker Armando Iannucci (APL Archive / Alamy Stock Photo).

that he should be paid for his livelihood. Dickens' own idealized notions of American liberty and justice for all were likewise permanently damaged.[2] Unlike the French critic Alexis de Tocqueville, who followed a similar route seven years earlier, Dickens was not psychologically prepared for what he encountered—a still-developing, rather young nation about to nearly tear itself apart over slavery while outright robbing Native Americans, Mexicans, and anyone less strong than the aggressive newcomers, of their preexisting possessions in the New World. It was also in the U.S. that Dickens unexpectedly encountered a blatant elevation of commerce over art, a vicious tabloid press, dubious pseudoscientific beliefs, and outright superstition disguised as fervent religion. After touring the American eastern coast from Boston to Richmond, Dickens headed west along the Ohio River Valley, intending to reach Chicago, but he never made it that far.[3] Homesick and disillusioned by the time he reached St. Louis, Dickens turned around and went north through Canada (via Niagara, Toronto, and Montreal), then down the Hudson River Valley to New York City where he shipped back to England.[4] Later writing of his experiences in *American Notes* and *Martin Chuzzlewit*, Dickens particularly disliked the state of Illinois where, ironically, both his brother Gus and son Francis would eventually live out their lives and be buried.[5]

Dickens' open disappointment with the United States may provide a clue as to why the topic has never been popular for a film industry centered traditionally in the U.S., or for that matter, never popular among viewers of that industry's biggest market share. And yet, this chapter of Dickens' life includes many interesting facets. The novelist traveled through the heart of the Ohio and Mississippi Valleys—the cradle of the American Civil War producing many of its outstanding personalities.[6] Although Dickens noticed slavery and easily condemned it, as an Englishman he failed to notice American regional prejudices of the subtle types so prevalent along the Ohio River and forming an essential part of the American social fabric.[7] For that matter, except for Richmond, Virginia, he completely avoided the South and the American West, control over which the Civil War itself would soon be fought. We also know from Dickens' letters that he met briefly in Philadelphia with a worshipful but struggling Edgar Allan Poe (1809–1849). Poe's tragic personal fate may well have entrenched Dickens' growingly strident view that artistic genius was not valued in the U.S., or at least certainly not paid a living wage. During the final leg of his tour, heading south down the Hudson Valley, Dickens visited the fabled Shaker Village of Mount Lebanon, New York, and came away decidedly underwhelmed by America's then-most famous home-grown religious sect. Dickens was more impressed by a brief, three-day (June 2–4) visit to West Point, where he noted both the physical beauty of the setting as well as a frightening American aptitude for waging warfare—this only a few years before the Mexican conflict of 1846. Unbeknownst to him at the time, a 20-year-old Ulysses S. Grant (class of 1843) was then a junior cadet at West Point.[8] There is no evidence the two ever met—nor was there any reason for them to—but had they met, Grant likely could have told Dickens a thing or two about the American national character then puzzling the English novelist.

American Notes for General Circulation was published by Chapman & Hall immediately upon the novelist's return to England in 1842. There were no illustrations, faint praise for the United States, and extensive criticism for the young republic raising eyebrows on both sides of the pond but producing good sales even as critics tore into it. Two centuries later, *American Notes* still makes informative reading. First and foremost, it is the written record of a 30-year-old literary idealist having his ideals shattered. This may help to explain why it has not captured the imagination of modern filmmakers delving into literary biography. American moviegoers want Charles Dickens to have been in love with the U.S., and he simply was not; worse, at the end of the day, he preferred England over the U.S. As much as he liked "New" England—and repeatedly said so in his writings—in the end he was happy to return to "Old" England. As for the American heartland and southland, at least to the limited extent he visited these two regions, the novelist made no bones about his disdain. In defense of Dickens, it should be remembered that, as usual, he wrote truthfully if sometimes unperceptively about what he saw and heard, and more importantly, by this point in his career needed to cultivate his growing reputation and public image as a quintessentially English writer, one permanently attached and unquestionably loyal to his own British homeland. One year later, in 1843, Dickens would continue his attack on, and grim view of, the American Midwest, this time in the form of fiction, with his oft-neglected novel *Martin Chuzzlewit*. After that, it would be another quarter century before he could be persuaded to return to America, this time for the sake of sheer financial profit.

Some two years later, in 1844–1845, Dickens set out for his first English Grand Tour of Italy via France, beginning in Genoa, followed by the major city-states of northern Italy and the Po Valley, and finally south to Rome and Naples.[9] Other than Naples, he skipped southern Italy, much as he had the American southland on his U.S. tour. It is a shame that Dickens never went to Sicily because if he had, his impressions of the place, post–Napoleonic era and pre–Risorgimento, would surely have been worthy of publication. Then in 1846, Bradbury & Evans of London published Dickens' travelogue *Pictures from Italy*, another delightful but lesser-known work.[10] Dickens later returned to northern Italy with friends in 1853, but not to southern Italy.[11]

Even more so than its predecessor *American Notes*, Dickens' *Pictures from Italy* has completely failed to attract the interest of modern filmmakers, despite its lively prose and many memorable observations from an English innocent abroad—innocent at least with respect to Mediterranean culture. His shock at the south Italian urban environment of Naples, which ends the book, by itself is priceless. Perhaps the idea of Dickens, the most English of English novelists, tramping up and down the slopes of Mount Vesuvius or through the festive streets of Rome is simply too much at odds with his long-established public image, especially in the United States.[12] At the time, however, he did find literary inspiration in the church bells of Genoa to continue his series of holiday novellas following the acclaim of *A Christmas Carol* in 1843. Also, after his second Italian trip, and during the mid-1850s, vivid images of affluent English tourists traveling through northern Italy found their way into Dickens' powerful social novel *Little Dorrit*, and some of these scenes have in turn made their way into modern film versions.

By 1860, Dickens had decided to make ongoing use of his well-honed journalistic talent for the picturesque in his latest magazine venture, *All the Year Round*. Titled as a regular feature, *The Uncommercial Traveller* took its moniker from the novelist's insistence that his signature brand of tourism should not be strictly for financial profit—a point of view he had no doubt heard in America—but rather for pleasure, personal growth, and self-edification.[13] Into this Dickens threw his favorite observations, not only of London town, but also for his extensive, ongoing travels throughout the British Isles, the European continent, and eventually, his return to the United States in 1867–1868. These vignettes became so popular that they were collected and published separately, first in 1863, then later updated further and re-published in 1866, then again posthumously in 1875 and beyond as the collection grew with more discoveries of unpublished pieces. The literary treasures of *The Uncommercial Traveller* are vast and yet, during the modern film era, make only oblique, vague appearances in the movies, usually those referring to England or America. Many, if not most, remain completely unexplored by filmmakers. One such incident took place on June 4, 1863, when Dickens spent several hours onboard the docked, outbound HMS *Amazon*, conversing with English Mormon immigrants to the United States, many from Merthyr Tydfil in Wales. This was during the height of a still-undecided American Civil War being fought out in Mississippi Valley, a journey Dickens himself would have declined making at the time. The Welsh Mormons were bound for St. Louis, Missouri, from which they would take wagon trains west to the Great Salt Lake. Dickens himself never made it past St. Louis in his own travels. He went onboard HMS *Amazon* no doubt intending to portray the Mormons as a laughingstock, much as he had portrayed the Shakers of upstate New York two decades earlier. Instead, he found himself, despite his inclinations (as was typical for him), empathizing with outcasts from English society, admiring their undaunted courage, unpretentious virtue, and dignified fortitude (see epigraph).

The first extended, notable film foray into Dickens' American travels was, fittingly enough, purely fictional in concept. On September 29, 1963, less than two months before the news cycle would be dominated by a presidential assassination, NBC's *Bonanza*, then one of the most popular television shows in the world, aired its Episode 2 of Season 5, titled *A Passion for Justice*, in which Charles Dickens, in the imaginations of viewers, visits the Ponderosa Ranch and Virginia City, Nevada, during his second American tour, circa 1868.[14] In reality, Dickens never once made it west of St. Louis and, in 1868, never went beyond New England. Dickens was portrayed by the highly underrated guest actor Jonathan Harris, some two years before he became a household name as interplanetary antagonist Dr. Zachary Smith in the hugely popular CBS television series *Lost in Space* (1965–1968). In *Bonanza*, the imaginary Dickens, while offending American fans with his monetary zeal and nearly being framed for a crime he did not commit, patiently explains to an attentive Hoss Cartwright (played by Dan Blocker) why international copyrights matter. In turn, Hoss convinces the rest of the Cartwright clan that Dickens may have good reasons for his strong feelings. The timing of the episode is suggestive. In April 1963, only five months before, the U.S. Court of Appeals for the Second Circuit decided the landmark case of *Shapiro, Bernstein and Co. v. H.L. Green Co.*, ruling unanimously that vicarious or secondary liability was justified in copyright situations. Initial reaction in the U.S. was predictably hostile, but British-born Hollywood screenwriter Peter Packer (1906–1987) wrote this teleplay for *Bonanza* in sympathy with the concept of extended copyrights, and no doubt helped to bring his good friend Jonathan Harris into the production to portray Charles Dickens, an important historical literary figure who would have financially profited from the court's decision, had he not in fact died some 97 years earlier.

The next biographical film work referencing Dickens' American travels was less impressive, at least in the artistic or popular sense. The massive, 13-episode, 13-hour miniseries *Dickens of London* was first aired in Great Britain by Yorkshire Television circa 1976 and then to American audiences in 1977 as part of Season 7 for the PBS hit series *Masterpiece Theatre*, the same season that saw the first airing of *I, Claudius* (based on the novels by Robert Graves and a screenplay by Jack Pulman) and *Our Mutual Friend*—the latter being the first Dickens novel dramatized by that notable franchise.[15] Doing yeoman duty in a double role of the elderly Charles Dickens and Dickens' father John was versatile British actor Roy

Dotrice. The big reveal at the end of the series is that Dickens based his character Wilkins Micawber on his father John, although this is not really a reveal since Dickens himself declared it so during his own lifetime. Unfortunately, this ultra-lengthy series also suffers from uncertain writing and plotting, both of which are too often clumsy, tedious, and hard to follow.[16] Structured as a series of flashbacks from Dickens' second American tour of 1867–1868, there are occasional allusions to *American Notes* but little or nothing referring to his extensive English and continental travels. Incredibly, there is no mention of Dickens' affair with Nelly Ternan—the series ends with the death of Dickens' father in 1851—although the novelist's inclinations towards younger women are hinted at frequently, while wife Catherine is portrayed very unsympathetically as being mentally unstable. Perhaps the most interesting episode is "Nightmare" in which Dickens meets Edgar Allan Poe under imaginary circumstances resembling a Poe horror story, but otherwise shedding little light on their mysterious 1842 interaction. The series is still widely available on DVD but requires plenty of patience and stamina from viewers, especially those newcomers to the life and works of Charles Dickens.

Quirkier, and half as long (10 episodes, five hours) but far more interesting, is the 2005 documentary *Dickens in America*, hosted by British Dickensian actor and enthusiast Miriam Margolyes.[17] Produced by Lion Television Scotland for the BBC, the series retraces the steps of Dickens in 1842 from England through the United States and Canada and back again to England, with special focus on the text of *American Notes*. The series suffers occasionally from its inability to bridge the huge cultural gap between the U.S. of the 21st century—an imperialist power still reeling from the horrors of 9-11—and the pre-Mexican War, pre-Civil War tinderbox that Dickens experienced in 1842. Nevertheless, thanks to a reliance on Dickens' own text, it often shines light on the novelist's priorities in a way seldom otherwise seen by viewers. For example, Dickens' admiration of the Perkins School for the Blind in Boston, or his revulsion at The Tombs penitentiary of New York City. A visit to the ruined remnants of The Octagon mental hospital on Roosevelt Island—a place known to Dickens—serves as a prelude to contemporary knowledge that the same site soon became a government-subsidized, mixed-income residential redevelopment, in many respects symbolic of New York City's more recent overall transformation. Above all, the mood is routinely lightened by the considerable humor and insights of Margolyes as narrator and visual tour guide. For viewers not familiar with *American Notes*, the miniseries serves as a handy introduction to this fascinating side of Dickens' genius and remains widely available on DVD.

It seems obvious (to this commentator, at least) that the travelogue aspect of Dickens' output deserves more exploration on film. This is especially true given the current vast oversupply of *A Christmas Carol, Oliver Twist, David Copperfield*, and other popular Dickens' novels on video, even as worthy as these other books are. In addition to daunting hurdles of audience false preconceptions about Charles Dickens the man and novelist, a bigger problem may be that literary biography does not matter to most audiences because, to them, literature itself hardly matters to begin with. In any event, there would seem to be plenty of room for more cinematic creativity in this regard. Dickens himself would surely have viewed it as an artistic challenge, such as the genre of historical novel which he eventually met to rousing acclaim in *A Tale of Two Cities*. By 1860, just as the United States was about to violently and temporarily break apart, the novelist was primed to meet yet another new challenge, this time eschewing "uncommercial" tourism in favor of a great interior journey of the self, and in the process would create one of the greatest fictional works in the English language. Pip, Dickens' semi-autobiographical hero from *Great Expectations*, is in no sense of the term a world traveler, that is, unless one counts from traveling a short distance from the marshes of Kent to the urban jungle of London town.

16

Great Expectations (1860–1861)

> "I had heard of the death of her husband ... and of her being married again to a Shropshire doctor ... and that they lived on her own personal fortune. I was ... in London, and walking along Piccadilly with little Pip—when a servant came running after me to ask would I step back to a lady in a carriage who wished to speak to me. It was a little pony carriage, which the lady was driving; and the lady and I looked sadly enough on one another.... I was very glad afterwards to have had the interview; for, in her face and in her voice, and in her touch, she gave me the assurance, that suffering had been stronger than Miss Havisham's teaching, and had given her a heart to understand what my heart used to be."[1]

In Dickens' *Great Expectations*, the longest physical journey is taken by Magwitch (as a convict) from England to Australia and back; however, an even longer interior journey is taken by the novel's eponymous hero, Philip Pirrip (II), aka Pip, who travels from innocent good intentions to sad wisdom and self-knowledge within the space of half a lifetime. Dickens the novelist has had more than his share of literary critics since his own day, but even his toughest critics usually concede that *Great Expectations* is work of unqualified genius. It is certainly the greatest among Dickens' six core novels (the ones by which he is best known) and, not surprisingly, has received a fair number of distinguished film adaptations during the modern era. Written when its 48-year-old author had less than a decade left to live, and in the immediate aftermath of his marriage and conventional family life being deliberately dismantled, the novel conveys a definite sense of hard-earned, critical self-assessment. As recently observed by biographer Claire Tomalin, "It did not come from research or the theatre but out of a deep place in Dickens's imagination which he never chose to explain, and perhaps never could, and it is all the better for that."[2]

After being published to since-unbated critical and commercial acclaim, *Great Expectations* was a book that Dickens (uncharacteristically for him) did not like talking about, quite unlike his earlier, semi-autobiographical blockbuster *David Copperfield*, in which the novelist became the hero of his own life.

Notoriously, the published ending of *Great Expectations* is not the ending of the story as written by Dickens in the original manuscript (see epigraph). In the original, after many years have passed, Pip, along with his namesake nephew, briefly meet Estella by chance only to realize that they are neither meant nor right for each other—in short, a highly bittersweet ending.[3] Then, on the eve of publication, Dickens' fellow Victorian novelist and older contemporary Edward Bulwer-Lytton (1803–1873) convinced him that a happy ending was better.[4] Dickens, always a good listener with respect to his admirers, quickly complied, and a more upbeat last chapter was added in which Pip foresees never again parting from a much-reformed Estella. This alternative ending was duly published, and has been published ever since, leaving readers to search obscure secondary sources to find the downbeat original.[5] Literary purists have, with justification, ever since viewed the newer, happier ending as a blot on Dickens' tremendous masterpiece. Notably, among the many subsequent film versions of *Great Expectations*, none use the original sadder ending, and almost all have Pip and Estella getting together at the end. Perhaps this is fitting, since Dickens himself apparently could not, in the end, face up to his own critical self-examination. In the final sentences of the novel, Pip, like David Copperfield before him, becomes the hero of his own life. In any event, after a serial run in 1860–1861, *Great Expectations* was immediately published in its complete form by Chapman & Hall of London, just as the American War Between the States was breaking out on the other side of the Atlantic Ocean.[6] Nearly unique among Dickens' novels—as if

Alec Guinness as Herbert Pocket in David Lean's *Great Expectations* (1946) (Masheter Movie Archive / Alamy Stock Photo).

16. Great Expectations (1860–1861)

to acknowledge its special, dark status—there were no illustrations in the serial run or original complete publication.

Like *David Copperfield* before it, *Great Expectations* utilizes an unusual (for Dickens) first-person narrative structure, strongly suggesting a semi-autobiographical element. Like many of the novelist's most seminal works, *Great Expectations* eschews a British Victorian setting mostly in favor of a nostalgic, pre–Victorian atmosphere of the early 1830s and Dickens' own troubled childhood within the small-town environs of rural Kent and Rochester, southeast of London. Beyond that, the two novels have little in common; in fact, readers may easily view *Great Expectations* as an anti–*David Copperfield*, with a bleak, pessimistic attitude towards its own narrator and the surrounding world—a hostile world in which goodness best survives by laying low and avoiding attention. There is little of Dickens' trademark social concerns, except pity for the incarcerated and the insane. As for characters, the novelist rolls out some of his more memorable and disturbing creations. While the portrayal of Miss Havisham is bizarre and tragic, Pip (especially the adult Pip) must rank as arguably Dickens' most unsettling hero or anti-hero. Abel Magwitch, who enters the story as a bogeyman, shockingly becomes Pip's surrogate father and true benefactor, leaving the stage almost in saintlike fashion. Magwitch and Havisham, in all their repulsiveness, do more than anyone else to shape Pip's personality and aspirations. Pip has none of Copperfield's pretentions to gentility; class-wise, he is the lowest of the low, a blacksmith's apprentice, albeit with a quick wit, handy fists, and a knack for literacy. Money exists merely to be spent acquiring things, including a spouse. Not until tragedy plays itself out near the end of the tale does Pip even consider finding a livelihood for himself. By then, his true surrogate parents and benefactors have become Joe Gargery, along with Gargery's second wife Biddy. Joe's exclamatory "What larks!" becomes a sort of rallying cry for a simple faith in success. Unlike the tragic Peggotty family from *David Copperfield*, Joe and Biddy in *Great Expectations* are not forced to immigrate and are always more than happy to save Pip from his worst instincts whenever necessary.

As one might expect, early 20th-century attempts to film Dickens' melancholy masterwork were tentative, despite the novel's ongoing popularity. Still surviving in film print, *The Boy and the Convict*, a 12-minute silent reel from 1909 condenses the Magwitch storyline but dispenses with Havisham and Estella, then tacks on a happy ending.[7] It has little in common with Dickens' original story. Then in 1917, during the height of World War I, came the first attempt at a full-length (five reels) silent adaptation by Paramount, now unfortunately lost except for some stills.[8] Italian American director Robert G. Vignola (1882–1953) worked with Jack Pickford (as the adult Pip), younger brother of the more famous Pickford sisters who worked with D.W. Griffith. In 1922, Danish Dickens enthusiast Anders Wilhelm Sandberg directed *Store Forventninger* ("Great Expectations"), to go along with his well-regarded silent versions of *David Copperfield* (1922) and *Little Dorrit* (1924), now preserved by the Danish Film Institute.[9] With the advent of sound, Universal Pictures produced the first talkie version of *Great Expectations* in 1934, directed by Stuart Walker (1888–1941). Though relatively undistinguished and taking significant liberties with Dickens' text, this movie starred several well-known American actors in lead roles, most notably, Francis L. Sullivan as Jaggers.[10] Twelve years later, following World War II, Sullivan would reprise this same role in arguably the most famous of all Dickens film adaptations, and certainly one of the most famous British films ever made.

The real story of *Great Expectations* on film, indeed the true story of Dickens' novels being adapted by modern film, began in 1939 London as England was on the cusp of entering World War II, two full years before the Japanese attacked Pearl Harbor. It was then that a relatively unknown, 25-year-old impoverished actor named Alec Guinness, along with his wife Merula Silvia Salaman, resolved to mount a super-low budget stage production of Dickens' novel at the 200-seat Rudolph Steiner House and Theatre near Regent's Park, with Guinness and Salaman cowriting an original script and Guinness himself playing Pip's adult confidant Herbert Pocket. Through an odd combination of circumstances, the tiny show was a big hit and the darling of London theater critics. David Lean, a 31-year-old British film editor who had never read Dickens, was dragged to the show against his will by his spouse but then was mesmerized by it, resolving to make a movie if ever given opportunity. After surviving a long tour of duty in the Royal Navy, Guinness returned to his love of acting after the war and soon found himself collaborating with now-head director Lean.[11] Of the 1946 *Great Expectations*, along with Lean's follow-up with Guinness in 1948, *Oliver Twist*, critic Joss Marsh has accurately written, "No Dickens films have had more impact on film history or more importance for Dickens's popular and critical reputation."[12] For the feature film, a new happy ending, partially based on the original text, was contrived by Lean's then-wife Kay Walsh, with a distinctive and haunting visual style painstakingly developed by Lean's unsung set designer, John Ryan.[13]

In addition to first-rate directing, writing, set design, and source material, the 1946 *Great Expectations* benefited enormously from arguably the best casting ever given to a Dickens adaptation. Exceptional performers included two members from the lauded 1939 stage version—Guinness in what proved to be his breakout film role as Herbert Pocket, plus a 46-year-old Martita Hunt in what many still consider to be the definitive movie portrayal of Miss Havisham. This was long before anyone could have remotely imagined Guinness in an iconic role for *Star Wars*. Controversially, the *Great Expectations* screenplay, like the stage play, eliminated lesser roles from the novel such as Pip's evil alter-ego Orlick or the relentlessly mocking Trabb's boy, although it was precisely these ruthless cuts that make such for a compelling two-hour viewing experience. Rounding out a stellar ensemble cast was stage and film veteran John Mills as the adult Pip, Francis L. Sullivan as Jaggers, Scottish-born Finlay Currie as Magwitch, Bernard Miles as Joe Gargery, Irish-born Valerie Hobson as the adult Estella, and perhaps most notably and certainly most visibly, a 17-year-old Jean Simmons as the young Estella.[14] Simmons' enacted disdainful treatment of the 14-year-old Anthony Wager (as the Young Pip) is one for the ages and made her into an immediate screen icon, a high status which she well retained for the next six decades.[15] Thus, what began seven years earlier as a pre-war patriotic act of do-it-yourself live theater, eventually became one of the loftiest masterpieces of modern Dickensian cinema, thanks mainly to Alec Guinness and David Lean. Following the commercial and critical triumph of the 1946 *Great Expectations*, produced unexpectedly by a British rather than American team, a template had been established both for this novel and other literary film adaptations lasting many years afterwards, and by which all subsequent productions would by some degree be measured.

It took American producers a few years to respond to this cultural challenge from Great Britain, and when they finally did it was in the newfangled medium of television. In 1954, the NBC series *Robert Montgomery Presents* ran a two-part, two-hour series of *Great Expectations* starring several British imported actors, including Estelle Winwood as Miss Havisham and a then-unknown Roddy McDowall as Pip.[16] The success of this modest venture was followed that same year by a similar production of *David Copperfield* as part of the same series. Within a few short years, the BBC responded back by taking the television miniseries concept to new, hitherto unknown heights, including a 13-part, six-hour version of *Great Expectations* in 1959, then again in 1967 with a 10-episode, nearly five-hour production.[17] The latter miniseries, ably adapted for the small screen by Hugh Leonard, featured British cult favorite Francesca Annis as Estella and Gary Bond as Pip (five years before Bond originated the lead role for Andrew Lloyd Webber's *Joseph and the Amazing Technicolor Dreamcoat* in 1972), is still available for viewing on DVD and makes an interesting artifact for its era. By the late 1960s, the BBC had firmly reestablished its supremacy as a producer of high-quality adaptations for the novels of Charles Dickens. This trend had been further propelled by the dizzying acclaim of Lionel Bart's *Oliver!* (i.e., *Oliver Twist*) both as a West End stage musical and English-produced blockbuster film. The unfortunate result was that, by the early 1970s, everyone trying to make a fast buck in the film industry was talking about turning Dickens' novels into musicals, no matter how inappropriate the subject matter. Fortunately, *Great Expectations* was never subjected to this fallacy, although it came disconcertingly close at one point.

Originally conceived as a musical with the annoying working title of *Pip!*, the 1974 version of *Great Expectations* was mercifully changed to a non-musical feature film in mid-production, and distinguished soundtrack composer Maurice Jarre (1924–2009) brought in to provide a conventional score.[18] According to lead star Michael York (as Pip), the decision to scrap the musical was made less than two months into shooting by director Joseph Hardy (b. 1929) because song-and-dance numbers would have interrupted the powerful narrative flow of the story—a polite way of saying that Dickens' dark tale of self-examination simply did not mix with a song-and-dance concept.[19] Fortunately, the marquee creative team assembled for the project decided to stick it out, including Sarah Miles as Estella, James Mason as Magwitch, Margaret Leighton as Miss Havisham, Robert Morley as Uncle Pumblechook, and Anthony Quayle as Jaggers. York worked on the film almost simultaneously with his participation in the famous 1974 adaptation of Agatha Christie's *Murder on the Orient Express* and admitted that he was drawn to *Great Expectations* by its autobiographical trajectory of obscurity to fame, as well as the high caliber of its professionalism.[20] York usefully observed that the first-rate cameraman utilized was David Lean's later cinematographer, Freddie Young (1902–1998), and the finished product itself represented a gloss on Lean's acclaimed 1946 version.[21] Although receiving a mixed critical reception from those who expected Lean's postwar adaptation to somehow be equaled or surpassed, the 1974 *Great Expectations* still makes enjoyable viewing on its own as a two-hour feature film and might well be considered a distant runner up in terms of quality to Lean's earlier classic.

In 1981, after a 14-year hiatus, the BBC decided to reboot *Great Expectations* as a six-hour, 12-episode miniseries.[22] For this latest effort, the BBC rolled out its Dickensian "A" Team of producer Barry Letts (1925–2009), director Julian Amyes (1917–1992), and screenwriter James Andrew Hall (b. 1939).[23] The results were somewhat mixed dramatically, although the 1981 production is still widely available for viewing on Prime and other platforms, and certainly no one can question its sincerity. British actors Gerry Sundquist, Sarah-Jane Varley, and Stratford Johns gave comparatively understated performances respectively as Pip, Estella, and Magwitch, while the redoubtable Joan Hickson, then 75 years old and her Agatha Christie-*Miss Marple* TV series still several years in the future,

16. Great Expectations (1860–1861)

gave a memorable and idiosyncratic portrayal of Miss Havisham. While mostly adhering to the original text, the expansive 1981 miniseries served mainly to remind television audiences that earlier feature films of *Great Expectations* from 1946 and 1974 had been brilliantly condensed into two-hour viewing experiences. The contrast suggests that Dickens' novels could still be made into compelling shorter dramatic versions—as proved by Alec Guinness in 1939—despite the many inherent advantages of the miniseries format as applied to the Dickens screen adaptation.

Two years later, in 1983, came the one and only animated version of *Great Expectations* from the irrepressible Burbank Studios of Sydney, Australia.[24] Utilizing even more radical cuts to make the bittersweet cartoon a little over one hour in length, Burbank's determined adaptation adheres to its usual excellent standards while at the same time providing some unusual surprises. Foremost among these surprises is an ending in which Pip and Estella do not come together, but rather part ways, making the 1983 animated *Great Expectations* the only film version of the novel (to our knowledge) in which Pip does not eventually "get the girl." Rather than adhere to Dickens' original manuscript, however, the cartoon offers its own conclusion in which Pip first takes leave of a chagrined Estella, then of the always-supportive Biddy, before returning to London to seek his fortune. Dickens' original ending, insofar as we know, has never been dramatized. The Aussie fascination with *Great Expectations* is understandable, given the forced immigration of Magwitch, sent to Australia as a convict, where he proceeds to amass a fortune, of which Pip later becomes the secret beneficiary before all is forfeited because Magwitch's illegal return to England. It is not surprising that a few years after this, in 1987, Australia saw a movie and television spinoff, *Great Expectations: The Untold Story*, in which the "untold" but prodigious rise of Abel Magwitch from prison to prosperity is duly dramatized.[25]

At the end of the decade, in 1989, Disney issued an expansive TV co-production of *Great Expectations* as a three-part, nearly six-hour extravaganza.[26] At the time, there was good reason for aficionados to be apprehensive, given that the year before (in 1988) Disney had made a small fortune with a preposterous, anthropomorphic animation of *Oliver Twist*, rebranded as *Oliver & Company*. To the astonishment of many, however, the 1989 Disney *Great Expectations* had much to recommend it, thanks mainly to some sensational casting decisions, primarily with British performers. For starters, a still very capable, 60-year-old Jean Simmons was brought in to play Miss Havisham, some 43 years after she had stolen the show as young Estella in David Lean's classic 1946 adaptation. Next, Anthony Hopkins, then at the top of his game as an actor, gave a nearly definitive portrayal of Magwitch. This was only two years before

Hopkins garnered worldwide attention for his performance as Hannibal Lecter in *The Silence of the Lambs* (1991). When Hopkins' Magwitch threatens to devour a young Pip, he is quite believable. Although Anthony Calf (Pip) and Kim Thomson (Estella) are less memorable in the lead romantic roles, secondary casting was rounded out with first-rate selections such as John Rhys-Davies (Joe Gargery), Frank Middlemass (Uncle Pumplechook), and Ray McAnally (Jaggers). Handsomely filmed, largely on location in rural Kent, the series was ably directed by Kevin Connor (b. 1937) and adapted for the screen by John Goldsmith (b. 1947). Surprisingly, perhaps even to Disney executives, the 1989 miniseries exceeded the 1981 BBC version in almost every respect.

While it is not the purpose of this study to delve into the endless dramatic riffs and spinoffs from Dickens' novels, one deserves special mention in reference to *Great Expectations*, which in 1998 became a big-budget, loose adaptation of the novel under the innovative supervision of a then still unknown, 37-year-old Mexican director, Alfonso Cuarón (b. 1961). This was two decades before Cuarón became the toast of the Academy Awards with *Roma* (2018), although his first two feature films in English had been adaptations of works by British novelists (Frances Hodgson Burnett and Dickens), in 1995 and 1998. For the 1998 *Great Expectations*, Ethan Hawke and Gwyneth Paltrow, both at the height of their celebrity, were cast within a modern-day Manhattan setting, along with several major character name changes, and substantial liberties taken with Dickens' plot, while the upbeat ending was retained. Distinguished Scottish composer Patrick Doyle (b. 1953) was recruited for the soundtrack. More interesting were the casting of the late Anne Bancroft and Robert De Niro as Dinsmoor (i.e., Havisham) and Lustig (i.e., Magwitch), but these key parts were so cut and altered as to be hardly recognizable. In hindsight, director Cuarón had reservations about the project, although the film retains a dedicated viewership and is easily located on video. In the final analysis, however, the 1998 *Great Expectations* is an example of the inherent dangers in "modernizing" Dickens while deviating too far from his original storyline.

Far more faithful to the novel was a four-episode, nearly-three hour BBC version of *Great Expectations* in 1999, its first attempt at a miniseries of the novel since 1981, airing on American television via *Masterpiece Theatre* that same year. Directed by Julian Jarrold (b. 1960) and adapted by Tony Marchant (b. 1959), this production featured the iconic Charlotte Rampling and always-excellent Bernard Hill in their respective roles of Havisham and Magwitch. The series also uniquely offered a Welsh-born lead, Ioan Gruffudd as Pip, and the British South African-born Justine Waddell as Estella. Despite its penchant for experimentation, the 1999 BBC version offered much to praise, and it retains the power of the original storyline, despite, like its predecessors, wrestling to deliver an upbeat ending. Gruffudd's lead performance, with its unapologetic Welsh accent, somehow seems to harmonize well with the fictional Pip's strictly working-class roots. Although variously criticized by purists at the time, this BBC update of a Dickens classic has retained its integrity over the years and is still easily accessible for viewing. Thus ended the 20th century for film adaptations of *Great Expectations*—but several other noteworthy productions were still yet to come.

In 2011, the BBC returned yet again to *Great Expectations*, this time delivering a three-episode, nearly three-hour miniseries seen by a large viewership and turning a nifty profit. The big news for this more recent production was American-born TV superstar Gillian Anderson (*The X-Files*) portraying Miss Havisham, at 43 years old possibly the youngest film actor to do this, although Martita Hunt had been even younger when she took the stage in the same role alongside Alec Guinness in 1939. After weathering initial skepticism, Anderson delivered a unique performance that has been rightfully praised, helping to establish her legitimacy as a serious dramatic actor. Rounding out a well-balanced, mostly British cast was Ray Winstone as Magwitch, Douglas Booth as Pip, Vanessa Kirby as Estella, and David Suchet as Jaggers. Making the job considerably easier for director Brian Kirk was an excellent screenplay by Sarah Phelps, a seasoned adaptor of works by Dickens, Agatha Christie, and J.K. Rowling, among others.[27] Filmed largely on location, the 2011 *Great Expectations* deservedly won four Emmy Awards and has a strong claim for being the best miniseries version of the novel made to date. It remains widely available for general viewership on various streaming services.

During the Dickens bicentenary birth year of 2012, and hard on the heels of the 2011 BBC miniseries, came yet another two-hour feature film version of *Great Expectations*, this one overseen by high-profile British director Mike Newell (b. 1942).[28] Leading an outstanding British cast was 46-year-old Helena Bonham Carter as Miss Havisham, continuing the trend of younger age portrayals for that character, and thus more emphasizing that character's early disappointments in life. Effectively cast as Magwitch was late-newcomer Ralph Fiennes, who reportedly had never previously read a Dickens novel but during production became so enthused that, for his next project, he directed and starred in a rare Dickens-biography drama, *The Invisible Woman* (2013). Scottish actor and Harry Potter-James Bond alumnus Robbie Coltrane introduced Dickens' Jaggers to a younger generation, as did Jeremy Irvine (Pip) and Holliday Grainger (Estella). Like the 2011 miniseries, the 2012 feature film created a new ending, but this version opted to keep the mood upbeat rather than utilizing the novelist's downbeat original manuscript. Although more than competently done, and financially successful to boot, the 2012 *Great Expectations* did not quite match the breathtaking artistry of David Lean's 1946 classic, or the skillfully performed and filmed (but underrated) 1974 update. Screenwriter David Nicholls (b. 1966) did, however, nicely delineate the complex backstories of Dickens' characters, and the film's Toronto Film Festival premiere additionally featured an independent work, *Magwitch* (2012), serving as a dramatic prequel for any viewers still confused or overwhelmed by older character motivations within Dickens' storyline.[29]

In examining the explosive popularity of Dickens' *Great Expectations* on film between 1946 and 2012—a mere 66 years—one is repeatedly drawn to the characters of Havisham and Magwitch, surely two of the novelist's greatest creations. The novel seems to be as much their story as it is Pip's and Estella's, in fact, probably more so. Havisham is deranged and her looks gone, but she stays with audiences, leaping off the printed page or video screen to inhabit our consciousness. She is a woman frozen in time. Magwitch represents the ultimate nightmare of capitalism—an uncouth criminal, brilliant and hardworking, who in the end is unable or unwilling to escape old grudges or previous missteps in life. Between Havisham and Magwitch, the fates of Pip and Estella are inevitably driven and perversely intertwined, although it should be clear to anyone paying half attention that the two cannot be a happy couple. Ultimately, Pip becomes a creature of Magwitch's aspirations, rather than his own person, while Estella, as observed by many, is one of Dickens' most thinly written heroines. And yet Dickens decided to oblige his readers by getting them together at the end of the story, after Havisham and Magwitch are long deceased.[30] For his next major work, however, Dickens would take a much closer look at mismatched romantic relationships, albeit stories with happy endings, combined with an uglier view of a proletariat class which he had otherwise championed in his fiction.

17

Our Mutual Friend (1864–1865)

> "'The book's name, sir?' inquired Silas.
>
> 'I thought you might have know'd him without it,' said Mr Boffin slightly disappointed. 'His name is Decline-And-Fall-Off-The-Rooshan-Empire.' (Mr Boffin went over these stones slowly, and with much caution.)
>
> 'Ay indeed!' said Mr Wegg, nodding his head with an air of friendly recognition."[1]

Our Mutual Friend holds the distinction of being the last fully completed novel by Charles Dickens, even though Dickens at age 53 still had five years left to live when the finished work hit London bookstalls in late 1865. At the time, the health of the indisputably greatest of all English novelists was beginning to fail for the first time, and his private life was in turmoil thanks to a self-inflicted divorce, tense relations with his legitimate children, and a secretive affair with a young former actress that appears to have ended in tragedy, loss, and disappointment for both.[2] Most of Dickens' remaining energies would be spent on a final unfinished novel, shorter fictional pieces, lucrative staged public readings, one last American tour in 1867–1868, and above all, coping with the reigning chaos in his personal affairs away from work. During its own day, *Our Mutual Friend* sold well enough commercially but critical opinions, especially American critical opinions, tended to be uncomprehending or outright hostile. In hindsight, the novel is clearly a work of experimentation, but also one of tremendous depth. During modern times, this dichotomy of opinion has reversed itself. General readership has declined (along with demand for film adaptations), but literary critical opinion of *Our Mutual Friend* has steadily improved since its original publication and currently runs quite high, with considerable justification. Initially, *Our Mutual Friend* first appeared in monthly serial form between early 1864 and late 1865, published by Chapman & Hall of London, with lavish illustrations by Marcus Stone (1840–1921), a noted English Pre-Raphaelite artist and old schoolfriend of Dickens' favorite daughter Kate (the future Mrs. Perugini), herself destined to become a Victorian painter of note.

In some respects, the plot of *Our Mutual Friend* represents a thematic continuation of its immediate predecessor, *Great Expectations*. Lead romantic characters John Harmon (aka "Rokesmith") and Bella Wilfer have many similarities with their more famous counterparts, Pip and Estella. Both couples have common origins but aspire to much more after being exposed to inherited wealth and privilege. Both appear destined for each other from childhood within an elaborate backstory, and like Estella's first impressions of Pip, Bella's initial expressed opinions of Rokesmith are strictly negative. Like Estella, Bella then seems to undergo a major personality shift, but unlike Estella, this change is gradual and begins early on as she gets to know Harmon-Rokesmith. There are, however, also important differences: Harmon (the "mutual friend" of the storyline) "gets the girl"—as well as his inheritance—while the free-spirited Bella is fully tamed into obedience and domesticity. Strikingly, *Our Mutual Friend*, quite unlike *Great Expectations*, has no nostalgia, no childhood flashbacks, and a rather complex view of good and evil in human nature—one that sees people as people, regardless of class, education, or breeding. Most of the characters are playacting away from their truer selves strictly to obtain more money or a higher station in life. Then Dickens introduces a second romantic plot between Eugene Wrayburn and Lizzie Hexam, an unlikely relationship starkly divided by class, wealth, and social status. In this case, however, it is the dissolute Wrayburn who gradually changes for the better while Lizzie, after some hesitation, remains steadfastly good and true. The prominent Wrayburn-Lizzie subplot quite likely introduces a strong autobiographical element into story for Dickens, representing the then-ongoing but socially condemned relationship between the novelist and Nelly Ternan, 27 years his junior, although the fictional Wrayburn and Lizzie do not have to overcome a similar large gap in age.

Like other Dickens novels, the eccentric characterizations of *Our Mutual Friend* are unique and unforgettable. Many other characters represent highpoints, even for Dickens, beginning with the villainous Bradley Headstone, who seems to be an extension of Orlick from *Great Expectations*, but with far more depth. Readers may disapprove of Headstone's villainy but can still fully empathize with his rage and resentment. The feigned snobbery of Noddy Boffin is so convincing that many commentators (including this one) believe Dickens intended the character to stay that way until changing course to tie up loose ends with a sudden conclusion to the novel. The pronounced money-grubbing theme is comically

17. *Our Mutual Friend* (1864–1865) 159

Promotional poster for Edison's silent film *How Bella Was Won* (1911), now lost, adapted from Dickens' *Our Mutual Friend*.

epitomized by Alfred and Sophronia Lemmle, who only marry each other in a mistaken belief that the other is wealthy and are deeply chagrined after learning otherwise. Silas Wegg, unlike Boffin, is literate and cultured in his own limited manner, but (unlike Boffin) is disfigured in body, mind, and moral values. Mr. Venus, on the other hand, is an odd fellow in most outward respects, including his eccentric appearance, but proves himself in the end to be morally upright compared to others. Fanny Cleaver (aka Jenny Wren), like Mr. Venus, is a social reject by conventional standards but beyond her appearance and marginal livelihood has far more integrity than her presumed social betters. The list goes on. In short, a Dickens novel without such wonderful characterizations would not truly be a Dickens novel, and the vivid characters springing from the pages of *Our Mutual Friend* have made it more than film-worthy during the modern age of cinema.

Two important circumstances surrounding the creation of *Our Mutual Friend* are rarely mentioned but deserve repeating. The first is that on June 9, 1865, Dickens, along with Nelly Ternan and her mother, were nearly killed while riding in a passenger train that crashed near Staplehurst, Kent, as they returned to London from France. Dickens survived the crash, tried to assist survivors, and scrambled to rescue the unpublished manuscript of *Our Mutual Friend*, but otherwise neglected his mistress and her mother—both unharmed as well—whom he wished to remain publicly unknown. This traumatic incident, along with the presumed or inferred recent death of their infant child in France, seemed to mark a significant cooling down in the ongoing relationship between Dickens and Nelly, as noted by recent biographers such as Claire Tomalin.[3] This sudden brush with mortality, among other things, appeared to spur Dickens to rapidly complete his latest novel, which indeed was then quickly wrapped up and published in final form later the same year. In addition to creating more distance between the novelist and his mistress, the Staplehurst train crash served to push *Our Mutual Friend* to a conclusion that in hindsight seems a bit rushed and contrived. After a brilliant set-up, many readers want the story to continue longer, but instead it comes to screeching halt with all conflicts neatly resolved, including the gradually developing romances between Harmon and Bella, as well as Eugene and Lizzie, overcoming all obstacles in their path.

The second important externality of 1865 is almost never mentioned by Dickensian critics. On April 9, exactly two months before the Staplehurst train crash, the American War Between the States concluded with General Lee's surrender to General Grant at Appomattox.[4] As a diligent if occasionally naïve student of American politics, Dickens would have been quite aware of the event, probably as he conceived the final chapters of

17. Our Mutual Friend (1864–1865)

Our Mutual Friend. Despite his staunch personal opposition to slavery, Dickens, like many of his English countrymen, was a severe critic of the American political-economic system, and probably harbored a common Anglo-American belief that the South would handily detach itself from any attempts at enforced federal union. When the opposite in fact came to pass, first with decisive federal victories in the American West, and finally within Virginia itself, Dickens reacted by taking a cold, hard look at the English political-economic system—something he was quite good at doing as a novelist. When Boffin pays Wegg to read out loud Edward Gibbon's *The Decline and Fall of the Roman Empire* (see epigraph), a book published less than a century before, his choice of material is quite appropriate. After 1865, Great Britain seemed to decline while the barbarous United States, now unified, was on the rise. *Our Mutual Friend* thus represents the novelist's final verdict on Victorian London—a verdict not favorable—but with Dickens still showing himself to be a steadfast defender of the common people, who are presented as realistic characters, however fictional, either good, bad, or mostly somewhere in between, accurately portrayed within their contemporary habitats.

Our Mutual Friend attracted interest from filmmakers early on, but its inherent complexity hindered outstanding production efforts for nearly a century. The years immediately prior to the Great War, especially those leading up to the Dickens centenary birth year of 1912, saw a flurry of ambitious adaptations for various Dickens novels by Edison, Thanhouser, Vitagraph, and other prominent film producers. In 1911, the Edison Company tackled *Our Mutual Friend* (as well as several other works by Dickens) but decided to divide the complicated work into two separate silent shorts, each dealing with the two main romantic plotlines, one for Harmon and Bella, the other for Wrayburn and Lizzie. The first of these was retitled *How Bella Was Won* and starred prominent American silent actor George Soule Spencer as John Harmon.[5] Little else is known about this adaptation which, unfortunately, is now considered lost. All that survives is a marvelous promotional poster featuring a rendering of Spencer, a portrait of Dickens hanging on the wall, and a quotation of endorsement from English poet Philip Sidney (1554–1586), conveniently overlooking the fact Sidney had died two centuries before Dickens was born.[6] That same year (1911) Edison also released *Eugene Wrayburn*, another silent short, this one starring the prolific American performer Darwin Karr as Wrayburn.[7] Co-starring with Karr was the American silent actor Bliss Milford (as Lizzie), who would go on the following year (1912) to appear in Edison's short adaptation of *Martin Chuzzlewit*. It would be another decade, three years after the Great War of 1914–1918, that any serious attempt would be made to adapt *Our Mutual Friend* as a unified set piece for a silent feature film.

In 1921, Danish silent auteur Anders Wilhelm Sandberg (1887–1938) directed *Vor Fælles Ven* ("Our Mutual Friend") for Nordisk Film of Copenhagen, the first in his notable series of four Dickens adaptations, the others being *Great Expectations* (1922), *David Copperfield* (1922), and *Little Dorrit* (1924).[8] Sandberg's landmark 1921 *Our Mutual Friend* is now partially lost but what remains has been carefully restored by the Danish Film Institute and is available on DVD through the New York Museum of Modern Art, among other specialized outlets.[9] Sandberg, who retired from making feature films after sound was introduced, must be given partial credit for helping to raise the Dickens adaptation movie form to the level of high art during an era when most studios viewed these works strictly as disposable commercial widgets. After Sandberg's backers, the innovative Nordisk Film, decided that such adaptations were too lavish cost-wise to continue, the decision appears to have played a major factor in Sandberg's self-imposed retirement. We are lucky to still have substantial remnants of his surviving work, thanks mainly to the dedication of Danish curators.

Thirty-seven years and yet another World War later, movie production techniques had changed considerably. Also, in the interim came David Lean's groundbreaking film work, the popularization of TV and pioneering of the miniseries format by the BBC, especially with respect to Dickens adaptations which seemed ideally suited for this new approach. Finally, in 1958–1959, came the first BBC adaptation of *Our Mutual Friend*, including a dozen half-hour episodes, roughly six hours total from start to finish.[10] This was the first time Dickens' last completed novel had been given an extensive miniseries adaptation. The late 1950s and early 1960s saw an explosion of BBC productions devoted to Dickens, and a good effort was made to tackle this elusive work. The influential Swedish-Anglo impresario Freda Lingstrom (1893–1989) was retained to produce a screenplay, while New Zealand-born Eric Tayler (1921–1997), who would later in 1962 direct *Oliver Twist* for the BBC, was brought in to direct. Among an experienced stage cast, of special note was Rachel Roberts as Lizzie Hexam, and a young and then unknown David McCallum as Eugene Wrayburn. McCallum would soon go on to worldwide TV fame as Illyia Kuryakin in *The Man from U.N.C.L.E.* (1964–1968), while Roberts would later play Pip's sister, Mrs. Joe, in the 1974 film of *Great Expectations*. The 1958–1959 BBC miniseries for *Our Mutual Friend* was recently (in 2017) released on DVD by Simply Media, and continues to hold up well for viewing, despite subsequent, far more acclaimed versions of the same novel produced by the BBC.

Our Mutual Friend also holds the distinction of being the first Dickens novel to be dramatized on American PBS's TV hit *Masterpiece Theatre*, being presented as part of that series' Season 7 in 1977–1978.[11] The nearly seven-hour miniseries (seven episodes), originally a BBC production in

1976, ran immediately after *Masterpiece Theatre*'s acclaimed adaptation of Robert Graves' *I, Claudius*, which in turn had run immediately after the biographical dramatization, *Dickens of London*, all part of the same Season 7. This probably represented the initial high-water mark in the American ratings popularity of *Masterpiece Theatre*, which found the now famous *I, Claudius* being bookended by two Dickens-related miniseries on the same show during the same season. Overseeing the project was the late British director Peter Hammond (1923–2011), with music provided by noted British composer Carl Davis (b. 1936). The adaptation is a bit stodgy, long, and slow-paced (as was typical for the mid–1970s BBC), but the casting is not without interest, beginning with the late John McEnery as Harmon and Jane Seymour as Bella. This was long before Seymour became widely acclaimed as a TV actor, and in 1976 she was best known as a 25-year-old former Bond girl (*Live and Let Die*, 1973). Poignantly, the short-lived Jack Wild, who portrayed the Artful Dodger in the 1968 smash hit musical film *Oliver!* becomes Lizzie's brother, the troubled and troublesome Charlie Hexam, while Warren Clarke, then not far removed from his memorable performance in Stanley Kubrick's *A Clockwork Orange* (1971), convincingly inhabits the villain Headstone. Also of note is the accomplished, Australian-born stage and screen actor Leo McKern as Boffin. Acclaimed at the time of its broadcast, the 1976 *Our Mutual Friend* in hindsight suffers somewhat from the conventional trappings of its era. It is still available for viewing, however, but only as a British import DVD, which is to say for home audiences possessing specialized access and equipment.

Fortunately for most other viewers, the end of the 20th century (in 1998) saw a BBC-produced, definitive miniseries version of *Our Mutual Friend* (four 90-minute episodes, six hours total), subsequently seen by a wide American audience on the 28th Season of *Masterpiece Theatre* in 1998–1999. Guiding the project was the highly experienced British duo of director Julian Farino (b. 1965) and screenwriter Sandy Welch (b. 1953), bringing a combination of formidable TV and costume drama expertise to the proceedings. The result was highly acclaimed and brought deserved recognition for its participants, including four BAFTA Awards. Because the production was so faithful to Dickens' complex original text, American audiences were a bit baffled but seemed to still understand that this story occupies a special place in the novelist's output. Acting was equally accomplished, although household names were generally not cast. Foremost among these was Steven Mackintosh as Harmon, Anna Friel as Bella, Paul McGann as Wrayburn, and Keeley Hawes as Lizzie. Friel and Hawes especially would soon go on to achieve more visibility in a wide variety of genres with both film and television audiences. Other notables rounding out the stellar cast included Peter Vaughan (Boffin), Pam Ferris (Mrs.

Boffin), Anthony Calf (Lemmle), and David Morrissey (Headstone).[12] Of special interest was Timothy Spall as Mr. Venus, giving both the definitive portrayal of that character, as well as helping to underscore Venus' generally underrated importance to the overall storyline.[13] Though he had been a familiar personage on screen for many decades, Spall's performance would earn him future Dickensian roles.[14] Overall, the ensemble casting employed was superb, with a de-emphasis of any potentially distracting star power, as well it should be for any faithful dramatic observance of the novelist's original intentions, particularly in his late fictional works.

The 1998 *Our Mutual Friend* also made a strong case that the more complex a Dickens novel, the more essential the need for a miniseries format in dramatization. Indeed, it is hard to reimagine the novel's subtle storyline without full character development of secondary figures such as Headstone, Venus, Wregg, Charlie Hexam, the Lemmles, and Jenny Wren. As for the major characters in the plot, most have complex development arcs intertwining with the minor characters (another distinctive Dickensian feature), requiring a more leisurely, episodic pace of storytelling. Bella and Wrayburn both seem to undergo gradual personality changes during course of events, while the Boffins vacillate so radically as to stretch reader credibility. Lizzie and Harmon are more consistent personalities, but even they must drastically change their surroundings and acquaintances as unexpected turn of events require. A coherent two-hour feature film of *Our Mutual Friend*, for these reasons, may be technically impossible, although the fine 1921 silent version by Sandberg might have pointed the way towards a solution.[15] The 1998 miniseries addresses all these potential pitfalls in more than competent fashion, adding crisp, dialogue-driven screenwriting, high production values with on location shooting for Kent-Chatham settings, a wide palette of cinematography (ranging from gritty to opulent to attractive), and careful attention to period detail.[16] In all quality respects, it exceeds previous miniseries for the same novel, and remains widely available on DVD, along with Amazon Prime and other streaming platforms.

Ultimately, for Dickens' last completed novel, viewers or readers must turn their attention back to its odd, unconventional romantic relationships—relationships very likely reflective of Dickens' own personal situation towards the end of his life. On one hand, the saga of Pip and Estella from *Great Expectations* seems to reach a resolution of sorts in *Our Mutual Friend* with the happy union of Harmon and Bella, that is, when combined with Bella's dramatic change in attitudes and values within the storyline while Harmon is heroically portrayed as a master playactor and benevolent manipulator of events.[17] On the other hand, the unsettling romance between Wrayburn and Lizzie is also consummated, one in

17. Our Mutual Friend (1864–1865)

which seemingly insurmountable class and cultural lines are first brazenly disregarded, then struggled against, and finally thwarted. The irresistible attraction between a privileged, educated cultural elite like Wrayburn and an underprivileged, under-educated daughter of a Thames River scavenger, in some respects, rings truer than anything else in the story. Wrayburn, however, must substantially change to achieve his goal, first by reluctantly admitting to himself what he really is, then by being beaten nearly to death by his villainous rival Headstone, then nursed back to health by the devoted, unfailing Lizzie. Whether reading or viewing, audiences get a definite sense that the novelist knew exactly what he was writing about, drawn directly from hard, personal experience. It is from the Wrayburn-Lizzie plot or subplot that the novel undeniably draws its strongest and most cinematic power.[18]

There have been no new video productions of *Our Mutual Friend* in the 21st century, or, for that matter, over the last 24 years. Perhaps it is now time to rectify that gap, although the intensely subtle, self-critical mood of the novel goes directly against current fashions in the Anglo-American world. In this broader sense, wide readership and viewership for the story is desperately needed, although less likely to be achieved as well, because of limited commercial appeal. *Our Mutual Friend* remains arguably Dickens most underappreciated work of fiction, written at a time in which the novelist sensed that his days were numbered, and his personal life had not worked out as planned, but his fame as a storyteller remained fully intact, if not more influential than ever, and deservedly so. During this same autumnal period of his life and career, Dickens began to dabble more with the short story format—an interest he consistently maintained from the beginning of a long commercial artistic career, and one never completely relinquished. Dickens was also probably later haunted by the memory of another famed author (long since deceased), one who had once defined the short story as a vehicle for the macabre, a writer that Dickens had once previously met in America.[19] This would have been especially true as he prepared to return to the United States in 1867–1868 for his second reading tour in that country—the first one being in 1842—one which in fact proved to be his own American swan song.

18

Later Short Stories (1859–1866)

> "'What is its [sic] warning against?" he said, ruminating, with his eyes on the fire, and only by times turning them on me. "What is the danger? Where is the danger? There is danger overhanging somewhere on the Line. Some dreadful calamity will happen. It is not to be doubted this third time, after what has gone before. But surely this is a cruel haunting of me. What can I do?"'[1]

Like Eugene Wrayburn in *Our Mutual Friend*, a lead character beaten nearly to death by his villainous rival, Charles Dickens had a serious brush with mortality in mid-1865, and in fact must have been continually reminded of his own mortality by other unhappy events throughout the 1860s. As noted in the previous chapter, on June 9, 1865, while traveling from Paris to London by cross-channel rail with his mistress and her mother, their train derailed near Staplehurst, Kent, killing 10 passengers and injuring at least 40 others, although the Dickens entourage, through pure luck, was not among these casualties. After this incident, Dickens traveled by train only with considerable reluctance and, according to his family, never recovered psychologically from the accident. His hesitancy was surely reinforced by knowledge that some four years earlier, in 1861, the deadliest train crash in British history had occurred at Clayton Tunnel near Brighton, killing 23 and injuring at least 176. Now that Dickens himself had narrowly escaped death, his previous enthusiasm towards rail travel, not surprisingly, seemed to wane. Then more bad things happened. The novelist's youngest brother Augustus "Gus" Dickens (1827–1866) died in Chicago, Illinois, on October 4, after living a hapless, turbulent life, leaving behind two separate families needing support on two different continents. It had been from his brother Gus that Dickens many years before had derived his popular pen name "Boz" as well as frequent, close sibling companionship. Other old friends and relatives were beginning to disappear as well. By the mid–1860s, Dickens was increasingly suffering physically from a host of undisclosed ailments often making the very act of walking, an activity crucial to his creative process, difficult or impossible. Lastly, it is strongly inferred from circumstantial evidence that sometime in 1863 the illegitimate infant son of Dickens and his mistress had died in France.[2] It is therefore safe to say that, by 1866, Dickens was beginning to think of his own personal demise, although (as far as we know) he chose not to discuss it with anyone, or at least not publicly.

Dickens had always been keenly interested in the short story format, beginning with his earliest days as a professional writer producing sketches under the adopted pseudonym of Boz. During the final decade of his writing career, this interest appears to have intensified, in part because creation of short stories was far less demanding on his time and energies than writing full-blown, serialized novels. His primary vehicle for

Laurence Harvey as Swiveller and Diane Cilento as the Marchioness in *The Small Servant* (1955), adapted from Dickens' *The Old Curiosity Shop*, from NBC television's *The Alcoa Hour* (Archive PL / Alamy Stock Photo).

publishing these tales was his self-owned, self-managed, and self-edited journal *All the Year Round*, first becoming a regular feature in London literary life between 1859 and 1870, then beyond Dickens' own lifetime, overseen initially by his eldest son Charley and then later by others. It did not cease publication until 1895 (25 years after Dickens' death) and included some of his lesser-known posthumous works. Auspiciously, *All the Year Round* had launched the serialization of Dickens' first "late" novel in 1859, *A Tale of Two Cities*, then, after this rousing success, became a permanent part of the novelist's creative activities moving forward, both for his own shorter works and those of other writers as well—in some cases, as collaborative ventures with these other writers. This was the same period as his close call with death on the English rail system, as well as Dickens' other mounting personal travails, all of which coincided with the initial heyday of *All the Year Round*. It is to this now-forgotten periodical that we must turn to closely examine Dickens' late period as a short story writer. Curiously, these short stories have never found a wide audience beyond their immediate Victorian contemporaries, and consequently, have not attracted significant interest from filmmakers nor film audiences during the modern era of combined recorded sound and vision.

As Dickens' creative mindset surely became darker in his unsettled, final years, his thoughts also likely turned to the works of another late genius, Edgar Allan Poe (1809–1849), whom Dickens had briefly met at the beginning of his first American tour in 1842, and with whom he later briefly corresponded. Although Poe's output had focused on gothic horror and produced the modern detective story, both Poe and Dickens shared a writer's interest in psychological phenomena, the grotesque, and the macabre. Dickens' own specialty, however, was the ghost story, a genre that Poe never precisely delved into. For that matter, the ghost story had been an integral part of Dickens' Christmas season output ever since his *Pickwick* days, and he effectively blended the two themes to immortal effect in *A Christmas Carol* (1843). Later, however, came "Hunted Down," a pseudo-detective short story (a genre invented by Poe) sold to the *New York Telegraph* for initial American publication in 1859, then again in 1860 for Dickens' *All the Year Round*.[3] Later that same year (1859), Dickens published his short story "The Haunted House," as a collaborative effort. Then, with personal calamities of the 1860s mounting for the novelist, he revisited the ghost tale genre in tandem with commercial publishing for the Christmas season, although the two themes were never again expressly combined, at least not as a short story. The first personal blow for Dickens came in early 1863 when his illegitimate infant son died in northern France, as inferred by surrounding circumstances and later confirmed by family testimony.[4] This tragedy may have prompted two short stories by

18. Later Short Stories (1859–1866)

Dickens appearing in *All the Year Round* circa 1863–1864, "Mrs. Lirriper's Legacy," and its sequel, "Mrs. Lirriper's Legacy," in which an illegitimate orphaned boy is adopted by a childless English couple, then taken to France to meet his dying, guilt-ridden natural father.[5] Next, in 1865, the supernaturally-tinged short story titled "The Trial for Murder," part of a collaborative series known as *Doctor Marigold's Prescriptions*, aka *To Be Taken with a Grain of Salt*, was published under Dickens' name. Finally in 1866, after the Staplehurst train derailment, Dickens seems to have had a premonition of his own death, as reflected by his next work of short fiction, dramatizing events not unlike those from the factual 1861 rail accident at Clayton Tunnel or the fictional, violent demise of the villain James Carker from Dickens' earlier novel *Dombey and Son* (1848).

The ghostly Dickens short story titled "The Signal-Man" was first published in 1866 as part of the Christmas edition for *All the Year Round*, and the collaborative writers' collection known as *Mugby Junction*. The name "Mugby" was likely inspired by the town of Rugby in Warwickshire, where Dickens had been briefly detained in early 1866—following another rail mishap, this one minor—and treated with comic indifference or provincial rudeness by the locals. Much later, in 2013, "The Signal-Man" was presented online by Project Gutenberg as the culminating work for Dickens' *Three Ghost Stories*, also including "The Haunted House" and "The Trial for Murder." Today, "The Signal-Man" is probably best known through Project Gutenberg, and is arguably the novelist's most polished work within a highly specialized genre. It tells the story of a nameless, haunted rail signalman, who relates to a skeptical English traveler (Mr. Barbox Brothers) how two previous visions of ghosts had immediately preceded fatal accidents along the line, before a final third premonition signals his own similar demise (see epigraph). Psychologically oppressed by the magnitude and monotony of his duties, the signalman is a doomed Poe-like figure straight out of the gothic literary tradition. Two years later, in 1868, English painter Henry Towneley Green (1836–1899), younger brother of future Dickens illustrator Charles Green (1840–1898), produced a single but memorable illustration for the work.[6] In some respects, H.T. Green's melancholy engraving was a harbinger of the foreboding mood that post–World War II filmmakers would later bring to adaptations of this underrated work.

Only 16–17 years after *All the Year Round* ceased publication, immediately leading up to the Dickens centenary birth year of 1912, came a bumper crop of silent shorts based on his fiction, including well-known titles such as *David Copperfield*, *Oliver Twist*, *A Tale of Two Cities*, *Nicholas Nickleby*, and *The Old Curiosity Shop*. Surprisingly, in addition to these famous stories, appeared *Mrs. Lirriper's Lodgers* and *Mrs. Lirriper's Legacy*, both from 1912, both produced by the historic Vitagraph Studios of Brooklyn, New

York, and both (sadly) now considered lost.[7] The loss is considered doubly unfortunate in that, besides being the only known adaptations, these tales seem to allude directly to Dickens' own personal life as he was writing them circa 1863–1864. All that is known for certain about these films as that both were directed by American-born Vitagraph auteur Van Dyke Brooke (1859–1921), also playing the role of the kindly Major Jackman, along with the prolific American-born silent star Mary Maurice as Mrs. Lirriper. In addition to screening the silent shorts, one would surely like to know how the famous Vitagraph studio came to choose these two obscure titles for production, although it might easily be guessed that more offbeat selections were made to set Vitagraph apart from its better-publicized competitors who were also making Dickens silent shorts during that same era, such as Edison, Thanhouser, and Hepworth.

Excepting the aberration of Vitagraph's two *Lirriper* silent shorts from 1912, Dickens' late-period short stories did not attract any activity of note among filmmakers until the post–World War II era. We can only guess at the reasons for this, given the material's generally high literary quality. One explanation may be that until the first "critical" Dickens studies of the late 1930s, and the first "serious" film adaptations of David Lean had appeared during the late 1940s, there was certainly little or no audience appreciation of literary biography, of which these short stories contain a revealing quantity.[8] Then during the 1950s and the age of television, things began to change, but at a slow pace. First, in 1952, Season 4 of the groundbreaking American CBS television series *Suspense* aired a 30-minute adaptation of "Hunted Down," starring John Baragrey.[9] Then in 1953, Season 5 of *Suspense* presented a half-hour version of "The Signalman," starring the famed, British-born Boris Karloff (aka William Henry Pratt) as Dickens' haunted railroad career man.[10] Frustratingly, the kinescopes for both Dickens productions by *Suspense* have not been preserved.[11] Possibly by coincidence, 1952 also saw the academic publication (among other revelations) of *Dickens and Ellen Ternan* by the respected American Dickens scholar Ada Nisbet.[12] By this time, some discerning readers were beginning to take a closer look at Dickens' personal life and how it may have affected his storytelling, including later, lesser-known pieces.[13] This was the same period during which the BBC began pioneering its TV miniseries format with particular application to Dickens' episodic, serialized novels. The period 1952–1953 would be neither the first nor the last time that revealing American academic research did not automatically generate American popular interest; however, some two decades later the BBC would help make up for the irretrievable loss of CBS television's 30-minute adaptations.

After hardly anyone took notice of the 1952–1953 CBS adaptations,

18. Later Short Stories (1859–1866)

another 20 plus years passed before any English-speaking filmmakers became interested in Dickens' later short stories, but then finally in 1974, seemingly out of nowhere, Anglia-ITV Television produced a half-hour color version of Dickens' "The Trial for Murder" as the 25th (and next to last) episode for the short-lived *Orson Welles Great Mysteries* (1973–1974).[14] The legendary Welles himself reportedly had little to do with the production except to record one of his trademark witty introductions; however, the rising, classically trained British actor Ian Holm, then 43 years old but still not yet internationally famous as a movie star, assumed the lead role of Dickens' haunted but decisive jury member in a dramatically-charged murder trial.[15] Also of considerable interest in this obscure TV production was the musical soundtrack, written by British composer John Barry (1933–2011), who by this time already had several Academy Awards under his belt, as well as numerous James Bond film scores.[16] Unfortunately, the 1974 Anglia "Trial for Murder" is nearly impossible to access in the United States at the present time, being only available as a British DVD import (and hence playable only with British-compatible equipment); moreover, according to those few who have managed to screen it, the 30-minute episode does not represent the best work by the artists involved in the project, however otherwise famous these names have since become.[17] In a similar manner, "Hunted Down" received a one-hour adaptation by British Thames TV in 1989 as part of its experimental *Storyboard* series, notably with a screenplay by Hugh Leonard.[18] Like the 1974 *Trial for Murder*, however, this video is currently only available through a British import DVD.

It could have easily been many more decades before moviemakers assayed this same material. Instead, only two years later, BBC television, perhaps spurred on by its old rivalry with Anglia-ITV, produced in 1976 perhaps the finest video version of the late Dickens short story "The Signal-Man," adapted by Welsh screenwriter extraordinaire Andrew Davies (b. 1936), representing perhaps his first in a long series of highly notable works.[19] In this full 40-minute color adaptation broadcast for its annual *A Ghost Story for Christmas* series, the BBC was fortunate in casting in the lead role the late British World War II combat veteran and character actor supreme, Denholm Elliott, then 54 years old, a role which he seems to inhabit as if he were born to play it, notwithstanding Elliott by then having well over a hundred screen appearances to his credit. The work was favorably received and reviewed at the time, and rightfully so, given its many unusual but memorable aspects. Among other qualities, at the time it was the first-aired BBC *Christmas* ghost story not based on a work by M.R. James (1862–1936), an accomplished writer whose life slightly overlapped that of Dickens and whose work was certainly influenced by Dickens. Today, this fine interpretation can easily be viewed on YouTube, among other platforms, as well as less easily accessible sources such as an import-only DVD anthology from the British Film Institute.[20]

The successful 1976 BBC production of *The Signalman* has an odd footnote to it. Three years later, in 1979, a 31-year-old Andrew Lloyd Webber (b. 1948), already a major commercial force on Broadway and the West End thanks in part to the mega-triumph of *Evita* (1976), became intrigued, if not obsessed, with this relatively unknown Dickens tale, and repeatedly but unsuccessfully tried to adapt it under his own name for the musical stage. Originally conceived as a twin bill with the small-scaled *Tell Me on a Sunday* (1979), Lloyd Webber decided instead to submit *The Signalman* as a full-blown music drama proposal for 1980–1981 season of the English National Opera (ENO), but the proposal was summarily rejected. Eventually, elements of Lloyd Webber's score for *The Signalman* found their way into his obscure 2004 stage musical *The Woman in White*, based on the 1859 novel by Dickens' friend and protégé Wilkie Collins (1824–1889). The end-result became one of Lloyd Webber's least commercially successful works. Even as his pet project was being rejected by the ENO, however, Lloyd Webber had yet again hit commercial paydirt with his adaptation of T.S. Eliot's *Cats* (1981), teaming as he had earlier on *Evita* with his favorite lyricist Tim Rice (b. 1944). Lost in all the commotion, confusion, and hype was the irony of Charles Dickens having first met Nelly Ternan while both performed in a now forgotten production of the Dickens-Wilkie Collins collaborative stage play *The Frozen Deep* over a century earlier in 1857.

Meanwhile, however, Dickens' "The Signal-Man" continued to find numerous cultural references throughout the contemporary era of film. These references have ranged from the lowbrow to the highbrow and all points in between. In 1996, the first season of Showtime's exploitive *Poltergeist: The Legacy* included an episode titled "The Signalman," which could be charitably categorized as an incoherent homage to the Dickens original. At the extreme opposite end of the cultural spectrum was a 2015 art house short feature, *O Sinaleiro* ("The Signalman"), by Brazilian director Daniel Augusto, premiering to short-lived acclaim at that year's Toronto International Film Festival. Even more recently, in 2019, the BBC successfully revived its old television franchise *A Ghost Story for Christmas*, beginning with an adaptation of "Martin's Close" by M.R. James, which, like many of James' popular ghost stories, owes its inspiration directly to Dickens, in this case specifically, "The Trial for Murder." The 30-minute production, directed by the English-born Mark Gatiss (b. 1966) and starring Scottish-born Peter Capaldi, was well-received and then repeated in 2020.[21] Notwithstanding this recent steady stream of Dickens and Dickens-inspired short fiction, viewing audiences seem to have little or no awareness of the source material. Part of this is surely due to Dickens' *A Christmas Carol*—the ultimate

18. Later Short Stories (1859–1866)

holiday ghost story—continuing to dominate movie market demand, although Dickens as a writer had been experimenting with supernatural material almost from the very beginning of his career as a professional storyteller. These single-minded audience perceptions are unlikely to change anytime soon, but through no fault of quality in the material itself. Dickens' other fine ghost stories may be consigned to oblivion as a result. The novelist himself may have likely shrugged the whole thing off by acknowledging professional storytelling's inherent hit-and-miss qualities—one thing on which he and Andrew Lloyd Webber would surely agree.

During his final years, Dickens was unquestionably aware of his own greatness as a storyteller and as a writer. So long as his published works turned a profit (which they invariably did) and pleased his audiences, he may not have cared what critics thought, especially critics coming two centuries later. Nevertheless, Dickens was also likely quite aware that Edgar Allan Poe, by that time tragically deceased for nearly two decades, would continue to be remembered and appreciated as a great storyteller and writer well into the foreseeable future. While shamefully ignored and neglected during his own short lifetime, Poe had, after his death, gradually come to represent the epitome of the American romantic era in several literary genres throughout the English-speaking world, including Dickens' home market of Great Britain. Thus, Dickens continued dabbling in short fiction, supernatural phenomena, psychological horror, and offbeat situations served to both fill a market demand and to satisfy his own artistic inclinations. It is a shame this part of his work is not better known, nor attracted much interest among filmmakers. Part of the problem may be that short stories are, by definition, shorter in length, and this may have slightly hindered Dickens' late writing style, which was becoming ever more expansive and episodic in structure. Then for his last but incomplete serious work of fiction, he turned once again to his wheelhouse, the Victorian serial novel, this time incorporating material that most any reader would consider dark and occasionally macabre, even by the standards of Charles Dickens.

19

The Mystery of Edwin Drood (1870)

> "Mr. Honeythunder expanded into an inflammatory Wen in Minor Canon Corner. Though it was not literally true, as was facetiously charged against him by public unbelievers, that he called aloud to his fellow-creatures: 'Curse your souls and bodies, come here and be blessed!' still his philanthropy was of that gunpowderous sort that the difference between it and animosity was hard to determine."[1]

While Edgar Allan Poe had already invented the modern detective story in 1841 with *The Murders in the Rue Morgue*, Charles Dickens subsequently experimented with the same genre in "Hunted Down" (1859), although for that later work Dickens' sleuth becomes an insurance claims investigator.[2] In a similar manner, Dickens' final but uncompleted, serialized novel, *The Mystery of Edwin Drood*, dramatizes a (presumed) murder puzzle without any professional detective to solve the case, but rather seemingly ordinary citizens left to their own devices while trying to sort out the truth and overcome the devious machinations of a clever villain. Then, almost exactly midway through writing this novel, on June 9, 1870, Dickens at age 58, after a lifetime of reasonably good health and non-stop productivity, died suddenly and, for many of his fans and associates, quite unexpectedly.[3] The "Great Inimitable" was no more. Within a matter of days, the premier novelist in all English literature was buried without question or objection in the Poet's Corner of Westminster Abbey, despite his expressed personal wish for a common grave, leaving behind an unchallenged literary legacy for storytelling, but also a large, unhappy family, along with a secretive and later controversial personal history. Dickens' *Edwin Drood* has proved to be controversial as well. As recently observed by biographer Claire Tomalin, "*Drood* has fascinated readers because it is a murder story left unfinished and unsolved."[4] A bigger problem, however, is that *The Mystery of Edwin Drood* is not really a mystery,

19. The Mystery of Edwin Drood (1870)

based on repeated statements Dickens made to those close to him before his death.[5] Drood has in point of fact been murdered and Jasper is definitely the murderer; it then only becomes a storytelling question of exactly how and when.

By the time that Dickens permanently fell unconscious on June 9, he had completed the first six installments (or 23 chapters) for *Edwin Drood*, several of which would be published in serial format through September 1870, then later as a bound but incomplete novel by Chapman & Hall of London. Illustrations were engraved by Luke Fildes (1843–1927), a noted pre–Raphaelite artist friend of Dickens' favorite daughter Kate, after Kate's ailing first husband (also an artist), Charles Collins (1828–1873), was unable to take on the task.[6] *The Mystery of Edwin Drood* outsold Dickens' previous novel, *Our Mutual Friend*, including as a serial well before Dickens' demise. Unlike its literary predecessor, *Drood* looks back with ambiguous nostalgia at a thinly disguised Rochester, Kent, the scene of Dickens' supposedly happy, early youth. Surprisingly, the Rochester of *Edwin Drood* is presented as a gloomy, disturbing, and rather creepy place. Drood, the namesake character of the novel, disappears without a trace on Christmas Eve, thus harking back to the novelist's known tendency for combining

Promotional poster for the silent film *The Mystery of Edwin Drood* (1914), based on the unfinished Dickens novel, with original ending by Tom Terriss, now lost.

holiday stories with psychological disturbance. Before Dickens was physically stopped in his tracks, he ended the text with Drood's maternal uncle, the sinister Anglican choirmaster John Jasper, back at his regular opium den and attracting suspicion from, among others, a routine drug supplier.

Jasper, the story's main character and protagonist, is a complex villain, a literary continuation of Bradley Headstone from *Our Mutual Friend*. Though respectable and pious in outward appearance, Jasper is in fact quite the opposite. By the end of his life, Dickens, for both personal and professional reasons, had pretty much had it with all sanctimony, especially sanctimony coming from the Church of England.[7] With exception of the unselfish Reverend Chrisparkle, Dickens' barely fictionalized Anglican church hierarchy is unsympathetic, beginning with Choirmaster Jasper as the implicated murderer, and continuing upwards through ranks, culminating unpleasantly with the church's financial backers, personified by the overbearing and hypocritical Mr. Honeythunder, himself the very embodiment of false piety (see epigraph). Jasper's nephew Edwin Drood is the prototypically unlikable, self-satisfied murder victim. More interesting and sympathetic are the Landless siblings (Neville and Helena) of British-occupied Ceylon, especially after Neville appears to be set up by Jasper as the fall guy for Jasper's probable crime. Nominal love interest Rosa Bud, on the other hand, ranks as one Dickens' least compelling female characters. Ultimately, readers, as well as viewers in later film adaptations, must ask why three grown men in the story (Edwin, Jasper, and Neville) all are, at one point, competing for her affections.

Movie adaptations of *Edwin Drood* began early, with an Anglo-French silent short by Gaumont in 1909, and then a few years later, an American silent version in 1914 by the historic World Film Company.[8] Regrettably, both films now appear to be lost.[9] All that survives for the American version are some stills, a delightful publicity poster, and shrill, hostile reviews from British critics. The 1914 adaptation in fact appears to have been rather interesting, featuring co-directing, writing, and a lead performance (as Jasper) by Tom Terriss, aka Thomas Herbert Lewin, who provided an unknown but original ending to the unfinished story. Terriss, along with his co-director, Herbert Blaché (1882–1953), had earlier that same year (1914) produced a rare movie version of Dickens' Christmas novella, *The Chimes*, now lost as well.[10] The 1909 Gaumont adaptation of *Edwin Drood* was directed by the relatively obscure British-born Arthur Gilbert, who earlier in 1906 had directed *Little Nell*, the very first film adaptation for Dickens' *The Old Curiosity Shop*. The Gaumont *Edwin Drood* is mainly notable for (apparently) having eliminated the central character of John Jasper altogether for purposes of its silent short format, although one can only guess what this adaptation precisely looked like. Since the novel itself was never completed by Dickens, film producers may well have felt justified in omitting all potential suspects, especially because of the shortened dramatic timeframe. Gaumont therefore seems to have reduced the story to a simple love triangle involving Edwin, Rosa, and Neville.

Twenty-one years later, in 1935, Universal Pictures, flush with success after inventing the sound-era monster movie genre, and fresh from producing the first talking movie version of Dickens' *Great Expectations* (1934), then somewhat unexpectedly released the first talking movie version for *The Mystery of Edwin Drood*.[11] To go directly from Dickens' most acclaimed novel to his final unfinished work was not a natural progression by early Hollywood standards. Ably directed by Kentucky-born Stuart Walker (1888–1941), who had also directed *Great Expectations* for Universal in 1934, the 1935 production was fortunate to land in the lead role of villain John Jasper the stellar, British-born Claude Rains, himself a newly type-casted offbeat star in the wake of Universal's hit, *The Invisible Man* (1933). A top-notch supporting cast included Francis L. Sullivan as the gregarious but likeable Septimus Crisparkle, Walter Kingsford as Rosa's suspiciously natured guardian Hiram Grewgious, the classically trained David Manners as Edwin, and Heather Angel as Rosa, along with Valerie Hobson and Douglass Montgomery as the Landless siblings.[12] Sullivan would go on to acclaimed major supporting roles in the two post–World War II Dickensian film classics directed by David Lean, *Great Expectations* (1946) and *Oliver Twist* (1948).

The Irish-born Valerie Hobson would later go on as well to play Estella in David Lean's landmark film adaptation of *Great Expectations* in 1946, while Montgomery circa 1935 portrays a very white, Anglo-looking Ceylonese. This was during the pre-war Hollywood era of *Gunga Din* (1939). Despite repeated references to "dark" skin, both Montgomery and Hobson come across more as exotic English foreign travelers. The boy "Deputy" harks back to *Oliver Twist* and the Artful Dodger, giving the film a distinctively Dickensian flavor. More importantly, the 1935 *Edwin Drood* completes the unfinished story in a manner doing the least amount of violence to the novelist's original intentions.[13] In this film version, the harassed Neville goes incognito to become the sleuth-like Datchery, a plot twist vaguely suggested within the manuscript itself. Rains' Jasper effectively comes across as another one of Universal's stock human monsters, before going straight to church while singing excerpts from George Frideric Handel's secular oratorio, *Semele*. This is all set within a moody, Edgar Allan Poe–like context, combined with an appropriately dark-hued style of cinematography.[14] Though the DVD can be difficult to find, the 1935 Universal production can still, after nearly a century, be called the best overall film adaptation of Dickens' last, uncompleted novel.

Despite Universal's notable achievement from 1935, the post–World War II era and the age of television saw a significant revival of interest in Dickens' intriguing, unsolved murder puzzle. In 1952, the CBS TV series *Suspense* aired a two-part, two-hour adaptation of *The Mystery of Edwin Drood*, starring John Baragrey, who soon afterwards also participated in an adaptation of Dickens' short story "Hunted Down" for the same series in 1953.[15] Kinescopes for both episodes have been long since lost. The CBS *Edwin Drood* had been adapted by director Robert Stevens (1920–1989) and *Suspense* regular screenwriter Halsted Welles (1906–1990). Then eight years later, in 1960, the London-based British ITV franchise Rediffusion unleashed an eight-episode, four-hour version of *Drood* featuring Donald Sinden as Jasper and an original ending credited to seminal American-born mystery writer John Dickson Carr (1906–1977), fully executed by British screenwriter John Keir Cross (1914–1967).[16] Notwithstanding this novelty, the production made little impression beyond London at the time and today is impossible to find on video anywhere. Given that these postwar film productions are no longer available for viewing, it is difficult to say what their precise merits or shortcomings may have been. Suffice it here to note, however, that these unnecessary adaptations demonstrated a clear demand for newer dramatic endings of *Edwin Drood* having little or nothing to do with the novelist's original conception of the work. A more faithful approach to the ending had in fact already been done quite effectively by Universal in 1935, yet some viewing audiences were still unsatisfied. Some of them felt a need, justified or not, to finish Dickens' Poe-like murder tale themselves, leading to results often proving, to put it kindly, unbelievably bizarre.

Strangely, in the mid-1980s, such a concept became a hit for the musical stage, the first of its kind since the tremendous acclaim received by *Oliver!* in the 1960s, and despite many failed similar attempts during the interim. The 1985 musical *The Mystery of Edwin Drood*, with music, lyrics, orchestrations, and book all by Rupert Holmes, aka David Goldstein (b. 1947), was a surprising smash success on both Broadway and London's West End, after debuting at the New York Shakespeare Festival that same year. Eventually, *Drood* the musical would garner an astounding 11 Tony Award nominations and five Tony wins, becoming the critical and commercial darling of that performing season. Twenty-seven years later, in 2012, the same work was successfully revived; moreover, original cast recordings from both 1985 and 2012 continue to sell robustly. No movie version has yet been made, but various amateur productions are still easily screened on YouTube. Probably the only reason a movie has not been made is that a movie audience cannot vote on a movie outcome, although this may well change sometime in the future. Holmes' concept considerably

19. The Mystery of Edwin Drood (1870)

lightens the foreboding mood of Dickens' tale by slightly changing the story and various characters, then borrowing heavily from English Music Hall traditions and adding the irresistible gimmick of the audience voting every night to determine how the story ends, with performers having to then adjust their lines accordingly. Long forgotten in this interactive process was Dickens' obvious intent on making John Jasper the villain-murderer, although the musical audience is allowed to vote him into that role if they so desire. To repeat, *The Mystery of Edwin Drood* is the only other stage musical of a Dickens work to date achieving widespread acclaim besides the ubiquitous *Oliver!* If it were not for the inescapable, inconvenient reality that Dickens did in fact complete his earlier novel *Oliver Twist*, one would not be surprised to see an interactive, musical version of that story as well, with an ending decided nightly by audience vote.[17]

Taking advantage of this unexpected, burgeoning popularity for Dickens' last but unfinished novel, England produced a new independent film version of *The Mystery of Edwin Drood* in 1993, featuring an unlikely cast of British character actors led by the quirky Robert Powell as the villainous John Jasper.[18] Much earlier in his long film career, Powell had played the lead role in Franco Zeffirelli's acclaimed *Jesus of Nazareth* (1977), and by this point in time had established himself as an offbeat audience favorite. Also appearing in the same film (as Edwin Drood) was Jonathan Phillips, who only a few years later became more widely known for a memorable bit part in the box office blockbuster *Titanic* (1997). Screenwriting services were supplied by another British cult favorite, Gwyneth Hughes, who finished the story much closer in spirit to the novelist's original setup, and similar with that of the 1935 Universal adaptation. Though not in the same quality league as the 1935 feature film or the 2012 BBC miniseries which came afterwards, the 1993 movie version of *Edwin Drood* has its own interesting, worthwhile aspects, including mostly onsite filming in Kent. At present, it can only be viewed in VHS cassette format (through A&E Home Video) for those able to find it, although excerpts occasionally appear on YouTube.

The Charles Dickens birthday bicentenary year of 2012 saw several fine film productions, including those for *Great Expectations* and a modernized version of *Nicholas Nickleby* (*Nick Nickleby*), but perhaps the most unexpected was that for the latest BBC miniseries adaptation of *The Mystery of Edwin Drood*. Directorial duties were handled by the late Diarmuid Lawrence (1947–2019), who just a few years previously had overseen a superb, definitive version of *Little Dorrit* (2008). For the new, updated screenplay, Gwyneth Hughes was brought back for the job, possessing the unique qualification of having written an earlier film script for the same novel in 1993. Filmed mostly on location in Kent (also like the 1993 film), the 2012 *Edwin Drood* soon aired on American television as a two-part, two-hour installment of the 42nd season for *Masterpiece Classics*, immediately following that same series' broadcast of *Great Expectations*. Unfortunately, neither Dickens nor Edgar Allan Poe would have likely approved of Hughes' overly sensitive, non–Dickensian ending for the story, which proves to be way too clever for its own good. As things turn out in the 2012 version, Drood is not really murdered, but has only gone into hiding. Accordingly, Jasper is not really a murderer and not as bad a guy as we originally had thought—only too stoned out of his mind with opium to remember whether he in fact murdered his secretly loathed nephew, Edwin. Except for this discordant solution to Dickens' unfinished storyline, the 2012 BBC miniseries offers many virtues and runs a close second in overall quality to the 1935 feature film of *Edwin Drood* by Universal Pictures. It is easily accessible on pay-per-view basis with Amazon Prime and other platforms.

The 2012 miniseries adaptation was fortunate in casting the Welsh-born superstar-on-the-rise Matthew Rhys into the leading role as John Jasper. Although the BBC miniseries is not considered definitive in and of itself, Rhys' highly nuanced, committed performance as Dickens' final would-be villain is in fact definitive. During this brief window of history (less than a decade ago), the talented Rhys was on the cusp of worldwide celebrity, soon to be secured by his performance in the acclaimed FX Network TV series, *The Americans* (2013–2018), widely considered one of the finest television productions of the decade.[19] Many of the supporting performances from 2012 are equally impressive. Refreshingly, Neville and Helena Landless finally become, visually and unapologetically, Ceylonese persons of color, played respectively by Sacha Dahwan and Amber Rose Revah. The ever-reliable Dickensian interpreter Alun Armstrong is highly effective as Grewgious, and Rory Kinnear equally memorable as the sympathetic Crisparkle.[20] Freddie Fox and Tamzin Merchant, both at the beginning of their promising film careers, portray Edwin and Rosa, who, in accordance with Dickens' original text, agree to break off their engagement before Edwin's sudden disappearance. As a bonus, the underrated Scottish composer John Lunn (b. 1956) was retained to provide a musical soundtrack, himself then on the cusp of winning two Emmy Awards (2012–2013) for his similar work on the hit PBS series *Downton Abbey* (2010–2015).[21] Overall, there is much to recommend for the recent BBC adaptation of *The Mystery of Edwin Drood*, that is, if one can look past the highly contrived and non–Dickensian ending for this version. Visually, the BBC production is stunning, although, for that matter, so is the 1935 Universal feature film.

There are not many continuous threads running throughout the

19. *The Mystery of Edwin Drood* (1870) 181

fiction of Charles Dickens, as he seemed to be constantly experimenting, changing, and moving forward in his art; however, what began with the Sexton Gabriel Grub in *The Pickwick Papers* ended with Anglican choirmaster John Jasper in *Edwin Drood*. Consistent for the novelist over a 34-year storytelling career was a marked hostility against officious sanctimony of any sort. Both Grub and Jasper, as dissimilar characters as they are, still are made to look bad despite their regular employment by the respectable Church of England. By 1870 and the end of Dickens' life, this same theme would have likely had even greater resonance for the novelist. Though highly protective of his benign public image, Dickens had, by the final decade of his life and career, effectively cast aside all conventional morality and respectability by discarding his longtime wife, along with his less favored biological children, in favor of a much younger mistress and an affected bohemian lifestyle. The truth behind his personal life had to be concealed in part because the truth would never be accepted by the church, nor many of his readers, hence divorce and remarriage was out of the question. Therefore, it is no wonder that a minor church official develops into the novelist's last fictional villain. For Charles Dickens, what could not be expressed in real life, could still at least be dramatized on the printed page.

20

Biographical and Apocryphal

"Instead of looking back, therefore, I will look forward."[1]

On June 5, 1870, some three days before Charles Dickens collapsed at his home in Gad's Hill near Rochester, Kent, never to rise again, he had a frank one-on-one conversation with his favorite child Kate, who, at 30 years of age and to Dickens' great delight, asked him for career advice. After wisely counseling her to rely on her keen intelligence rather than her good looks, Dickens gave his regrets to his daughter that he had not been a been a better father or a better man. Then he expressed doubts that his health would allow him to finish his last (and ultimately incomplete) novel, *The Mystery of Edwin Drood*. Their emotional parting the next day on June 6 was the last time they would see each other, with the novelist's sudden death occurring on June 9.[2] Vivid memories of these two days would stay with Kate for the rest of her long life—the next 59 years, to be precise. Their conversation that night in early June of 1870 highlighted a dilemma which Kate would much later seek to rectify, namely, the irreconcilable gap between her father's public image as an artist and the realities of his private personal life. Several decades later, during the late 1890s, she vented her frustrations to a younger George Bernard Shaw (1856–1950), probably hoping the distinguished playwright would use his talents to rectify a dominant but false public perception of her father as "a joyous, jocose gentleman walking about the world with a plum pudding and a bowl of punch."[3] Shaw prudently wrote nothing of the kind, but much later, in 1923, Kate shared her turbulent family history with Gladys Storey, an aspiring writer. A decade after Kate's death in 1929, Storey published *Dickens and Daughter* (1939), a book universally panned until a still living Shaw informed a dismayed press that the scandalous truth was in fact old news to him.[4] What followed was a stalemate in Dickens' literary biography for the rest of the century, which to a large extent, continues to the present day.

20. Biographical and Apocryphal

As the bicentenary of Charles Dickens' birth came and went in early 2012, the prevailing mood, even among the reading public, was at best indifferent. This represents quite a contrast from Dickens' own milieu in Victorian England, an age not knowing of video entertainment, and one in which the hard-working novelist held true celebrity status, financially compensated with a lifestyle that today would be considered, at least, upper middle class. The root cause of this comparative modern indifference is possibly that the wider public, including much of the general reading public, does not likely care as much about serious literature of the distant past. An important corollary to this problem is that today's wider, literate public does not likely care as much about literary biography. Many people are now too preoccupied with personal concerns, although a healthy appetite remains for quality entertainment. The same problem is equally applicable to the legacy of Charles Dickens and all similarly important figures in English literature, including Dickens' hero William Shakespeare.[5] Dickens himself would have recognized the dilemma. Nonetheless, today even the most indifferent, illiterate audiences still watch television, and many still go to the cinema. Here they frequently view images of Dickens' old stories reinterpreted and reimagined by talented actors and directors. As a result, familiar names like Ebenezer Scrooge, Oliver Twist, Uriah Heep, David Copperfield, Fagin, Pip, and many others continue to live within the modern consciousness, even for those who cannot name the storyteller inventing them—assuming they realize these are fictional inventions rather than historical figures.[6]

Kate Perugini, *née* Dickens (1839–1929): The novelist's favorite child, artistic in temperament, determined that future biographers should have a more accurate though less flattering image of her father. Mid–19th century painting by Carlo Perugini (Charles Dickens Museum, London).

After Kate's death in 1929, the novelist's last surviving child was Sir Henry Fielding Dickens (1849–1933), named after the famed 18th-century English novelist, and by far Charles Dickens' most financially successful offspring. Henry confirmed Kate's controversial recollections of their father, although he defended their mother less and was far more critical of their father's "radical" political views than his messy personal life and bouts of depression.[7] Henry's differing emphases were telling in many respects. As a respected Barrister, a designated King's Counsel, and a Tory-leaning establishment figure, Henry liked to joke that his more controversial father (the novelist) should have been born French instead of English, and hence found more to apologize for in a decidedly leftist political outlook (as well as its spectacular expression in fiction) than in the stark fact that his father had left his family in favor of a mistress 27 years his junior.[8] For over the last century, politically conservative critics of Charles Dickens, especially those unhappy with the ardently socialist message of his storytelling, may have a more accurate image of the man and the artist than those admirers who want the novelist to be strictly "joyous" and "jocose"—as Kate once ironically described her famous father.[9] Then six years after Henry's passing in 1933, Gladys Storey's sensational exposé (based on Kate's recollections) went public, luridly confirming similar suspicions by earlier biographers, and this was openly defended by none other than the leading English literary figure of the day (Shaw). Still, however, the revealed truth about Dickens' untidy personal life met with tremendous resistance from his fans.

This dichotomy in Dickens' long-established public image—the perceived jolliness versus the documented turbulence—has gradually translated onto film, particularly during the 21st century, with some interesting results. What began as mere continuation of the false image during the silent era slowly morphed into a jumbled uncertainty by the *Masterpiece Theatre* period of the mid–1970s, before finally becoming a full-blown critical revaluation after the bicentenary year of 2012, then lastly, a partial reaction against and retrenchment by 2017. When writing his Preface to the semi-autobiographical *David Copperfield* circa 1849–1850, Dickens himself hinted at awareness of his own restless spirit and unwillingness to rest on past laurels, even at the height of his commercial success and artistic fame (see epigraph). He seems to be trying to let go of nostalgia, although it would be several more years before he could stop thinking of himself as the character David Copperfield and begin to see himself more like Pip of *Great Expectations* or Eugene Wrayburn from *Our Mutual Friend*.[10] What now remains is a curious situation in which academia long ago discarded any notions of the premier English novelist as "the hero of his own life" while simultaneously, a still-significant segment of the Dickens fan base tenaciously clings to whatever is left of a benign image long since debunked by serious scholarship. In short, the myth of Charles Dickens the man appears to be dying a rather slow and stubborn death.

As previously noted, this long process of facing up to the hard truth in Dickensian biography, including its later manifestation as film entertainment, appears to have unpromisingly begun during the early 20th century and the dawn of the silent era. General indifference to English literature appears to have been far less of a problem in 1912, the year of Dickens' birth centenary, although during this era the first silent shorts touching upon the novelist's biography were little more than travelogue promos for the false public image cultivated earlier by Dickens himself. Many of these are listed—or in some instances may be screened—through the excellent website of *The Bioscope* under the entry for Charles Dickens.[11] Snippets of these short but highly diverse works may also be viewed at the website for British Pathé or on the imported DVD *Dickens Before Sound*.[12] While most of these preserved pieces are quite interesting as historical video documents from the early 20th century, none provide any meaningful insight into the novelist's life such as would later come from academia during the 1930s and continue, oftentimes controversially, into the present day. Not until the surviving children of Dickens, most notably Kate and Henry, began rather late in life to confirm some of the troubling rumors about their father, would academia begin to seriously consider revision of the old standard biography. It would take even longer before these unpopular revisions to the traditional image (or disguise, one might say) would attempt to filter through into the realm of popular entertainment, and only then very gradually and with much resistance every step of the way.[13]

With respect to filmmaking, the first highly tentative step in this long process began in 1976 with the elaborate *Masterpiece Theatre* production for *Dickens of London*. At 13 hours and 13 episodes, *Dickens of London* attempted to present to the American television-viewing public (at least for those tuning in to *Masterpiece Theatre* on PBS), a far edgier version of the novelist's biography, or edgier than anything previously seen. Remarkably, there is no mention of Dickens' extra-marital affair with Nelly Ternan, conveniently so since the dramatization ends in the year of 1851 when Dickens' father John dies, and the son did not begin his relationship with Nelly Ternan until 1857 at the earliest. Roy Dotrice plays dual roles as the adult Charles Dickens and his father John Dickens.[14] Scripted by Wolf Mankowitz, who later noted that he had written an additional 11 episodes never produced, the lengthy, somewhat cumbersome series delves into several aspects of Dickens' biography that went against the conventional grain, such as his unhappy marriage, a bittersweet relationship with his biological family, a flirtatious attitude towards younger women, and a bizarrely re-imagined interaction with Edgar Allan Poe during Dickens' first American tour of 1842. One would love to know if any of the unproduced episodes written by Mankowitz in fact delved into the Ternan affair.[15] In either case, Mankowitz later admitted the series was too long to begin with, and that which was produced suffered mediocre ratings.[16] At the time, *Masterpiece Theatre* was only in its seventh season, and 1976 also saw ratings blockbusters such as *I, Claudius* produced on the same show, against which *Dickens of London* was bound to suffer by comparison.[17] It is also notable that during the mid–1970s, an age in which salacious material was commonplace on TV, even for primetime, the possibility of dramatizing a Dickens biography in which the novelist is not portrayed as a moral paragon appears to have been a ratings non-starter.

It would be nearly four decades before another attempt would be made to present a biographical sketch of Charles Dickens on screen for television audiences. First in 2005 came the documentary *Dickens in America*, ably narrated by British Dickensian expert Miriam Margolyes, with a focus on the novelist's first American tour of 1842. Like the earlier 1976 *Masterpiece Theatre* extravaganza, there is little or no mention of Dickens' messy private life, although the documentary effectively debunks any stubborn notions that the novelist unequivocally loved the United States or preferred it to his British homeland. In this critical respect, it is more akin to the completely fictionalized version of Dickens in Virginia City, Nevada, from *Bonanza*, televised in 1963.[18] Then, in close conjunction with his fine performance as Grandfather Trent in the 2007 ITV production of *The Old Curiosity Shop*, Derek Jacobi took the lead in two other Dickens-related works, the first being the independent British film *The Riddle* (2007), playing a dual role as Dickens himself (in flashback) and a modern-day homeless man living near the Thames River in London. A convoluted plot involves a murder committed over a lost-and-found Dickens manuscript containing elements that are obviously autobiographical, pointing to a much darker side of the novelist's personality. Unfortunately, the movie is not well made, was not financially successful, and Jacobi's high-profile appearance comes across more as a personal favor to young aspiring theatrical colleagues. Two years later, in 2009, Jacobi then served as narrator for the documentary *Charles Dickens's England*, an attempt to bolster the contemporary London tourist industry, much like the first silent shorts of the early 20th century. Reviews were mostly negative and distribution spotty, while Jacobi looks and sounds mostly bored. Indeed, there is yet again little or no suggestion of Dickens' extensive personal demons. While not nearly as bad as *Anonymous*, the 2011 muddled attempt at alternative-Shakespeare biography (also involving Jacobi), *The Riddle* and *Charles Dickens' England* both seemed to unsuccessfully test the waters for public reception of a non-traditional interpretation and more true-to-life story for the famous novelist's life. All in all, the lead-up to the bicentenary year of 2012 was by this point in time shaping up to be even more bland than the centenary year of 1912.

20. Biographical and Apocryphal

Things then appeared to take a turn for the better. In tandem with the well-received updated, 2011 revisionist biography by Claire Tomalin (*Charles Dickens: A Life*), came the fascinating short documentary *Dickens on Film* (2012), as part of the influential and long-running BBC *Arena* series. It made the strong case that Dickens thought about his stories cinematically many years before the invention of cinema. The astounding diversity of the adaptations speaks for itself and strongly against any over-simplified notions of Dickens as a writer. Next (and precipitously), in 2013, came the British-produced *The Invisible Woman*, an overt, all-out dramatization of Dickens' late life affair with Nelly Ternan, in the format of a star-studded feature film. Film rights to Tomalin's initial biography on Dickens (from 1990) had been acquired earlier, but Tomalin herself—by then an established English literary biographer—had little interest in participating other than in a consulting role.[19] Rising British star Felicity Jones was quickly cast as Nelly. Then, crucially, in 2010, British celebrity Ralph Fiennes was persuaded first to direct, then to take on the lead role as Charles Dickens, soon after he had similarly overseen an acclaimed film version of Shakespeare's *Coriolanus* (2011). Fiennes' acting colleague Kristin Scott Thomas was also brought in to portray Nelly's mother, along with a stellar cast of supporting players.[20]

The Invisible Woman should have been a game-changer, but it proved not to be. Despite mostly positive reviews and obviously being a labor of love, the film found a limited audience at best. In the final analysis, the stark fact remained that gross box office receipts were a mere fraction of high production costs. It is tempting to conclude that the movie's still-controversial message ran directly into a brick wall of public preconceptions or misconceptions. The Charles Dickens portrayed by Ralph Fiennes in the film is profoundly unlike the Dickens normally envisioned even by his most devoted followers: he is troubled, unhappy, restless, moody, and feeling trapped by a marriage and self-created image as an artist when he first works with Nelly Ternan in the fateful 1857 production of the Dickens-Collins stage play, *The Frozen Deep*. In some respects, any truthful depiction of Dickens' life, especially the later years, runs into the same roadblock that Dickens oftentimes ran into as a novelist—that is, a formidable barrier between routine audience expectations and a tangible, irresistible need to expand artistic horizons. Commercially, Pip and Estella need to get together at the end, if not in real-life then at least in fiction, figuratively speaking. Fortunately, *The Invisible Woman* remains easily accessible on DVD or on a pay-per-view basis and is well worth screening for viewers able to tolerate an alternative image of the novelist.[21]

Four years later, in 2017, after *The Invisible Woman* had floundered commercially despite high artistic quality and to the considerable disappointmet of its joint Anglo producers, the Americans, Canadians, and Irish showed the Brits how to turn a profit with a similar type of entertainment widget. Tapping into the rising star power of British-born actor Dan Stevens (*Downton Abbey*) as a young Charles Dickens, *The Man Who Invented Christmas* also featured, just to play it safe, a bevy of marquee-quality names for co-stars, including the late Christopher Plummer as the fictional Scrooge of Dickens' fired imagination, and the still-active Jonathan Pryce as Dickens' troublesome, inopportune father John, along with more specialized, highly experienced players such as Simon Callow and Miriam Margolyes in minor roles. British-East Indian HBO alumnus Bharat Nulluri (b. 1965) was retained to direct, while screenwriting veteran Susan Coyne (b. 1958) delivered a bankable script. For filming, Dublin, Ireland, substituted for Victorian London, while a fictional Irish housemaid named Tara was inserted to be Dickens' creative sounding board as he slowly wrote the most famous holiday tale in all English literature. The movie plot tapped into the established scholarly notion that Dickens the novelist reshaped the way in which most people think about the Christmas holidays, embellished by many clichés central to a polished biographical image created and promoted by Dickens himself. Scandalous dramatization was limited to a gentle suggestion that Dickens' genius may have been fueled by childhood resentments over his family's poverty—not much of a revelation since Dickens' close friend and chosen biographer John Forster (1812–1875) had presented similar details back in 1872–1874 (after the death of the novelist), in no small part because Dickens himself had shared these supposed secrets with him.

As literary biography, *The Man Who Invented Christmas* triumphantly concludes in December of 1843, with the publication of *A Christmas Carol* (when Dickens was 31 years old), implying that his fortune was forever made by this future blockbuster, which in fact was far from the truth. It would be at least another five years before Dickens achieved financial security as writer, although sales for *A Christmas Carol* were strong enough to keep the novelist writing now near-forgotten holiday novellas for another five years. Disparaging references are made to some of Dickens' previous but lesser known and underrated works such as *Martin Chuzzlewit* (first entirely published in 1844 after *A Christmas Carol*), *Barnaby Rudge*, and *American Notes*. Little or no mention is made of game-changing books already written by Dickens such as *Oliver Twist* and *The Old Curiosity Shop*, or unqualified commercial successes such as *Nicholas Nickleby* and *The Pickwick Papers*. No matter. *The Man Who Invented Christmas* grossed over $8 million in its initial run, almost quadruple the amount of *The Invisible Woman*. It clearly told a story that modern audiences wanted to hear, even for those not counting themselves among the

20. Biographical and Apocryphal

dedicated fans of Dickens, over two centuries after his birth. Four years after its release, the movie remains easily accessible in a wide variety of platforms and still makes pleasant enough viewing. Unfortunately, anyone seeking insight into the troubled, restless genius that was Charles Dickens the novelist, at least as video entertainment, will need to look elsewhere.

Based on the receptions of these two films, one should naturally ask whether the real Charles Dickens—the one now well known to scholarly biographers—will ever find full acceptance among enthusiasts of his fiction. Another question is how long can the two competing biographies of Charles Dickens, the factual one versus the concocted image, coexist as they appear to do at present? In a sense, Dickensian biography has come full circle over the last two centuries, beginning with the pseudonymous "Boz" of 1836 being revealed as Charles Dickens, imagined Victorian jovial man about town, in *The Pickwick Papers* and subsequent early novels. From there, Dickens became the "hero of his own life" from *David Copperfield* circa 1850, only to devolve into the more disturbing character of Pip from *Great Expectations* around 1860. And yet, almost as an afterthought, Pip gets the girl (Estella), leading us back to the imaginary Charles Dickens, or at a minimum, making his transformation into something more real, a very slow and still ongoing process. Within the motion picture industry, a similar process seems to be currently playing out. Perhaps we should recall that Samuel Pickwick undergoes a dramatic (but fictional) transformation as well, from comical laughingstock to heroic figure of stoicism, with considerable help, that is, from his cockney sidekick and alter-ego, Sam Weller. In the final analysis, it might be argued that the "real" Charles Dickens of serious literary biography becomes so only in relation to those closest around him, including his chosen friends and extended family.

Summary

"A little learning is a dangerous thing, but a little patronage is more so."[1]

In 1836, shortly before becoming world famous as a novelist, the 24-year-old Charles Dickens, while writing one of his *Sketches* under the pseudonym "Boz," humorously noted that misguided charitable intentions can often cause unintentional but substantial harm (see epigraph). This sentiment would remain a constant theme in Dickens' storytelling art for the next 34 years, right up until his death in 1870 while writing *The Mystery of Edwin Drood*. This theme included the notion that benevolent appearances can disguise malevolent intent; in short, appearances can be deceiving—especially appearances cloaked with piety. And yet the novelist himself often engaged in the process of personal image making and, over the course of a long career, significant image rebranding for sheer commercial purposes. As noted in previous chapters, what began as the humorist "Boz" later became a David Copperfield–like version of Charles Dickens, still later reshaped into an image resembling Pip Pirrip from *Great Expectations*. With possible exception of Pip, none of these images had much to do with Charles Dickens as a real-life, intensely fallible human being. Thus, the apocryphal Charles Dickens became publicly confused with reality at a very early stage. Later writing a Preface or Apology for *Sketches* during his *David Copperfield* period, Dickens critically re-evaluated his own work with the observation, "I am conscious of their often being extremely crude and ill-considered."[2] In hindsight, it seems fair to say, for this novelist, good storytelling involved a constant, relentless tension between cold, hard reality and pure imagination. To give only one example, are the life-changing, nocturnal ghosts appearing to Ebenezer Scrooge in *A Christmas Carol* real visions or strictly Scrooge's own guilt-ridden dreams?

The above psychological query is indeed worthy of a fictional tale by Edgar Allan Poe, whom Dickens had briefly met in America shortly before writing *A Christmas Carol*. Like his own literary creation (Scrooge), Dickens the novelist seems to have embodied multiple, contradictory personalities found within a single individual of tremendous ability. For purposes of this survey, and in faint imitation of the Greco-Roman moralist-historian Plutarch, the virtues and vices of Charles Dickens should be weighed and compared in relation to his artistic output. Although Dickens was one man rather than two (as typically examined by Plutarch), the dual or multiple personalities of the novelist will serve to try and make sense of his world-changing storytelling art, an art which succeeded in saying so many different things to so many different people. On one hand there was Charles Dickens, the great reformer of British society, a public role which he relished throughout his career, one finding forceful expression both in his commercial storytelling and in the many charitable endeavors of his personal life.[3] In stark contrast stood Dickens, the ordinary, highly flawed man, a view he seems to have leaned towards during the latter part of his life. This opposite, far less attractive side of the novelist has always found less traction among his devoted fans and the reading public, although it undoubtably has gained more acceptance during modern times and the era of filmmaking. Currently, there appears to be an audience debate as to whether they prefer a false biographical image of the Great Inimitable, or maybe something less sympathetic and more realistic, or perhaps both images simultaneously. In any case, there can be little or no argument that, as an artist, Dickens was always trying to step outside of his comfort zone and expand his horizons, a process that continued until his dying day.

Though hardly an original observation, it should be duly reiterated within these pages that the Christmas holidays frequently played a central role in Dickens' storytelling, both as a backdrop and integral thematic concern. Moreover, the novelist would often blend this pervasive Christmas theme with individual, psychological disturbances, thus giving his tales a very distinctive quality seldom found elsewhere in English literature. This is true not only for *A Christmas Carol*, but also was an ongoing Dickensian device for over three decades, from *Sketches by Boz* ("A Christmas Dinner") through *The Mystery of Edwin Drood* in which Edwin vanishes on Christmas Eve, presumably having been murdered by his jealous uncle. Returning to *Sketches*, Dickens, circa 1835, as a narrator exclaimed: "Christmas time! That man must be a misanthrope indeed, in whose breast something like a jovial feeling is not roused—in whose mind some pleasant associations are not awakened—by the recurrence of Christmas."[4] The centrality of this Christian holiday to the novelist's mindset was thus established early on, and would continue strongly into his breakthrough, serialized work of 1837, *The Pickwick Papers* ("A Good-Humoured

Christmas") For Dickens, Christmas held considerable moral significance, as well as a time of year for merrymaking and gift giving. And because most of Dickens' commercial fiction was originally conceived for a specific moral purpose—especially, to change prevalent public attitudes towards the poor and disadvantaged—utilizing Christmas as both a setting and context for these moralistic stories suited his artistic needs perfectly. It need hardly be added that this very same quality lent itself well to encouraging later film adaptations of Dickens' work on a prolific scale during the following century, beginning and foremost with *A Christmas Carol*, the numerous film interpretations of which could easily fill a critical book by itself (and in fact already have).[5]

In surveying the vast quantity of Dickensian film adaptations over the last century or more, several generalizations become readily apparent. First and foremost, dramatizing the fabulous characters of Charles Dickens on video has proven to be a consistent springboard to much greater fame for ambitious professional performers. Examples of this phenomenon are legion, but one coming readily to mind is that of Alec Guinness, who, long before becoming part of the *Star Wars* franchise, was an unknown and relatively impoverished British thespian, that is, until partnering with director David Lean in 1946–1948 to portray Herbert Pocket and Fagin on the big screen. After that, Guinness would never again have trouble finding screen roles, although it would be another three decades before he found financial security.[6] Another previously unknown performer to benefit enormously from Lean's grand artistic vision of Dickens' *Great Expectations* was a teenaged Jean Simmons (as the young Estella), who went on later to become a true Hollywood icon of the 1950s and 1960s, but also revisiting the same Dickens novel on screen after achieving stardom. The spectacular examples of Guinness and Simmons inspired other ambitious Anglo performers following in their wake and continues to do so. In more recent years, some of these British actors have included Claire Foy as Little Dorrit in 2008 and Matthew Rhys as John Jasper in 2012, both of whom soon achieved much wider recognition and acclaim. Perhaps the most notable recent exemplar, however, was the 10-year-old Daniel Radcliffe portraying a young David Copperfield circa 1999, immediately before becoming a household name as Harry Potter in 2001.[7] An even more dramatic example might be that of Tom Wilkinson, first coming to widespread attention with his bracing performance as Seth Pecksniff in *Martin Chuzzlewit* from 1994, a full three years before *The Full Monty* (1997) would turn him into a household name. Numerous similar examples of this abound and are detailed throughout this survey.

Less obvious perhaps has been a consistent trend in which completely established performers have used Dickens as means to fulfill old creative ambitions. Famous actors have chosen to perform Dickens long after they had anything left to prove. Possibly the most unusual example is (again) that of Alec Guinness, who four decades after first gaining visibility through David Lean's film adaptations, and a decade after *Star Wars* had turned him into a wealthy man, opted to return to Dickens for Christine Edzard's historic production of *Little Dorrit* in 1987, simply because he wanted to. Another striking case is the 86-year-old Michael Caine, although his motivation appears to have been far more obvious: after being denied a chance at a breakthrough singing stage role in *Oliver!* the musical from 1960, Caine opted to play a Fagin-like reincarnation in the dubious 2021 reboot of the same Dickens novel (*Twist*). This was long after the aging superstar had anything substantial to gain by taking such a risk.[8] Other similar examples abound. During the 1930s era of talkies, comedian W.C. Fields proved to many surprised audiences that he was a serious actor by taking on the role of Wilkins Micawber in *David Copperfield* (1935), while that same year (1935), British matinee idol Ronald Colman reminded American movie fans of his highbrow training by landing the part of Sydney Carton in MGM's *A Tale of Two Cities*, a role that he had been secretly preparing for his entire career, even though by that time he was too old by conventional industry standards to play such a character. In a like manner, there are countless examples of established players taking on memorable Dickensian film roles near the end of successful careers in which these roles were seemingly selected by the performers for personal reasons rather than through normal, competitive auditions. A sampling of these have included the distinguished likes of Christopher Plummer (Ralph Nickleby), Jean Simmons (Miss Havisham), Nigel Stock (Samuel Pickwick), Paul Scofield (Martin Chuzzlewit), and Derek Jacobi (Grandfather Trent).[9]

Less glamorous but no less significant has been the Dickens film adaptation as an ongoing device to expand personal artistic horizons for performers breaking out of typecasts. Very recently, prominent examples have included Dev Patel's portrayal of David Copperfield in Armando Iannucci's innovative 2019 feature film, or megastar Lena Headley (*Game of Thrones*) as a female version of Sikes in the 2021 reimagining of *Oliver Twist*. One of the more noteworthy examples over the past decade, however, has surely been the (then) 43-year-old Gillian Anderson's decision to play Miss Havisham in the BBC's latest go at *Great Expectations* (2012). Anderson had no doubt been encouraged to take a bolder leap into the world of Dickens storytelling after her lauded, adventurous portrayal of Lady Dedlock in the earlier BBC *Bleak House* (2005).[10] Seven years later, Anderson as Miss Havisham forcefully reminded audiences that the key to Havisham's eccentric personality is in her past as a young adult, very much like the more youthful approach of Martita Hunt as Havisham, both in the 1939 stage production and the landmark 1946 David Lean film version. With respect to sound pictures, the original prototype for this kind of ambitious career move may well have been Claude Raines' startling leap from unconventional Hollywood stardom in *The Invisible Man* (1933) to a more nuanced Dickensian villain, John Jasper, in Universal's *The Mystery of Edwin Drood* (1935). Under the old studio contract system, Raines might have been required to take this career risk against his will, but it nonetheless was successful and established a template from which later performers have frequently benefited.

Lastly, the ongoing, viable market for screening Charles Dickens has, in many respects, made itself into a specialist genre, providing steady employment for performers using this film type as a specialty niche. In recent years alone, many fine actors have fallen into this category, some of which have included Alun Armstrong, Miriam Margolyes, Timothy Spall, and Simon Callow, to name only a few. Although actors are the artists most visible to movie audiences for these productions, the genre has also inspired many non-actors who work behind the scenes, especially directors, possibly beginning in 1909 with the famed D.W. Griffith and his short silent take on Dickens' popular holiday tale, *The Cricket on the Hearth*. In more recent times, prominent directors to willingly take on the challenge of a Dickens storyline have ranged the full gamut from all-out satirists such as Armando Iannucci (*The Personal History of David Copperfield*) to foreign arthouse auteurs such as Alfonso Cuarón (*Great Expectations*). This continuing interest from high-profile directors, producers, and actors has ensured that market demand for this genre will, at least occasionally, be very well served. Furthermore, it appears certain that the ever-popular storylines of Dickens will be competently reinterpreted for both present times and modern audiences.[11]

Unfortunately lost in all these competing interests and motivations of the movie industry is the unmistakable fact that Dickens the novelist originally created these works not only to entertain but also to subtly instruct. Everyone quickly recognizes Scrooge, but no one wants to be like him, at least not before his reformation.[12] The English novel as a vehicle for social change was practically invented by Dickens during the mid–1800s, or at least raised to an extraordinarily high qualitative level not previously known and hardly known since. Sadly, neither public opinion nor the body politic is any longer influenced in its views by *Oliver Twist*, *Bleak House*, or for that matter, any written novel. The printed word no longer seems to hold political sway except for a small group of social and economic elites, a group constantly shrinking in number. During the contemporary era, such changes no longer seem possible. When a Dickens classic does manage to find its way into video format, viewers certainly still want to be entertained, but to what extent the author's original reformist intentions are honored can vary in the extreme. Even a clever mashup such as the 2015 Netflix series *Dickensian* only serves to demonstrate that Dickens' characters, once stripped of their underlying social message, come across mainly as incoherent or unsympathetic, no matter how otherwise innovative, brilliant, and eccentric. Nonetheless, it is now through the video dramatization of Dickens' stories that remnants of his revolutionary social messages still survive, however imperfectly, and, as we should remind ourselves, this special aspect of his art primarily motivated him as a young man in leaving a promising journalistic career to become a professional storyteller in serialized printed format.[13]

Given over 124 years of non-stop interpretive film activity (see Filmography), it is thankfully probable that the works and life of Charles Dickens will continue to be adapted for film audiences well into the foreseeable future. Each generation needs its own versions of Copperfield, Pip, Heep, Scrooge, and Fagin (among many others), proving yet again the durability and indestructibility of Dickens' storytelling art. Another good reason for hope is that, when one considers all the trauma and disruption endured by the civilized world since 1897 (*Death of Nancy Sykes*), as well as a wealth of Dickens film adaptations during that same period, it seems reasonable to suppose that, artistically at least, this long-term trend will continue. The Dickens of the future may not look the way his stories have in the past, and these may not look the way we expect them to, but they will surely continue to proliferate, unless mankind somehow tragically loses the ability to retell old stories. Charles Dickens himself lived through an epoch witnessing Great Britain's transition from the Napoleonic Wars and the War of 1812, through the American War between the States, to the superficial prosperity and prestige of the British Victorian era. The novelist was no doubt keenly aware of this illusion, being a master illusionist himself, and that difficult theme found its way into his fiction as well. Perhaps this will be the side of Dickens emphasized to future movie generations: Charles Dickens the consummate illusionist, but an illusionist who never forgets the true nature of reality.

Filmography

(Film Adaptations of Charles Dickens Material—Selected Highlights)

1897—*Death of Nancy Sykes* (Paul, lost)
1898—*Mr. Bumble the Beadle* (Paul, lost)
1901—*The Death of Poor Joe* (Smith)
   Mr. Pickwick's Christmas at Wardle's (Paul, lost)
   Scrooge: or Marley's Ghost (Paul)
1903—*Dotheboy's Hall: or Nicholas Nickleby* (Gaumont)
1906—*Oliver Twist* (Gaumont, lost)
   Dolly Varden (Gaumont, lost)
   Little Nell (Gaumont, lost)
1908—*A Christmas Carol* (Essanay, lost)
1909—*The Cricket on the Hearth* (Griffith)
   The Old Curiosity Shop (Essanay, lost)
   Oliver Twist (Vitagraph)
   The Boy and the Convict (Williamson)
   The Mystery of Edwin Drood (Gaumont, lost)
1910—*A Christmas Carol* (Edison)
1911—*The Old Curiosity Shop* (Thanhouser)
   The Early Life of David Copperfield (Thanhouser)
   Little Em'ly and David Copperfield (Thanhouser)
   The Loves of David Copperfield (Thanhouser)
   A Tale of Two Cities (Vitagraph)
   How Bella Was Won (Edison, lost)
   Eugene Wrayburn (Edison)
1912—*Nicholas Nickleby* (Thanhouser)
   Oliver Twist (Bentley, lost)
   Martin Chuzzlewit (Edison, lost)
   Mrs. Lirriper's Lodgings (Vitagraph, lost)
   Mrs. Lirriper's Legacy (Vitagraph, lost)

1913—*The Pickwick Papers* (Vitagraph)
David Copperfield (Bentley)
Little Dorrit (Thanhouser, lost)
Mr. Horatio Sparkins (Vitagraph, lost)
1914—*The Old Curiosity Shop* (Bentley, lost)
The Chimes (Bentley, lost)
The Chimes (Blaché-Terriss, lost)
Martin Chuzzlewit (Biograph)
The Cricket on the Hearth (Biograph)
The Mystery of Edwin Drood (Blaché-Terriss, lost)
1915—*Barnaby Rudge* (Bentley, lost)
Hard Times (Bentley, lost)
1916—*Oliver Twist* (Lasky, lost)
1917—*Dombey and Son* (Elvey)
A Tale of Two Cities (Lloyd)
Great Expectations (Vignola, lost)
1920—*Bleak House* (Elvey)
1921—*The Old Curiosity Shop* (Bentley, lost)
Our Mutual Friend (Sandberg)
1922—*Tense Moments from Great Plays: Bleak House* (Parkinson)
Tense Moments with Great Authors: A Tale of Two Cities (Parkinson, lost)
David Copperfield (Sandberg)
Great Expectations (Sandberg)
Oliver Twist (Lloyd)
1923—*The Cricket on the Hearth* (Johnston)
1924—*Little Dorrit* (Sandberg)
1926—*The Only Way* (Wilcox)
1928—*Grandfather Smallweed* (B. Williams)
Scrooge (B. Williams, lost)
1931—*Rich Man's Folly* (Paramount)
1933—*Oliver Twist* (Monogram)
1934—*The Old Curiosity Shop* (Bentley)
Great Expectations (Universal)
1935—*David Copperfield* (MGM)
A Tale of Two Cities (MGM)
Scrooge (Twickenham)
The Mystery of Edwin Drood (Universal)
1938—*A Christmas Carol* (MGM)
1946—*Great Expectations* (Lean)
1947—*Nicholas Nickleby* (Cavalcanti)

Filmography

1948—*Oliver Twist* (Lean)
The Only Way (BBC)
1950—*A Christmas Carol* (B. Williams)
1951—*Scrooge* (Sim)
1952—*The Pickwick Papers* (Langley)
The Pickwick Papers (BBC)
The Cricket on the Hearth (NBC)
Hunted Down (Baragrey, lost)
1953—*A Tale of Two Cities* (ABC)
The Signalman (CBS, lost)
1954—*A Christmas Carol* (CBS)
Great Expectations (NBC)
David Copperfield (NBC)
1956—*A Charles Dickens Christmas*, from *The Pickwick Papers* (Britannica)
The Stingiest Man in Town (NBC)
David Copperfield (BBC)
The Mating of Watkins Tottle (NBC)
1957—*Nicholas Nickleby* (BBC)
A Tale of Two Cities (BBC)
1958—*A Tale of Two Cities* (Rank)
Our Mutual Friend (BBC)
1959—*Bleak House* (BBC)
Great Expectations (BBC)
1960—*Barnaby Rudge* (BBC)
The Mystery of Edwin Drood (Lawton)
1962—*Oliver Twist* (BBC)
The Old Curiosity Shop (BBC)
1964—*Martin Chuzzlewit* (BBC)
1965—*A Tale of Two Cities* (BBC)
1966—*David Copperfield* (BBC)
1967—*Great Expectations* (BBC)
The Cricket on the Hearth (Rankin Bass)
Mr. Dickens of London (ABC)
1968—*Oliver!* (Reed)
Nicholas Nickleby (BBC)
1969—*David Copperfield* (Mann)
Pickwick (BBC)
Dombey and Son (BBC)
1970—*Uneasy Dreams: The Life of Mr. Pickwick* (Marre)
Scrooge (Finney)

1971—*A Christmas Carol* (R. Williams)
1973—*Smike!* (BBC)
1974—*David Copperfield* (BBC)
  Great Expectations (Hardy)
1975—*Mister Quilp* (Newley)
1976—*Dickens of London* (Masterpiece Theatre)
  Our Mutual Friend (BBC / Masterpiece Theatre)
  The Signalman (BBC)
1977—*Hard Times* (Granada)
  Nicholas Nickleby (BBC)
1979—*The Old Curiosity Shop* (BBC)
1980—*A Tale of Two Cities* (BBC)
  A Tale of Two Cities (Hallmark)
1981—*Great Expectations* (BBC)
1982—*Oliver Twist* (Donner)
  Oliver Twist (Burbank)
  A Christmas Carol (Burbank)
  The Life and Adventures of Nicholas Nickleby (Primetime/RSC)
1983—*Dombey and Son* (BBC)
  David Copperfield (Burbank)
  Great Expectations (Burbank)
1984—*A Christmas Carol* (Donner)
  The Old Curiosity Shop (Burbank)
  A Tale of Two Cities (Burbank)
1985—*Bleak House* (Masterpiece Theatre)
  Oliver Twist (BBC)
  Oliver Twist (Burbank)
  The Pickwick Papers (BBC)
  The Pickwick Papers (Burbank)
  Nicholas Nickleby (Burbank)
1986—*David Copperfield* (BBC)
1987—*Little Dorrit* (Edzard)
1988—*Tempos Difíceis* (Botelho)
  Scrooged (Donner)
  Oliver & Company (Disney)
1989—*A Tale of Two Cities* (Granada)
  Great Expectations (Disney)
  Hunted Down (Thames)
1992—*The Muppet Christmas Carol* (Henson)
1993—*The Mystery of Edwin Drood* (A&E)

1994—*Hard Times* (Masterpiece Theatre)
Martin Chuzzlewit (BBC)
1995—*Ebbie* (Lucci)
The Old Curiosity Shop (Hallmark)
1997—*Ms. Scrooge* (Tyson)
Oliver Twist (Disney)
1998—*Great Expectations* (Cuarón)
Our Mutual Friend (BBC / Masterpiece Theatre)
1999—*David Copperfield* (BBC)
A Christmas Carol (Stewart)
Oliver Twist (ITV)
Great Expectations (BBC / Masterpiece Theatre)
2000—*David Copperfield* (Hallmark)
The Chimes (Xyzoo)
2001—*The Life and Adventures of Nicholas Nickleby* (Whittaker)
2002—*Nicholas Nickleby* (McGrath)
2004—*A Christmas Carol: The Musical* (Hallmark)
2005—*Bleak House* (Masterpiece Theatre)
Oliver Twist (Polanski)
Dickens in America (Margolyes)
2006—*Dickens Before Sound* (BFI)
2007—*The Old Curiosity Shop* (ITV)
Oliver Twist (miniseries)
The Riddle (Jacobi)
2008—*Little Dorrit* (Masterpiece Classic)
2009—*A Christmas Carol* (Disney)
2011—*Great Expectations* (BBC)
2012—*Nick Nickleby* (BBC)
Great Expectations (Newell)
The Mystery of Edwin Drood (BBC)
Dickens on Film (BBC)
2013—*The Invisible Woman* (Fiennes)
2015—*Dickensian* (Netflix)
2017—*The Man Who Invented Christmas* (Nalluri)
2019—*The Personal History of David Copperfield* (Iannucci)
A Christmas Carol (BBC)
2020—*A Christmas Carol* (Morris)
2021—*Twist* (Owen)

Chapter Notes

Introduction

1. Introduction to MoMA exhibition titled *Dickens on Film*. See https://www.moma.org/calendar/film/1314. The Museum of Modern Art presented its film series in late 2012 and early 2013 as part of the Charles Dickens birth year bicentenary.

2. Smith's *The Death of Poor Joe* was only recently discovered in 2012 (see Chapter 12). Iannucci's *The Personal History of David Copperfield* appeared at film festivals in late 2019, but its 2020 theatrical release was delayed due to the pandemic crisis (see Chapter 10).

3. The first known silent film adaptation of Dickens (now lost) was reportedly *The Death of Nancy Sykes* [sic] in 1897, a scene taken from the novel *Oliver Twist*.

4. Roughly a quarter of known Dickens' screen adaptations will be covered by this survey. Many others are considered now lost or unavailable for general viewing.

5. This 1996 published survey in fact appears to cut off at the year 1994; hence, strictly speaking, it is currently 26 years out of date.

6. The 2013 biographical film *The Invisible Woman* was largely based upon Claire Tomalin's work *Charles Dickens: A Life* (Penguin Books, 2011).

7. Dr. Marsh is currently Associate Professor Emeritus of English at Indiana University.

8. See https://www.theguardian.com/film/2020/jun/13/streaming-best-dickens-adaptations-film-tv-personal-history-david-copperfield-armando-iannucci.

9. Pointer, p. 123.

10. These two lost works will be discussed in Chapter 18.

11. Pointer, p. 152.

12. Pointer, pp. 103, 170.

13. Published by Bradbury & Evans of London, *Household Words* was the immediate predecessor to Dickens' more famous periodical *All the Year Round*. Like other Dickens short stories from the period, *The Seven Poor Travellers* may have been a collaborative work between the novelist and Wilkie Collins, the same writer with whom Dickens worked on the stage play *The Frozen Deep* three years later in 1857. It was the first holiday short story associated with Dickens' name since *The Haunted Man* of 1848.

14. Pointer, p. 170.

15. Eisenstein's essay was translated into English by Jay Leyda in 1949.

16. The most eminent of these recent biographers, Claire Tomalin, has been highly critical of Dickens the man while maintaining the greatness of his fiction.

17. Dickens also wrote forcefully against American slavery in his *American Notes* (1842), while traveling through the Ohio River Valley.

Chapter 1

1. *The Pickwick Papers*, Chapter LVII.

2. The successful collection *Sketches by Boz*, representing the young Dickens' first efforts as a humorist, written between 1833 and 1836, appeared about one month before the initial installment of *The Pickwick Papers* in early 1836, with illustrations by George Cruikshank (see Introduction).

3. Tragically, the original illustrator of *Pickwick*, Robert Seymour (1798–1836),

committed suicide as it became soon apparent that his plates would be designed to suit an original storyline by Charles Dickens. After several candidates came forward to fill the vacancy, but were rejected by novelist, including *Vanity Fair* author William Makepeace Thackeray (1811–1863) and noted painter Robert William Buss (1804–1875), Hablot Knight Browne (1815–1882), aka "Phiz," was selected and became Dickens' main illustrator for the next two decades.

4. Thanks to Marion Buckley for this insight.

5. Dickens' final public reading on the Ides of March 1870, less than three months before his death, included "The Trial of Pickwick." See Tomalin, pp. 386–387.

6. Pointer, p. 112.

7. This contrasts with Pickwick's literary predecessors such as Cervantes' Don Quixote or Shakespeare's Sir John Falstaff, who are (respectively) either crazy or dishonest.

8. English critic and Dickens afficionado W.H. Auden aptly described Samuel Pickwick as "a pagan god wandering through the world imperviously." See Tomalin, p. 63.

9. Pointer, p. 117. See also https://thebioscope.net/2012/01/11/charles-dickens-filmmaker/.

10. Pointer, pp. 15–16, 117. Stills from this production are still extant and can be viewed in U.K.-available-only DVD *Dickens Before Sound*.

11. Pointer, pp. 117, 119.

12. Pointer, pp. 25, 33–34, 122.

13. Pointer, p. 123. Only two of the original three reels survive.

14. Pointer, p. 124. Director Wilfred Noy happened to be the maternal uncle of his better-known nephew, British actor Leslie Howard. Several stage plays based on the *Pickwick* trial scene were developed after Dickens' death in 1870. Some of these plays may have formed additional basis for now lost films utilizing the same subject matter.

15. Pointer, pp. 45, 49, 130.

16. See https://www.britishpathe.com/video/news-in-a-nutshell-mr-pickwick-rides-to-rochester.

17. The first English operetta based on *Pickwick* (by Burnand and Solomon) had appeared as early as 1889.

18. Pointer, p. 145.

19. Pointer, pp. 75, 145–146.

20. Pointer, pp. 70–71, 138–139. Film director-writer Noel Langley is perhaps best remembered for his major script contributions to *The Wizard of Oz* (1939).

21. Pointer, pp. 76, 148–149.

22. Pointer, pp. 76, 149.

23. Pointer, pp. 77, 151.

24. Program host Lilli Palmer (1914–1986), born Lilli Marie Preiser, was an American German-Jewish refugee from Nazism. At the time of this broadcast (1956), she was also Mrs. Rex Harrison.

25. Pointer, pp. 71, 139.

26. Pointer, pp. 79–80.

27. Pointer, pp. 158–159.

28. Pointer, pp. 86, 171. A YouTube except exists of Harry Secombe performing this segment of *Pickwick* from *The Ed Sullivan Show*, circa 1965.

29. Pointer, p. 165.

30. Pointer, pp. 79, 163, 167, 171.

31. Pointer, p. 140. *Uneasy Dreams* helpfully suggests or reminds viewers that the character of Samuel Pickwick and his fictional childhood roots were essentially formed within the Enlightenment period of the late 18th century, a period explored directly by Dickens in *A Tale of Two Cities* and *Barnaby Rudge*.

32. Pointer, pp. 96, 187. Nigel Stock is perhaps best remembered today for his portrayal of Dr. Watson in the BBC production of *Sherlock Holmes* from the late 1960s. British actress Jo Kendall (b. 1938) played the Widow Bardell.

33. Pointer, p. 189. Burbank Films Australia later became Burbank Animation Studios. After production was moved to China in 1994, the copyright status of its holdings became notoriously uncertain. All of its Dickensian animations, however, are still widely available in various platforms.

34. Pointer, p. 190.

35. Setting trends and standards for animation, *The Simpsons* premiered in 1989, two years after *Ghost Stories*, although the latter did not reach American audiences until 1990.

Chapter 2

1. *Oliver Twist*, Chapter LI.

2. British commentator Michael Pointer, writing during the mid–1990s, ranked *Oliver Twist* and *A Christmas Carol* as Dickens' two most popular books with filmmakers, then supported this assertion with detailed filmographies. See Pointer, p. 112. This high status of *Oliver Twist* for movie adaptations has been maintained over the last quarter century. The subtitle of the original novel is an overt reference to John Bunyan's late 17th-century allegory, *A Pilgrim's Progress*.

3. The fictional town of Mudfog is possibly based on the English town of Kettering, whose workhouse may have also been a real-life model for *Oliver Twist*. Kettering is located 75 miles from London, approximately the same distance Oliver must walk in the novel; moreover, the name "Tulrumble" has a disconcerting resemblance to "Bumble" from the later fictional narrative.

4. Pointer, pp. 7, 117.
5. Pointer, pp. 8, 117.
6. Pointer, pp. 16–19, 117. During the previous year (in 1905), a UK-produced silent, now lost, *A Modern Day Fagin*, also reportedly attempted to update this aspect of Dicken's novel.
7. Pointer, pp. 20, 118.
8. Pointer, pp. 119–120. The French version from 1910, *L'enfance d'Oliver Twist*, is lost. The Italian version from 1911 is alternatively known as *Storia di un orfano*.
9. Pointer, pp. 29–30, 122.
10. Pointer, pp. 30–31, 122.
11. Irreverent, burlesque-style featurettes using *Oliver Twist* also appeared during war years in 1915 and 1917, now lost, thankfully so, most likely. See Pointer, pp. 126–127.
12. Pointer, pp. 39–40, 126.
13. Pointer, pp. 42–43, 129–131.
14. Pointer, pp. 45–46, 131–132.
15. Pointer, pp. 50–51, 134.
16. Pointer, pp. 51, 65–70, 138.
17. Director Lean and actor Guinness (like Dickens before them) were both questioned at the time for seeming too anti-Semitic. Defensively, both pointed to similarly disturbing original illustrations of Fagin by George Cruikshank as justification. As for Dickens after publication, he shrugged off accusations of anti-Semitism by replying that he was merely portraying real people he once knew.
18. These lines are paraphrased directly from the text. See *Oliver Twist*, Chapters L and LII. The mob reference to English King William IV (1765–1837) is yet another reminder in the text that the action is set during pre-Victorian times.
19. Today the same London venue is known as the Noël Coward Theatre.
20. *Oliver!* won six Oscars in 1968. Pointer, pp. 85–87, 139.
21. Pointer, p. 86.
22. Pointer, p. 85.
23. A number of these included foreign-language features with exotic settings, such as the *Manik* (1961) and *Chitti Tammudu* (1962), both from different regions of the East Indian subcontinent and receiving considerable critical praise.
24. Pointer, p. 158.
25. Pointer, pp. 80–81, 83–84, 163.
26. Pointer, p. 85.
27. Strictly speaking, the first Oliver-themed animated film receiving major distribution had been the ABC television-produced *Oliver and the Artful Dodger* (1972) by William Hanna and Joseph Barbera. More precisely, however, the action portrayed in this work was a sequel to the Dickens novel.
28. Pointer, p. 190.
29. Pointer, pp. 109, 143
30. Pointer, p. 141.
31. Pointer, p. 97, 188–189.
32. The toned-down Disney *Oliver Twist* also may have been a reaction to the rather scandalous *Twisted* (1996), loosely based on Dickens but turning the story into a post–AIDS-era cautionary tale set in the gay underworld of New York City. *Twisted* received considerable attention in part because of its high-profile creative team, which included actor William Hickey and director-writer Seth Michael Donsky.
33. British actor Edward Hardwicke (1932–2011), like Nigel Stock before him, was well known and widely admired for his portrayal of Dr. Watson in the British TV series *Sherlock Holmes*. Prolific Dickensian Alun Armstrong seemed more comfortable in a role originally written by Dickens, versus his earlier performance as a later-added character from the 1997 Disney version of *Oliver Twist*. Composer Rachel Portman was coming off her recent success of scoring the soundtrack for *Nicholas Nickleby* (2002).

34. The 2007 BBC *Oliver Twist* aired on PBS Masterpiece Classic in 2009.

35. The title is not to be confused with a 2003 Canadian independent film of the same name, based very loosely on the Dickens novel.

36. https://deadline.com/2019/10/twist-michael-caine-lena-headey-rita-ora-raff-law-sky-movie-charles-dickens-1202761507/.

Chapter 3

1. *Nicholas Nickleby*, Author's Preface.
2. *Cambridge Companion*, p. 25.
3. With the published portrait by Maclise, as perceptively noted by Patten, "Boz" had now unequivocally become Charles Dickens for the reading public. See *Cambridge Companion*, pp. 30–32.
4. Tomalin, pp. 93–94.
5. *Cambridge Companion*, p. 26.
6. Tomalin, pp. 89–90.
7. *Cambridge Companion*, p. 26.
8. *Cambridge Companion*, pp. 26–27.
9. Tomalin, pp. 28–30, 95.
10. *Cambridge Companion*, p. 28.
11. *Cambridge Companion*, pp. 29–30. See also Tomalin, pp. 90–91.
12. Pointer, pp. 15, 117.
13. Pointer, pp. 25, 119.
14. Pointer, pp. 28, 121–122.
15. Pointer, pp. 65, 69–70, 137.
16. Cecil Hardwicke's son Edward Hardwicke would later play Mr. Brownlow in the 2005 film version *Oliver Twist*, as well as Mr. Wickfield in the 2000 film version of *David Copperfield*.
17. Critic Joss Marsh charitably tags the 1947 *Nicholas Nickleby* as "processional." See *Cambridge Companion*, p. 211.
18. Pointer, p. 154.
19. Pointer, pp. 170–171.
20. Derek Francis portrayed Ralph Nickleby in the 1968 miniseries and later Wackford Squeers in the 1977 film. See Pointer, pp. 91–92, 178.
21. Pointer, pp. 103, 174–175.
22. Pointer, pp. 94–96, 183–184.
23. https://www.theguardian.com/media/2001/apr/09/tvandradio.television2.
24. https://www.nytimes.com/2002/12/27/movies/film-review-the-pure-at-heart-at-a-hardhearted-boarding-school.html.
25. https://www.theguardian.com/tv-and-radio/tvandradioblog/2012/nov/08/nick-nickleby-daytime-dickens.
26. *Nicholas Nickleby*, Author's Preface.

Chapter 4

1. *The Old Curiosity Shop*, Chapter 72.
2. Tomalin, p. 111.
3. For example, a reference in Chapter 29 of the novel is made to the recent death of English poet Lord Byron in 1824. Other chronological references are somewhat ambiguous, but in sum these suggest another pre-Victorian setting, as in Dickens previous three novels.
4. Dickens became acquainted with the Hogarth sisters of Edinburgh during the early 1830s. He married Catherine Hogarth (1815–1879) in 1836, the year before Dickens' first novel, *The Pickwick Papers* (1837), was published, while younger sister Mary Hogarth also died in 1837. Later in 1842, another younger sister, Georgina ("Georgy") Hogarth (1827–1917), became Dickens' housekeeper for life, even after he separated from Georgina's sister Catherine circa 1857–1858. There is no indication of scandalous relations between Dickens (who had a mistress) and Georgina, other than she chose employment by him over siding with her elder sister Catherine and biological family after the latter's separation from the novelist.
5. Dickens' manuscript indicates that the Marchioness was the illegitimate daughter of Mrs. Sally Brass and the villain Daniel Quilp, but this background was not included in the published text.
6. Pointer, pp. 19–20, 118.
7. Pointer, p. 121.
8. Pointer, pp. 27–28, 120.
9. Pointer, pp. 44–45, 124, 130.
10. Pointer, pp. 51–53, 134–135.
11. British Pathé has preserved a 1930 silent film re-enactment of a scene from *The Old Curiosity Shop* performed publicly for Dickens' birthday. See https://www.britishpathe.com/video/the-old-curiosity-shop.
12. Pointer, pp. 80, 151.
13. Pointer, pp. 80, 161–162.
14. Pointer, pp. 83, 164.
15. Pointer, pp. 19–20.
16. Pointer, pp. 88–89, 92, 141.

17. Pointer, pp. 92–93, 180.
18. See https://www.imdb.com/title/tt0227938/.
19. See https://www.charlesdickenspage.com/charles-dickens-old-curiosity-shop.html.
20. *The Old Curiosity Shop* from 2007 aired in 2009 on PBS Masterpiece Classic.
21. Mendes' *1917* would be deservedly nominated for Best Picture in 2019, in no small part because of MacKay's stunning lead performance.
22. The miniseries begins misguidedly by moving most of the action and characters forward in time. At one point during the first episode, reference is made to the dead English king, thus implying a Victorian setting, when in fact the original novels are mostly set during the mid-1820s and mid-1830s when the king was still alive, before Victoria's accession to the English throne in 1837.
23. In reference to screenplays for televised miniseries, Constance Cox perceptively wrote, "if one is too mysterious they [viewers] may become weary of the effort to follow a tortuous plot from week to week." See Pointer, p. 83.
24. In American literature, Edgar Allan Poe's *Murders in the Rue Morgue* (1841) receives credit for introducing the first detective in the character of C. Auguste Dupin.
25. Chicago sculptor Lorado Taft (1860–1936) was one of the most influential artists of his time.

Chapter 5

1. *Barnaby Rudge*, Chapter 37.
2. *Barnaby Rudge* was eventually published by Chapman & Hall after Dickens broke off earlier promises made to separate publishers John Macrone and Richard Bentley. The genesis of *Barnaby* had a comparatively lengthy history, with the working title *Gabriel Varden*.
3. Tomalin, p. 122.
4. The Gordon Riots of 1780 were named after Lord George Gordon (1751–1793), a prominent anti-Catholic agitator (who makes an appearance in Dickens' novel), but later legally acquitted of encouraging the riots. As it became apparent that the American Revolution would be a long, drawn-out affair, the English sought to diffuse American support by European Catholic countries such as France, Spain, and Austria. The Papist Act of 1778 was designed to aid this effort by granting more toleration to English Catholics, but only succeeded in stirring up opposition from a growing class of economically oppressed Englishmen, a group well represented by several characters in Dickens' novel.
5. By contrast, American Catholics were often tolerated, with Freedom of Religion becoming a shared value among colonials. For example, the state of Maryland became an early center for American Catholicism.
6. For one good discussion on this fascinating topic, see Tomalin, pp. 3–6.
7. Tomalin, p. 122.
8. Hugh, who has no surname, gets his moniker from the Maypole Hotel where he is employed by the Willet family as a hostler.
9. Pointer, pp. 19, 117–118.
10. Pointer, pp. 25, 123–124.
11. The most visually arresting of these promotional materials were printed for an American company, the Aborn Opera, dating from 1906, the same year as the Gaumont silent short.
12. *Cambridge Companion*, p. 207.
13. Pointer, pp. 38–39, 126.
14. *Cambridge Companion*, pp. 206–208.
15. Powers' distinguished career on the stage later included roles in works by Shakespeare, George Bernard Shaw, and Eugene O'Neill.
16. Chrissie White was coming off her performance in a 1913 film adaptation of *The Vicar of Wakefield* by Oliver Goldsmith, reportedly one of Dickens' favorite novels by another writer.
17. Pointer, p. 162. Morris Barry, along with many other accomplishments, later became associated with the highly popular *Doctor Who* BBC series, like many other Dickensian film specialists of that same era.
18. The flamboyance and cleverness of Dolly in the novel are never effectively conveyed, although this may have been due to factors not related to the performance, such as direction or writing.
19. Hugh, on the contrary, encouraged

in his misdeeds by his biological father Sir John Chester and the unwitting instigator of the riots, Lord George Gordon, eventually becomes a convenient scapegoat for the unrest after the riots are suppressed.
   20. *A Christmas Carol*, Stave III.

Chapter 6

1. *A Christmas Carol*, Stave III.
2. Add to this the growing phenomenon of child hunger, even within the United States, and the underlying message of Dickens' *A Christmas Carol* becomes even more urgent and timely.
3. *A Christmas Carol*, Stave III.
4. The unique tombstone scene has been included in nearly every film adaptation of *A Christmas Carol*. Novelist Jane Smiley has written that "Dickens in Edinburgh in the middle of his thirtieth year is an original without a progenitor"—in other words, with no precedent for his innovation. See Smiley, p. 63.
5. Tomalin, pp. 147–150.
6. *A Christmas Carol*, Stave I.
7. Smiley, p. 64.
8. Caricaturist John Leech (1817–1864) had been introduced to Dickens by George Cruikshank, Dickens' illustrator for *Oliver Twist*. Leech's images for *A Christmas Carol* would go on to influence most film adaptations of the work.
9. *Cambridge Companion*, p. 204.
10. To give just one example (out of hundreds), it has been pointed out that the 1946 holiday movie classic *It's A Wonderful Life* by director Frank Capra is a modern variation of *A Christmas Carol* from the viewpoint of Bob Cratchit (or George Bailey as played in the film by James Stewart). A fine full-length survey of film adaptations for Dickens' *A Christmas Carol* (as of the year 2000) has in fact been written. See Guida, Fred, *A Christmas Carol and Its Adaptations: A Critical Examination of Dickens' Story and Its Production on Screen and Television* (McFarland, 2000).
11. Another fine work on this subject with respect to films made through the 1980s, is by the wide-ranging commentator Paul B. Davis in his *The Lives and Times of Ebenezer Scrooge* (Yale University Press, 1990).
12. Pointer, pp. 8–13, 117.
13. Pointer, pp. 13, 124.
14. Pointer, p. 119.
15. Some of these have alternative titles, such *The Right to Be Happy*, aka *Scrooge the Skinflint* (1916), and *Scrooge* (1923). *A Christmas Carol* (1908) was produced by Chicago's historic Essanay Studios and starred British-born silent star Thomas Ricketts as Ebenezer Scrooge. See Pointer, pp. 118, 126–127, 132.
16. Pointer, pp. 14–15, 75, 133, 147.
17. Pointer, p. 136.
18. Pointer, pp. 102, 136–137. Joseph Mankiewicz was the younger brother of Herman Mankiewicz who, along with his collaborator Orson Welles, would soon viciously caricature the corporate culture of MGM from this period with their collaboration on *Citizen Kane* (1940). Later, in 1964, Joseph Mankiewicz directed a modernized version of Dickens' tale, *A Carol for Another Christmas*, written by Rod Serling and featuring an all-star Anglo-American cast that included Sterling Hayden, Robert Shaw, Peter Sellers, Ben Gazzara, Eva Marie Saint, and Britt Ekland, among others, plus music by Henry Mancini. Sellers and Ekland were recently married at the time.
19. Pointer, p. 138. The 1951 *Scrooge* was retitled *A Christmas Carol* for its initial U.S. release.
20. Many of the early television versions of *A Christmas Carol* (mostly from the 1940s and 1950s) were broadcast live and have not survived, although some of these productions featured distinguished casts playing leading roles, including that of Scrooge. Perhaps the most notable of these was a BBC production titled *Christmas Night* (1946), including a ballet and musical score written by British composer Ralph Vaughan Williams (1872–1958). See Pointer, p. 146. The idea of combining ballet with *A Christmas Carol* has been recently revived for a 2020 feature film.
21. For an example of recent chamber opera, see *The Passion of Scrooge* (2018), by American composer Jon Deak and filmed by H. Paul Moon around the same time.
22. Pointer, pp. 150–151. Later, in 1959, Rathbone played Scrooge in an abbreviated, non-musical production by UK-ABC. See Pointer, p. 161.
23. Pointer, p. 153.
24. Pointer, p. 179. Earlier, producers

Rankin and Bass had helped to effectively invent the television Christmas special for American audiences, beginning in 1964 with the now somewhat notorious *Rudolph the Red-Nosed Reindeer*. See https://www.theatlantic.com/magazine/archive/2020/12/rankin-bass-rudolph-the-red-nosed-reindeer/616932/.

25. Not to be outdone, American Broadway composers Jule Styne and Bob Merrill provided original song-and-dance material for the animated TV special *Mister Magoo's Christmas Carol* (1962), with the inimitable American performer Jim Backus providing voiceovers for Magoo-Scrooge. Not surprisingly, this animated version has often been praised for its music. See Pointer, pp. 164–165.

26. Pointer, pp. 140, 174, 176.

27. Pointer, p. 174.

28. DIC Productions (1997) featured voiceovers from Tim Curry, Whoopi Goldberg, Michael York, and Ed Asner, among others, while Illuminated Films (2001) secured similar services from Simon Callow, Kate Winslet, and Nicolas Cage, to name just a few.

29. Notoriously, Scott won the Oscar for Best Actor in *Patton* (1969) but declined accepting the award on personal principle. Donner had been a film editor for *Scrooge* (1951).

30. Pointer, p. 142.

31. Two year later in 1990, Murray told critic Roger Ebert during an interview that *Scrooged* could have been much better movie but was hindered by poor directorial choices. See https://www.rogerebert.com/interviews/bill-murray-quick-change-artist.

32. Pointer, p. 143. See also *Cambridge Companion*, p. 211.

33. One immediate forerunner to *Scrooged* (1988) was probably the made-for-TV *An American Christmas Carol* (1979), starring Henry Winkler (of *Happy Days*) as Scrooge, and setting the action in Depression-era Concord, New Hampshire. Another was Rod Serling's *A Carol for Another Christmas*, from 1964.

34. See https://www.boweryboyshistory.com/2011/12/pre-scrooged-ghost-of-new-york.html.

35. Pointer, p. 143.

36. Tomalin, p. 387.

37. The late British theater director Mike Ockrent (1946–1999) wrote the book for the successful 1994 stage production, on which the 2004 film was based.

38. Impressively, Gary Oldman voiced over parts for both Jacob Marley and Bob Cratchit, as well as performing the motion capture movements of Tiny Tim. Later Oldman won an Oscar for Best Actor in *Darkest Hour* (2018). Lesley Manville has been associated with the films of British director Mike Leigh.

39. For a typical negative review, see *Variety*: https://variety.com/2019/tv/reviews/christmas-carol-fx-guy-pearce-andy-serkis-1203433602/.

40. https://www.theguardian.com/film/2020/dec/04/a-christmas-carol-review-jacqui-david-morris.

41. Andy Serkis does the voiceover for Marley's ghost in the 2020 film production. Previously, in 2019, Serkis had played the Ghost of Christmas Past in the FX Network miniseries of *A Christmas Carol*.

Chapter 7

1. *Martin Chuzzlewit*, Chapter 16.
2. Tomalin, p. 145.
3. Unlike *Martin Chuzzlewit*, sales figures for *Barnaby Rudge* were relatively healthy at the time, despite general agreement that the earlier experimental novel was not up to Dickens' usual high standards.
4. Tomalin, p. 145.
5. Like many of Dickens' most eccentric "fictional" characters, Mrs. Gamp was reportedly based on a real person known to Dickens' benefactor Mrs. Coutts, the dedicatee of *Martin Chuzzlewit*.
6. *Martin Chuzzlewit*, Chapter 23.
7. Future Confederate President Jefferson Davis was born in Fairview, Kentucky (not far from Cairo, Illinois) and by 1842 was just becoming prominent in pre-Civil War Southern politics.
8. Young Martin's American associate Bevan expresses concern over Tapley's habit of frank speech among pre-Civil War Americans and advises the three of them to stay together during transit: "He [Tapley] may get into some trouble otherwise." See *Martin Chuzzlewit*, Chapter 17.
9. Pointer, p. 121.
10. Bioscope and other sources report

the film to be lost. Others report that copies or partial copies may exist. See https://thebioscope.net/2012/01/11/charles-dickens-filmmaker/. For rumors of continued existence, see https://www.imdb.com/title/tt0002346/. Photographic stills of the 1912 Edison production can still be viewed online.

11. Pointer, pp. 28–29.

12. This statement applies to all four known attempts at filming the novel.

13. Pointer, pp. 28–29.

14. Pointer, p. 125.

15. Alan Hale, Sr., specialized in action and swashbuckler genres. He was also the father of Alan Hale, Jr., perhaps best known for his role as the Skipper in the American hit TV series *Gilligan's Island*.

16. The close timeline between the two, however, is suggestive.

17. Pointer, pp. 83, 166.

18. See https://www.imdb.com/title/tt0423697/.

19. One notable exception had been Scofield's narration of a now treasured 1960 sound recording of Dickens' *A Christmas Carol*, in collaboration with Ralph Richardson as Scrooge.

20. Pointer, p. 194.

21. Elizabeth Spriggs (1928–2008) had a long career on both stage and screen as a character actor and was highly respected by her professional colleagues.

22. Earlier in 1994, Postlethwaite had raised his screen profile considerably by portraying the villain-antagonist in "Sharpe's Company" and "Sharpe's Enemy," both episodes part of the hit PBS TV series starring Sean Bean.

23. Villainy disguised by outward appearances of piety was one of Dickens' favorite dramatic devices.

Chapter 8

1. *The Chimes*, Third Quarter.

2. The other two illustrators for *The Chimes* (besides Daniel Maclise and John Leech) were Richard Doyle and Clarkson Stanfield.

3. In the play, Falstaff tells Justice Shallow "We have heard the chimes at midnight, Master Shallow" (Shakespeare, *Henry IV, Part II*, Act 3, Scene 2).

4. Tomalin, p. 157.

5. Pointer, pp. 37, 125.

6. Other notable Dickens-related Hepworth-Bentley film productions from this same era include *Oliver Twist* (1912), *David Copperfield* (1913), *The Old Curiosity Shop* (1914), and *Barnaby Rudge* (1915).

7. Pointer, pp. 37, 125.

8. Earlier in 1845, Dickens proposed starting a periodic home journal titled *The Cricket*, an idea rejected by John Forster and other associates, but sowing the idea for a similarly titled novella later appearing that December. See Tomalin, p. 169.

9. Tomalin, p. 175.

10. Tomalin, p. 295.

11. *The Cricket on the Hearth*, "Chirp the Third."

12. Pointer, pp. 20–22, 118.

13. At the time (1909) Pickford had just introduced herself to Griffith and was taking any walk-on film roles she could find, however brief or insignificant. Her future first husband, Owen Moore, was also on the set. Pickford may be one of the tavern performers in the film, but this has not yet been proven.

14. Pointer, p. 125.

15. See https://thebioscope.net/2012/01/11/charles-dickens-filmmaker/.

16. Pointer, p. 125.

17. See https://thebioscope.net/2012/01/11/charles-dickens-filmmaker/.

18. Pointer, pp. 146–147. NBC's *Your Show Time* was the first filmed television series, focusing on short adaptations of significant literary works, and winning the first Emmy Award for its efforts in 1950.

19. See https://cinema.library.ucla.edu/vwebv/search?searchArg=your+show+time&searchCode=FTIT*&setLimit=1&recCount=50&searchType=1&page.search.search.button=Search.

20. Pointer, p. 148.

21. Pointer, p. 170.

22. The Christian emphasis of this production was surely influenced in part by co-producer Thomas' Lebanese Maronite Christian background. As a philanthropist, Thomas was a co-founder of the St. Jude's Children's Hospital charity. Daughter Marlo Thomas at the time starred in her own hit TV series *That Girl*. Her voice portrayal of Bertha in the animated film is a composite of Dickens' characters Bertha Plummer and May Fielding.

23. Setting Dickens' novella to music

was not a new idea; in fact, it had earlier inspired two operas, one in German by Karl Goldmark in 1896, and another in Italian by Riccardo Zandonai in 1908.

24. The opening credits acknowledge that the film is merely "Suggested by" the Dickens novella.

25. Notably a successful 1862 Christmas Eve production of *The Haunted Man* included the technical innovation of projecting a ghost image on stage, known as "Pepper's Ghost," and named for its inventor, John Henry Pepper. Given modern cinema's preoccupation with special effects, this factor alone would seem to invite updated efforts using this novella.

26. Tomalin, pp. 172–178.

Chapter 9

1. *Dombey and Son*, Chapter 1.
2. A "twaddling manifestation of silliness" wrote one hostile London reviewer with respect to *The Cricket on the Hearth*. See Tomalin, p. 175.
3. Tomalin, p. 169.
4. The work was begun near Lake Geneva. See *Dombey and Son*, Preface of 1867.
5. Tomalin, p. 185.
6. Fanny Dickens was a successful concert pianist in her youth. Later, in 1837, she married Ignaz Moscheles, who had been a pupil of Ludwig van Beethoven.
7. Paul Sr. is said to be 48 years old when the story begins. See *Dombey and Son*, Chapter 1.
8. Tomalin, p. 413.
9. Tomalin, p. 415.
10. Both McKinnel and Braithwaite later appeared an early silent effort directed by Alfred Hitchcock, *Downhill* (1927).
11. Pointer, pp. 40–41, 127.
12. Pointer, pp. 40–41. See also https://thebioscope.net/2012/01/11/charles-dickens-filmmaker/.
13. Pointer, pp. 50, 133–134.
14. Pointer, p. 50.
15. In an open letter to the public, Shaw asserted that Dickens' daughter Kate had told him everything in Storey's book some 40 years earlier, adding some new information of his own. The first Dickens biography to drop the bombshell of his affair with Nelly Ternan was *The Life of Charles Dickens* (1936) by Thomas Wright. Storey's biography came three years later in 1939, underscoring the validity of Wright's claim with testimony from Dickens' own daughter Kate. See Tomalin, p. 414.

16. Pointer, pp. 171–172.
17. Pointer, pp. 96, 185–186.
18. Kate Flint has written: "Dombey's taking of a second wife is, effectively, the purchase of a potential breeding partner." Edith Dombey represents one example of Dickens "strong, often angry women" characters. See *Cambridge Companion*, pp. 40–41.
19. For many Anglo-American audiences, the older image of Charles Dickens as a strictly jovial, benevolent figure still prevails, although a truer, more troubling picture of the novelist continues to make inroads.

Chapter 10

1. *David Copperfield*, Chapter 48.
2. The 1966 film version of *Fahrenheit 451* was directed by François Truffaut (1932–1984), and starred Oskar Werner as Montag and Julie Christie, the latter playing dual roles as Montag's wife and girlfriend. The film was financed and produced in large part because of the Academy Award–winning Christie, then coming off her recent high-profile performance as Lara in *Doctor Zhivago* (1965), directed by another Charles Dickens enthusiast, David Lean.
3. The screenwriting credits for these changes in the first film version of *Fahrenheit 451* went to Truffaut and his frequent collaborator Jean-Louis Richard (1927–2012). A distinctive soundtrack was provided by American composer Bernard Herrmann (1911–1975).
4. Dickens maintained this high opinion of *David Copperfield* for the rest of his life: "Of all my books, I like this the best." See Preface to the 1869 "Charles Dickens" Edition.
5. Pointer, p. 112.
6. Dickens critical biographer Claire Tomalin writes, "The first fourteen chapters, covering David's early childhood, stand on their own as a work of genius." See Tomalin, p. 217.
7. *David Copperfield*, Chapter 1.
8. Cleverly, as a storyteller, Dickens

kills off David's biological parents early in the novel and transfers all the positive qualities of Dickens' parents to the Micawbers. See Tomalin, pp. 219–220.
  9. Tomalin, p. 221.
  10. Tomalin, p. 220.
  11. Pointer, p. 119.
  12. Pointer, p. 121.
  13. Pointer, pp. 120–121. Excerpts from these films are reportedly preserved in Museo Nazionale del Cinema of Turin. See https://thebioscope.net/2012/01/11/charles-dickens-filmmaker/.
  14. Pointer, p. 123. Excerpts from the 1913 *David Copperfield* may be viewed on the DVD British-import *Dickens Before Sound* (2006).
  15. Pointer, pp. 44, 132. Clips of this production are available for viewing at the website of the Danish Film Institute. See https://www.dfi.dk/viden-om-film/filmdatabasen/film/david-copperfield.
  16. Pointer, p. 135.
  17. Pointer, p. 150. The Emmy-winning series *Robert Montgomery Presents* aired on NBC between 1950 and 1957, often featuring adaptations of serious literary works for mass American TV audiences.
  18. Reportedly, the series can be found within the UCLA Film and Television Archive.
  19. Pointer, pp. 152–153.
  20. Pointer, pp. 168–169.
  21. Episode titles included "David and His Mother," "David and Mr. Micawber," "David and Betsey Trotwood," "David and Dora," "David and Dora Married," and "Uriah Heep." See Pointer, pp. 159–161.
  22. Pointer, p. 140.
  23. Pointer, p. 175.
  24. Pointer, p. 185.
  25. One cannot help but believe that these anthropomorphic animations were influenced, indirectly at least, by the astounding popularity of the 1981 musical *Cats* by Andrew Lloyd Webber, then in the middle of its record-breaking theater run on Broadway.
  26. Pointer, pp. 189–190.
  27. Letts, Dicks, and Hall brought an impressive combined resumé to the 1986 *David Copperfield* as producers, directors, and writers. These included several outstanding film adaptations of Dickens novels, most recently for Letts (as a producer), the 1983 BBC *Dombey and Son*.

  28. Originally, the production had John Sullivan (1946–2011) as its screenwriter, but Sullivan left early to develop his own separate, spinoff comedy series *Micawber* for ITV in 2001.
  29. The Iannucci-Blackwell screenplay utilizes several clever time-saving innovations, such as suddenly writing David's first wife Dora out of the story because she does not fit, rather than slowly killing her off as in the novel and many other film versions.
  30. London's Ealing Studios have hosted important film works for over a century, from the advent of the silent era to the present day. In 1947, the first feature adaptation of Dickens' *Nicholas Nickleby* was filmed at Ealing.
  31. For one recent, typical, positive review, see https://www.rogerebert.com/reviews/the-personal-history-of-david-copperfield-movie-review-2020.
  32. Sometimes this continuing image of Dickens assumes surprising forms; for example, a search for "David Copperfield" through an internet search engine will more likely yield results for the famous contemporary magician of that name rather than the novel or films based upon the novel.

Chapter 11

  1. *Bleak House*, Chapter XLVII.
  2. Dickens in the text refers to the court case as *Jarndyce and Jarndyce*.
  3. Many of these law students had undergraduate backgrounds in English literature.
  4. Dickens' last "Christmas" novella, *The Haunted Man and the Ghost's Bargain*, was published in 1848.
  5. Tomalin, p. 246.
  6. Tomalin, p. 244.
  7. Tomalin, p. 242. The fictional Esther Summerson belonged to Dickens' own younger generation of the times. Both would have been in their twenties during the 1830s.
  8. Tomalin, p. 243.
  9. Of Jo, biographer Claire Tomalin observed, "when it comes to Dickens's outburst of rage and sorrow that follows Jo's death there is no doubt that it is linked to a reality well known to him, and he is writing from head as well as heart." See Tomalin, p. 244.

10. Tomalin, p. 241.
11. See https://www.bbc.com/news/entertainment-arts-17298021.
12. Pointer, pp. 119, 128.
13. Pointer, pp. 129, 131.
14. See https://thebioscope.net/2012/01/11/charles-dickens-filmmaker/.
15. Pointer, p. 133. The primitive sound technology used for *Smallweed* (1928) can typically be found on the YouTube platform.
16. For Constance Cox, as a BBC screenwriter, following in quick succession were *Bleak House* (1959), *Oliver Twist* (1962), *The Old Curiosity Shop* (1962), *Martin Chuzzlewit* (1964), and *A Tale of Two Cities* (1965). See Pointer, pp. 83–84, 157–158.
17. The BBC-produced *Mr. Guppy's Tale* (1969), was a one-hour episode from the series *Detective*, having little to do with the Dickens novel except to borrow a character name. See Pointer, p. 172.
18. Pointer, p. 188.
19. The highly accomplished Diana Rigg passed away in 2020. Her last screen role was as Mrs. Pumphrey in the newest PBS production of *All Creatures Great and Small* (2020).
20. The 2005 production of *Bleak House* is often cited as one of the most popular series to ever appear on *Masterpiece Theatre*. For Amazon Prime, the same series was reformatted to eight edited episodes, approximately one-hour each in length.
21. Thanks to Marion Buckley for this insight.
22. So dark and tragic is the fate of Poor Jo that the 2005 *Bleak House* reduces the extent of this subplot to an optional outtake status, depending on which cut viewers are screening.

Chapter 12

1. *Hard Times*, Book the Third, Chapter One.
2. Both Elizabeth Gaskell and her frequently provocative fiction would later be better appreciated by modern readers and critics than during her own lifetime.
3. Tomalin, p. 250.
4. Economic activity and growth in the northern mill towns of England had, a generation earlier, greatly impressed Adam Smith, helping to inspire his classic work, *The Wealth of Nations* (1776). Many years later, Dickens was far less impressed by what he saw in places like Preston, especially the hard plight of the mill workers.
5. Tomalin, p. 251.
6. By the time that *Hard Times* was written by Dickens, its dedicatee Thomas Carlyle had publicly broken with the philosophy of John Stuart Mill, which perhaps helps to further explain the book's dedication.
7. In *A Christmas Carol*, Dickens had earlier attacked both Smith and Malthus in a similarly indirect manner. Scrooge rails against surplus population in a Malthusian vein, while Scrooge's very name is likely derived from that of Ebenezer Scroggie, the Scottish grandnephew of Smith.
8. Pointer, pp. 39, 49, 126.
9. See https://thebioscope.net/2012/01/11/charles-dickens-filmmaker/.
10. Pointer, p. 39.
11. Pointer, pp. 84–85, 110, 113, 178. Arnold had previously scored the music for the 1969 film version of *David Copperfield*. Hopcraft would go on to be the screenwriter the 1985 BBC production of *Bleak House*.
12. Pointer, pp. 84–85.
13. See https://www.nytimes.com/1977/05/11/archives/tv-hard-times-is-true-to-dickens.html.
14. Pointer, pp. 107–108, 142–143.
15. Pointer, pp. 142–143.
16. *Cambridge Companion*, p. 204.
17. During Dickens' own time, for example, it was well remembered that Portugal had fought on the side of England during the Napoleonic Wars, which also played a crucial role in the early military career of Arthur Wellesley, the future Duke of Wellington.
18. The 1994 miniseries of *Hard Times* originally ran four one-half episodes, or roughly two hours total, versus nearly four hours for the 1977 miniseries. See Pointer, p. 194.
19. *Remains of the Day* was adapted from the prize-winning 1989 novel by Kazuo Ishiguro.
20. The most recent of these appears to have been the 2018 stage production of *Hard Times* by the Northern Broadsides Theatre company of Halifax, West Yorkshire, thus bringing authentic regional

dialects to Dickens' fictional storyline. See https://www.theguardian.com/stage/2018/apr/15/hard-times-northern-broadsides-observer-review.
21. Tomalin, p. 251.

Chapter 13

1. *Little Dorrit*, Chapter Two.
2. Tomalin, p. 256.
3. Tomalin, p. 257.
4. Tomalin, p. 259.
5. Tomalin, p. 260.
6. *Little Dorrit*, 1857 Preface. See also Tomalin, p. 263.
7. Tomalin, p. 260.
8. Tomalin, p. 264.
9. The identity of Arthur Clennam's unnamed and deceased but true biological mother is gradually revealed during the story, also providing motivation for Mrs. Clennam's unconcealed resentment against her late husband and adoptive son.
10. Tomalin, p. 262.
11. Dickens had briefly corresponded and reunited with Maria Beadnell in 1856, by then known as the widowed Mrs. Winter, but was taken aback by her unattractiveness and immediately broke off contact. See Tomalin, pp. 266–267.
12. Pointer, pp. 28, 123.
13. See https://www.thanhouser.org/TCOCD/Filmography_files/con1gi6wc.htm.
14. Pointer, p. 129.
15. See https://screenarchive.brighton.ac.uk/detail/3473/.
16. Pointer, pp. 132–133.
17. Sandberg's four Dickens film adaptations (English titles) included *Our Mutual Friend* (1921), *Great Expectations* (1922), *David Copperfield* (1922), and *Little Dorrit* (1924).
18. See https://thebioscope.net/2012/01/11/charles-dickens-filmmaker/.
19. Pointer, p. 43.
20. An early German-language, silent version of the novel, remarkably made during World War I, *Klein Doortje* (1917) is now considered lost. See Pointer, pp. 127, 134.
21. Edzard and Goodwin have each received numerous nominations for Academy Awards, Golden Globes, and BAFTAs for their film work over the years.
22. Pointer, pp. 106–107, 142.
23. *Cambridge Companion*, pp. 209–210.
24. *Cambridge Companion*, p. 209.
25. Pointer, p. 106.
26. For its 38th season in 2008, *Masterpiece Theatre* was rebranded as *Masterpiece Classics*.
27. Freema Agyeman's performance as Tattycoram was especially provocative, transforming the unhappy female servant of Mr. and Mrs. Meagles into a person of color. In this sense, the 2007 *Little Dorrit* is a forerunner of future multi-racial adaptations of Dickens novels. Also startling in hindsight is the minor but challenging role of Maggie effectively played by then unknown, future Welsh superstar Eve Myles.
28. Alun Armstrong may aptly be described as a veteran of the BBC Dickens miniseries, having also played major supporting roles in *David Copperfield* (1999), *Oliver Twist* (2005), and *Bleak House* (2005).

Chapter 14

1. *A Tale of Two Cities*, Book the Third, Chapter XIV.
2. Tomalin, p. 415.
3. Dickens himself acknowledged the change and the accuracy of the portrait, one generally despised by his most loyal supporters. See Tomalin, p. 305.
4. Tomalin, p. 308.
5. Tomalin, pp. 283–284, 307–308.
6. Dickens' favorite child Kate originally played the same role in *The Frozen Deep* later assumed by Ellen Ternan. They were about the same age. Dickens' friendship with Collins later cooled considerably when Kate married Collins' invalid brother, an unhappy marriage that soon ended upon the brother's death.
7. Queen Victoria requested and received a royal command performance, one indication of the play's popularity and influence on the British general public.
8. Tomalin, p. 307.
9. Dickens had dropped Chapman & Hall as his publisher in 1844 after disappointing net royalties for *Martin Chuzzlewit* and *A Christmas Carol*, even though the latter was a best-seller.

10. Tomalin, p. 309.
11. When not actively engaged in doing evil, Madame DeFarge is constantly knitting, like the Fates or *Moirai* of ancient Greek mythology.
12. Dickens' ongoing theme of incarceration in *A Tale of Two Cities* continues to resonate with younger African American readers, as brilliantly highlighted in the YouTube series *Thug Notes* by educator Sparky Sweets, Ph.D., aka comedian Greg Edwards.
13. The Selig Company is perhaps most famous for also being the first to attempt filming *The Wizard of Oz*.
14. Pointer, pp. 20, 118.
15. Pointer, pp. 26–28, 34, 120. See also *Cambridge Companion*, p. 208. The success of the 1911 production led to another Vitagraph silent version of *A Tale of Two Cities* in 1920, titled *Birth of a Soul*, now considered lost. See also Pointer, p. 128.
16. Pointer, pp. 41, 127.
17. In 1921, Charles Dickens-enthusiast D.W. Griffith directed *Orphans of the Storm*, starring the Gish sisters, which also had a French Revolution setting and showed a strong influence from Dickens' work. The Griffith version of a similar story, however, was not commercially successful.
18. Pointer, p. 131.
19. Pointer, pp. 47, 133. See also *Cambridge Companion*, p. 208. *The Only Way* was based on a popular 1899 play by Freeman Wills and Frederick Longbridge (starring John Martin Harvey in its premier), and the 1925 film version was released in 1926. Interestingly, a BBC version of this same stage drama in 1948 became the first post-World War II sound version of the novel produced. See Pointer, pp. 75, 146.
20. See https://thebioscope.net/2012/01/11/charles-dickens-filmmaker/.
21. Pointer, pp. 59–60, 136. To help disguise his age, Colman agreed to shave (something he otherwise never did) then had his facial close-ups filmed in soft focus.
22. Michael Pointer shared the view of most critics when he wrote that the MGM *A Tale of Two Cities* represented "one of the best performances of Ronald Colman's career." See Pointer, p. 59.
23. *Cambridge Companion*, p. 208.
24. *Cambridge Companion*, pp. 208–209.
25. My late father, at the time an idealistic college student in Chicago, once mentioned seeing this film.
26. The 1936 Academy Award for Best Picture went to the now relatively forgotten and more critically assessed MGM biopic, *The Great Ziegfeld*.
27. Pointer, pp. 76–77, 149.
28. Pointer, p. 154.
29. Pointer, pp. 71, 78, 139. Addinsell had earlier also provided film music for *Scrooge* (1951).
30. Pointer, p. 155. Robert Mulligan would go on four years later to direct the film adaptation of *To Kill a Mockingbird* (1962), probably his best-known work.
31. See https://ctva.biz/U.S./Anthology/DuPontShowOfMonth_01_(1957-58).htm.
32. Pointer, pp. 83, 167–168.
33. Pointer, pp. 93, 181.
34. Nigel Stock would soon go on to star as Samuel Pickwick in the BBC miniseries for *The Pickwick Papers* (1985).
35. Pointer, p. 181.
36. Pointer, p. 187.
37. Pointer, pp. 109–110, 191.
38. Thanks (once again) to Marion Buckley for this important observation.
39. *A Tale of Two Cities* (the opera) was first heard on BBC radio in 1953, then had its stage premier in 1957. In 1958, the full opera was televised by the BBC with a first-rate cast, including a young Heather Harper singing the role of Lucie Manette. See Pointer, pp. 102, 156.

Chapter 15

1. *The Uncommercial Traveller*, Chapter XXII ("Bound for the Great Salt Lake").
2. Miriam Margolyes, in her documentary, perceptively notes that Dickens had previously idealized the United States, very much like he often idealized young women, and then turned against it (or them) after these ideals were shattered by firsthand experience.
3. In Washington, D.C., Dickens was granted a brief interview with then-President, Virginia-born John Tyler, which he later wrote about. See Tomalin, p. 134.
4. Dickens reportedly loved Canada (of the British Commonwealth), just as he had hated the state of Illinois during the same trip.
5. Brother Augustus "Gus" Dickens

(1827–1866) from whom Charles borrowed the nickname "Boz," is buried at Graceland Cemetery in Chicago. Son Francis Dickens (1844–1886) is buried at Riverside Cemetery in Moline, Illinois.

6. Some of these key personalities included Abraham Lincoln, Jefferson Davis, Ulysses S. Grant, William T. Sherman, and Philip H. Sheridan, to name just a few.

7. Although Dickens, like most Europeans, condemned American slavery, he was muted towards the entrenched English class system and always kept personal servants about his family, including one, Anne Brown, during his American tour of 1842.

8. In June of 1842, Junior Cadet Ulysses S. Grant was struggling with both his health and his studies at West Point. We know from Grant's *Memoirs* that he enjoyed novels and was aware of famous people visiting West Point, but he makes no mention of Charles Dickens, although later Grant alludes to *David Copperfield* (a novel written by Dickens years later in 1850) by comparing an inept Confederate General to Wilkins Micawber.

9. Tomalin, pp. 166–168.

10. *Pictures from Italy* was sparsely illustrated (perhaps to save costs) but did include some engravings by the noted Victorian artist Samuel Palmer (1805–1881).

11. Tomalin, p. 252.

12. Dickens' walking ascent of Mount Vesuvius, along with his wife and sister-in-law, was especially audacious given that during this period in history, the volcano was highly active.

13. Dickens' magazine *All the Year Round* first appeared in 1859. The initial set pieces under the subtitle *The Uncommercial Traveller* were included between 1860 and 1861. Dickens did not consider returning to the United States until the American War between the States (1861–1865) had concluded.

14. Pointer, pp. 102, 165.

15. Pointer, pp. 91, 177.

16. British-born screenwriter Wolf Mankowitz (1924–1998) later revealed that he had drafted an incredible number of 24 episodes for this series, of which 13 were filmed. See Pointer, p. 91.

17. Margolyes gave perhaps the definitive portrayal of Flora Finching in the 1985 landmark film production of *Little Dorrit*. That same year (1985), she also portrayed a memorable Mrs. Corney/Mrs. Bumble in the BBC miniseries of *Oliver Twist*.

Chapter 16

1. *Great Expectations* (original ending), based on the proof slip reproduced by Edgar Rosenberg in the W. W. Norton (1999) edition, p. 492. See https://www.victorianweb.org/authors/dickens/ge/ending.html.

2. Tomalin, p. 309.

3. Pip the younger is not the biological nephew of Pip the elder, but rather the son of Pip's boyhood brother-in-law Joe Gargery and his second wife, Pip's childhood friend Biddy.

4. Tomalin, p. 315.

5. Dickens' friend and first serious biographer, John Forster, published the original manuscript ending in his biography. Forster shared the opinion that the original ending was better.

6. Like *A Tale of Two Cities* before it, *Great Expectations* first appeared as a serial run in Dickens' own journal, *All the Year Round*.

7. Pointer, p. 119. See also https://thebioscope.net/2012/01/11/charles-dickens-filmmaker/.

8. Pointer, pp. 40, 127.

9. Pointer, pp. 43, 128.

10. Pointer, pp. 51–52, 135.

11. During World War II, Lean had progressed to the front ranks of British film directors. *Brief Encounter* (1945), his film immediately before *Great Expectations*, is widely considered to be a classic as well.

12. *Cambridge Companion*, p. 211.

13. *Cambridge Companion*, pp. 213–217.

14. Pointer, pp. 65–68, 92, 137.

15. Simmons later became especially known for her romantic leads in sword-and-sandal epics of the 1950s, beginning with *The Robe* (1953).

16. Pointer, pp. 77, 150.

17. Pointer, pp. 79, 157, 169.

18. Pointer, pp. 87–88, 140–141. Jarre was a veteran film composer, having recently provided an outstanding soundtrack for *Ryan's Daughter* (1970),

directed by David Lean, also starring Sarah Miles.
19. *Accidentally on Purpose: An Autobiography*, by Michael York (Simon & Schuster, 1991), p. 290.
20. Welsh actor Rachel Roberts, who played Mrs. Joe in the 1974 *Great Expectations*, also performed with York in *Murder on the Orient Express*. See York, pp. 288–290.
21. York, p. 290.
22. Pointer, pp. 94, 182.
23. Amyes had ably directed the 1979 version of *The Old Curiosity Shop*, and Hall would go on to script well-received BBC productions of *Dombey and Son* (1983) and *David Copperfield* (1986). Letts was a veteran producer of Dickens adaptations for the BBC.
24. Pointer, p. 185.
25. Pointer, pp. 109, 190.
26. Pointer, pp. 110, 192.
27. Sarah Phelps' screenwriting credits to date include Dickens' *Oliver Twist* (2007), five adaptations of works by Agatha Christie between 2015 and 2020, and, following her 2011 *Great Expectations*, an HBO miniseries adaptation for J.K. Rowling's adult novel, *The Casual Vacancy* (2015).
28. Newell first came to widespread attention as a director with *Four Weddings and a Funeral* (1994).
29. The relatively unknown British production of *Magwitch* (2012) was directed by Samuel Supple and distributed by Viola Films.
30. The published concluding chapter of *Great Expectations* moves the action forward about 11 years after the deaths of Magwitch and Havisham.

Chapter 17

1. *Our Mutual Friend*, Chapter 5.
2. Many biographers, including Claire Tomalin, believe that Dickens was carrying on a secret, long-distance affair with Nelly Ternan in France during this same period, culminating in the birth and death of an illegitimate child, after which their relationship seems to have cooled. As presented by Tomalin, the evidence for this scenario is circumstantial but cumulative and compelling.

3. In the published epilogue to *Our Mutual Friend*, Dickens writes of the train wreck and the saved manuscript, but not of his mistress.
4. More strictly speaking, the American Civil War ended hostilities in mid–April 1865 with the surrender of Confederate General Joseph Johnston to Federal General William Tecumseh Sherman in North Carolina.
5. Pointer, pp. 25, 120.
6. "A tale which holdeth children from play and old men from the chimney corner" proclaims the endorsement, taken from Sidney's *Defence of Poesie* (c. 1581).
7. Pointer, pp. 25, 120.
8. Pointer, pp. 43, 129–130.
9. See https://thebioscope.net/2012/01/11/charles-dickens-filmmaker/.
10. Pointer, pp. 79, 156.
11. Pointer, pp. 84, 92, 176–177.
12. Anthony Calf had previously appeared as Pip in the 1989 *Great Expectations*. The well-known David Morrissey gave perhaps the definitive portrayal of the complicated villain, Headstone. Peter Vaughan and Pam Ferris (as the Boffins) both had prominent, long careers on film, television, and stage.
13. The prolific Spall's portrayal of Mr. Venus earned him a BAFTA nomination.
14. Future prominent Dickensian appearances on film for Spall would include *Nicholas Nickleby* (2002) and *Oliver Twist* (2007).
15. The problem is further complicated by the fact that approximately half of the concluding portion for the 1921 Sandberg film is now lost.
16. See https://kentfilmoffice.co.uk/filmed-in-kent/1998/03/our-mutual-friend-1998/.
17. Famously, in *Great Expectations*, Dickens rewrote the ending to make it more upbeat. It seems likely that he was still less than completely certain how the relationship between Pip and Estella should conclude, even after completing the novel and beginning *Our Mutual Friend*.
18. The promotional image for the 1998 miniseries fittingly portrays the characters Wrayburn and Lizzie (played by McGann and Hawes), rather than Harmon and Bella.
19. This other writer being Edgar Allan Poe (1809–1849).

Chapter 18

1. *The Signal-Man*.
2. Tomalin, pp. 331–332.
3. In addition to the groundbreaking detective fiction of Edgar Allan Poe, Dickens' *Hunted Down*, like many of his short stories from this same period, reflects the influence of Wilkie Collins, with whom Dickens had collaborated three years earlier on the stage play *The Frozen Deep* (1856), during which time he also first became involved with Nelly Ternan.
4. Dickens' son Henry confirmed the fact to an early biographer. See Tomalin, pp. 332, 415.
5. Tomalin, p. 330.
6. Charles Green produced numerous engravings for later, posthumous editions of Dickens' works, beginning with *The Old Curiosity Shop* (1876), along with illustrations for the works of English novelist Thomas Hardy (1840–1928)
7. Pointer, pp. 29, 122–123.
8. Thomas Wright's *Life of Charles Dickens* was published in 1935, while *Dickens and Daughter* by Gladys Storey was published in 1939. These were the first two biographical works to publicly reveal Dickens' affair with Nelly Ternan, and both were heavily criticized for it. See Tomalin, p. 414.
9. Pointer, pp. 76, 148.
10. The CBS production co-starred Alan Webb as Barbox Brothers. See https://www.imdb.com/title/tt0041061/episodes?season=5&ref_=tt_eps_sn_5. See also Pointer, p. 149.
11. By this point in his long career, Karloff had been a professor performer for over four decades, helping to define the American Hollywood monster film genre with his recurring roles in the *Frankenstein* films of the 1930s and beyond.
12. Tomalin, p. 334.
13. Other significant revisionist biographies of Dickens from the early 1950s acknowledging the affair included *Charles Dickens* (1953) by J.K. Fielding and *Charles Dickens: His Tragedy and Triumph* (1952) by Edgar Johnson. See Tomalin, p. 470, note 28.
14. Pointer, p. 175.
15. Mainstream movie audiences would not become more familiar with Holm until his role in Ridley Scott's *Alien* (1979). Before that, he was mainly known as a character actor in period dramas, not including his more serious work on the stage, which had included Shakespeare.
16. Barry had won his first two Oscars (Best Original Score and Best Song) in 1966 for his soundtrack work on the popular film *Born Free*.
17. See the DVD import release *Orson Welles Great Mysteries: Volume One* (2019).
18. Pointer, p. 192. The Irish-born Leonard was an experienced adaptor of Dickens' works for television. For the 1989 adaptation of *Hunted Down*, distinguished British actor Alec McCowan played the narrator Aeneas Sampson.
19. Pointer, p. 177.
20. See the DVD import *Ghost Stories: Classic Adaptations from the BBC* (2012).
21. The accomplished Capaldi around this same time memorably portrayed Wilkins Micawber in Armando Iannucci's film *The Personal History of David Copperfield* (2019).

Chapter 19

1. *The Mystery of Edwin Drood* (Chapter VI).
2. Poe invented a fictionalized but brilliant amateur detective, C. Auguste Dupin, while Dickens utilized a retired chief manager of an insurance company, known as Mr. Sampson.
3. The date of death, June 9, 1870, was exactly five years after Dickens survived a rail crash at Staplehurst, Kent. For a good summary of Dickens' final hours, including somewhat contradictory accounts, see Tomalin, pp. 395–397.
4. Tomalin, p. 389.
5. Although the novel was left unfinished, Dickens before his death purportedly laid out his intentions to his illustrator, his son, and his biographer, all of whom later concurred in their accounts. We see no reason to challenge this alleged authorial intent, especially given the novel's consistent set-up of events.
6. Fildes later in 1880 made a notable sketch of Kate Dickens Perugini, who sometimes modeled for pre-Raphaelite artists in her younger years.
7. Dickens' skeptical attitude towards the church strongly calls to mind the

famous quote from the French humanist Montaigne, who wrote, "I know no quality so easy to counterfeit as piety." See Montaigne, *Essays* ("Of Repentance"), Translated by Donald Frame (Stanford University Press, 1957), p. 617.

8. Pointer, pp. 20–21, 38, 125, 148. The short-lived but significant World Films was founded by Louis J. Selznick (1869–1933), father of MGM film producer, David O. Selznick (1902–1965), another Dickens enthusiast.

9. See https://thebioscope.net/2012/01/11/charles-dickens-filmmaker/.

10. By 1914, Terriss was a seasoned Dickens performer, having earlier played Scrooge on stage.

11. Pointer, pp. 62–63, 111, 135–136.

12. Heather Angel later appeared in Alfred Hitchcock's *Lifeboat* (1944), among her many other well-known film roles.

13. The screenplay for the 1935 Universal adaptation is credited to John Balderston and Gladys Unger, the latter also writing the 1934 screenplay for Universal's *Great Expectations*.

14. Previously, Universal had successfully pioneered the genre with *Dracula* (1931), *Frankenstein* (1931), *The Mummy* (1932), and *The Invisible Man* (1933), the latter with Rains. Universal had also loosely adapted several works by Edgar Allan Poe, including the detective-thriller *Murders in the Rue Morgue* (1932) and *The Black Cat* (1934).

15. Pointer, pp. 76, 143–144.

16. Pointer, pp. 80, 162.

17. Dickens was himself famously attentive to the whims of his reading audience. For example, his conclusion to *Great Expectations* was altered in consequence of these perceived preferences. Nevertheless, there is a big difference between that and allowing the audience to vote every single night on a broad menu of possible outcomes.

18. Pointer, pp. 111, 143–144.

19. Matthew Rhys began his rise to film acting fame in 1999, portraying the villainous Demetrius from Julie Taymor's *Titus*, a notable adaptation of Shakespeare's *Titus Andronicus*. For *The Mystery of Edwin Drood* in 2012, Rhys returned to playing a villainous archtype as John Jasper.

20. Alun Armstrong's previous credits on television as a distinctive interpreter of Dickens material included *David Copperfield* (1999), *Bleak House* (2005), and *Little Dorrit* (2008).

21. Earlier, Lunn had earned a BAFTA nomination for his soundtrack to the acclaimed 2008 BBC adaptation of Dickens' *Little Dorrit*.

Chapter 20

1. *David Copperfield*, 1850 Preface.
2. Tomalin, p. 393.
3. Tomalin, p. 414.
4. The first biography to reveal Dickens' affair with Nelly Ternan was *Life of Charles Dickens* (1934) by Thomas Wright, a year after the death of Dickens' last surviving child, Henry. See Tomalin, p. 414.
5. The Shakespeare Authorship Question, like the truth or falsity of Dickens' public image, continues to rage on at the present, despite frequent claims to the contrary.
6. In this sense, Dickens' achievement is akin to that of Shakespeare's so-called history plays—the blending of fact and fiction.
7. Tomalin, p. 416.
8. Henry no doubt had to occasionally cope with allegations that he was betraying his father's liberal political legacy, to which Henry liked to counter with his father's well-documented pleasure at the advancement of Henry's professional and academic career.
9. At least the political critics of Dickens get that aspect of the artist's personality correct (as well as his storytelling art), which many of his most ardent admirers somehow fail to do.
10. In these two late, completed novels, *Great Expectations* and *Our Mutual Friend*, Dickens seems to wrestle with a more accurate self-image through the art of storytelling.
11. See https://thebioscope.net/2012/01/11/charles-dickens-filmmaker/.
12. See https://www.britishpathe.com.
13. There can be little doubt that Dickens did not want anyone, then or now, to know the details of his personal life, other than perhaps isolated details filtering through into his storytelling art.
14. Pointer, p. 177.

15. Following the broadcast of *Dickens of London* in 1976, interest grew in the groundbreaking research of Gladys Storey, who died in 1978. See Tomalin, p. 334.

16. Pinter, p. 91.

17. *Dickens of London* was immediately followed on *Masterpiece Theatre* by a production of Dickens' final completed novel, *Our Mutual Friend*, the first Dickens story presented by that historic series.

18. Though completely fictionalized, the 1963 *Bonanza* episode presents Dickens (played by Jonathan Harris) as a successful writer who is extremely unhappy with the then prevalent American custom of not observing international copyrights.

19. Claire Tomalin's initial foray into the topic came with the prize-winning book, *The Invisible Woman: The Story of Nelly Ternan and Charles Dickens* (1990). Much of the material was later incorporated into Tomalin's full biography of Charles Dickens in 2011.

20. Ralph Fiennes and Kristin Scott Thomas had famously co-starred in the Oscar-winning film *The English Patient* (1996). Welsh playwright Abi Morgan (b. 1968), working with Fiennes, helped persuade him to take on the lead role of Charles Dickens, of whom Fiennes knew relatively little beforehand. Around the same period (circa 2011), Morgan was also writing a screenplay for an acclaimed Margaret Thatcher biopic, *The Iron Lady*, ultimately starring Meryl Streep.

21. Tomalin's well-regarded books on the same subject are also highly recommended.

Summary

1. *Sketches by Boz* ("Our Parish"), Chapter VI.

2. *Sketches by Boz*, Preface.

3. Dickens' extensive personal contributions to charity, the only big outlet for social change during that time and place, are well documented.

4. *Sketches by Boz* ("A Christmas Dinner").

5. See Guida, Fred, *A Christmas Carol and Its Adaptations: A Critical Examination of Dickens' Story and Its Production on Screen and Television* (McFarland, 2000).

6. Guinness' successful negotiation for 2.25% of box office receipts from *Star Wars* with producer George Lucas has become the stuff of legend.

7. The first Harry Potter film was *Harry Potter and the Philosopher's Stone* (2001).

8. *Twist* has been near-universally panned by critics since its release, despite containing many clever innovations, as well as the participation of Michael Caine.

9. The case of Jean Simmons is especially interesting, given that she, like Alec Guinness, first came to widespread public attention in David Lean's *Great Expectations* (1946), but much later returned, out of choice, to playing a Dickensian role, and in her case, a different role (Havisham) from the same story.

10. By the time the BBC *Bleak House* was made in 2005, Gillian Anderson was an established television superstar, thanks to her ongoing performance as Agent Dana Scully in the American hit science fiction TV series *The X-Files* (1993–2002).

11. As noted earlier, this survey does not begin to take account of numerous, indeed countless, other movie storylines inspired by Dickens or borrowing elements from his novels.

12. The same may be said for many of Dickens' character creations, such as Pickwick, Fagin, Havisham, and Heep, to name just a few. These characterizations, however, are always, without exception, employed to further an entertaining storyline with a very subtle, underlying social message.

13. The word "revolutionary" continues to be appropriate in this context. The best critics of Dickens' work, whether sympathetic or hostile, are quick to recognize and acknowledge this central aspect of his storytelling art, even as it continues to be toned down or submerged by modern film adaptations.

Select Bibliography

Bioscope. https://thebioscope.net/2012/01/11/charles-dickens-filmmaker/.

Davis, Paul B. *The Lives and Times of Ebenezer Scrooge* (Yale University Press, 1990).

Eisenstein, Sergei. "Dickens, Griffith and the Film Today." Edited and translated by Jay Leyda, *Film Form: Essays in Film Theory* (Harcourt Brace, 1944, 1949, 1977).

Forster, John. *The Life of Charles Dickens* (Cambridge University Press, 1872, 1873, 1874, 2011).

Gross, John, and Gabriel Pearson, eds. *Dickens and the Twentieth Century* (Routledge/University of Toronto Press, 1962).

Guida, Fred. *A Christmas Carol and Its Adaptations: A Critical Examination of Dickens' Story and Its Production on Screen and Television* (McFarland, 2000).

Johnson, Edgar. *Charles Dickens: His Tragedy and Triumph* (Simon & Schuster, 1952).

Jordan, John O. *The Cambridge Companion to Charles Dickens* (Cambridge University Press, 2001).

Lodge, Guy. "Streaming: The Best Dickens Adaptations." *The Guardian*, June 13, 2020.

Nisbet, Ada. *Dickens and Ellen Ternan* (University of California Press, 1952).

Pointer, Michael. *Charles Dickens on Screen: The Film, Television, and Video Adaptations* (Scarecrow Press, 1996).

Smiley, Jane. *Charles Dickens: A Life* (Viking Penguin, 2002).

Storey, Gladys. *Dickens and Daughter* (F. Muller, 1939).

Tomalin, Claire. *Charles Dickens: A Life* (Penguin, 2011).

Tomalin, Claire. *The Invisible Woman: The Story of Nelly Ternan and Charles Dickens* (Knopf Doubleday, 1992).

Wright, Thomas. *The Life of Charles Dickens* (Charles Scribner's Sons, 1936).

York, Michael. *Accidentally on Purpose: An Autobiography* (Simon & Schuster, 1991).

Index

Addinsell, Richard 60, 134, 218
Adrian, Max 134
Les Adventures de M. Pickwick (1964 serial) 16
The Adventures of Mr. Pickwick (1921 film) 14
Adventures of Oliver Twist (1996–1997 animated) 27
Affaire Bardell Contre Pickwick (1962 film) 16
The Age of Innocence 119
Agyeman, Freema 127, 214
Ahern, Lynn 66
Albery, Donald 25
Alexander, Jason 66
Alien 218
All Creatures Great and Small 213
All My Children 64
All the Year Round 130, 143, 168–169, 213, 216
Allan, Elizabeth 133
Allen, Douglas 98
Allen, Karen 64
Allen, Patrick 117
An American Christmas Carol (1979 TV special) 209
American Notes (travelogue) 59, 73, 141–142, 145, 188, 203
The Americans 180
Amuka-Bird, Nikki 103
Amyes, Julian 152, 217
Anderson, Gillian 110, 155, 193, 220
Anderson, Maxwell 61
Andrews, Anthony 102
Angel, Heather 177, 219
Annis, Francesca 151
Anonymous 186
Anthony, Lysette 28, 92
Apfel, Oscar C. 73
Armstrong, Alun 28, 101, 110, 128, 180, 194, 214, 219
Arnim, Elizabeth von 118
Arnold, Malcolm 99, 116, 213
Asner, Ed 209
Atkins, Eileen 102
Attenborough, Richard 99

Auden, W.H. 204
Augusto, Daniel 172
Aumont, Jean-Pierre 136
Austen, Jane 48, 127
Avenue 5 102

Backus, Jim 209
Baddeley, Angela 74
Balderston and Unger (screenwriters) 219
Bancroft, Anne 154
Bancroft, George 90
Baragrey, John 170, 178
Barbera, Joseph 205
Bardell Against Pickwick (1938/1946 TV broadcast) 15
Bardell v. Pickwick (1955 TV episode) 15
Bardell Versus Pickwick (1959 TV episode) 16
Barnaby Rudge (1915 film) 53–55, 198, 210
Barnaby Rudge (1960 miniseries) 54, 91, 134, 199
Barnaby Rudge (novel) 48–57, 70, 86, 128, 131, 188, 204, 207, 209
Barnes, Justus D. 33
Barnes, Peter 65, 118
Baron, Alexander 27
Barry, Christopher 34
Barry, John 171, 218
Barry, Morris 54, 207
Barrymore, Lionel 98
Bart, Lionel 16, 25, 151
Bartholomew, Freddie 96, 98
Bassett, Linda 37
Bateman, Victor 33
Bates, Alan 119
The Battle of Life (novella) 83–84
Bax, Arnold 25
Bayley, Laura 108
Beach, Michael 65
Beadnell, Maria 96, 103, 123, 214
Beale, Simon Russell 67
Beckett, Samuel 135
Beethoven, Ludwig van 211
Bell, Jamie 37
Belmore, Lionel 24

224 Index

Benjamin, Arthur 137
Bennett, Rodney 92
Bennett, Tony 16
Benson, Elaine 42
Bentley, Richard 21, 207
Bentley, Thomas 14, 23, 31, 42, 46, 53–54, 97, 115, 210
Bernard, Dorothy 78
Bernstein, Elmer 44
Bettany, Paul 102
The Birth of a Nation 53, 81
Birth of a Soul (1920 film) 215
Blaché, Herbert 79, 176
The Black Cat 219
Blackton, J. Stuart 23
Blackwell, Simon 102, 212
Bleak House (1920 film) 108, 198
Bleak House (1922 film) 108, 198
Bleak House (1959 miniseries) 26, 74, 109, 199, 213
Bleak House (1985 miniseries) 109, 125, 136, 200, 213
Bleak House (novel) 6, 38, 104–113, 121, 138, 194
Bleak House (2005 miniseries) 110, 193, 201, 213–214, 219–220
Bleasdale, Alan 28
Blitzer, Bill 81
Blocker, Dan 144
Bogarde, Dirk 134
Bonanza (TV episode) 144, 186, 220
Bond, Gary 151
Bonham Carter, Helena 155
Booth, Douglas 155
Booth, Walter R. 12, 22, 59
Born Free 218
Botelho, João 117
Boublil, Alaine 136
The Boy and the Convict (1909 film) 149, 197
Boyd, William "Stage" 24
Brabin, Charles 53
Bradbury, Ray 94
Bradbury & Evans (publishers) 80, 83, 86, 95, 105, 113, 212, 130, 142, 203
Braithwaite, Lilian 90, 211
Bricusse, Leslie 16, 62
The Bridge on the River Kwai 134
Brief Encounter 216
Broadbent, Jim 37
Brooke, Van Dyke 4, 170
Brown, Anne 216
Brown, James 16
Browne, Hablot Knight 9, 13, 22, 30, 32, 48, 69, 86, 95, 105, 113, 212, 130, 204
Brydon, Rob 28
Buckstone, J.B. 130
Bugs Bunny's Christmas Carol (1979 animated) 63
Bulwer-Lytton, Edward 148
Bunny, John 10, 13

Bunyan, John 205
Burdett-Coutts, Angela Georgina 69, 130, 209
Burge, Stuart 98
Burgon, Geoffrey 75
Burke, Edmund 50
Burnand and Solomon (composers) 204
Burnett, Frances Hodgson 154
Buss, Robert William 204
Butler, Alexander 108
Bygraves, Max 25
Byron, Lord 97, 206

Cage, Nicholas 209
Caine, Michael 25–26, 29, 58, 64–65, 193, 220
Calf, Anthony 154, 164, 217
Call the Midwife 37, 127
Callow, Simon 84, 101, 188, 194, 209
Capaldi, Peter 103, 172, 218
Capra, Frank 208
Carlyle, Thomas 105, 113, 130, 213
A Carol for Another Christmas (1964 film) 208–209
Caron, Leslie 67
Carr, John Dickson 178
Carrey, Jim 66
Carroll, Lewis 83
Carson, John 91
Cary, Tristam 62
The Casual Vacancy 217
Cats 172, 212
Cattermole, George 39, 48
Cavalcanti, Alberto 33
Cervantes, Miguel 204
Chadwick, Justin 110
Chambers, Emma 75
Chaney, Lon 20, 24
Chaplin, Charlie 23–24, 66
Chaplin, Geraldine 66
Chapman & Hall 9–10, 30, 39, 48, 59, 69, 78, 130, 142, 158, 175, 207, 214
A Charles Dickens Christmas (1956 TV episode) 15, 199
Charles Dickens's England 186
Charles Dickens' Ghost Stories (1987 animated film) 17–18, 204
A Child's History of England (non-fiction) 105
The Chimes (1914 British film) 53, 79, 198
The Chimes (1914 American film) 79, 176, 198
The Chimes (novella) 2, 78–80, 84, 210
The Chimes (2000 film) 80, 201
Chitti Tammudu (1962 film) 205
Christie, Agatha 55, 152, 155, 217
Christie, Julie 211
Christmas at Dingley Dell (1959 TV episode) 16
A Christmas Carol (novella) 2, 6, 12, 56–69, 72, 75–80, 83, 107, 143, 146, 168, 172, 188,

Index

190–192, 205, 208, 213–214; *see also The Right to Be Happy*; *Scrooge*
A Christmas Carol (1908 film) 59, 197
A Christmas Carol (1910 film) 53, 197
A Christmas Carol (1923 film) 59, 203
A Christmas Carol (1938 film) 60, 198
A Christmas Carol (1954 TV special) 64, 199
A Christmas Carol (1960 sound recording) 210
A Christmas Carol (1971 animated) 62, 200
A Christmas Carol (1982 animated) 63, 100, 200
A Christmas Carol (1984 film) 63, 200
A Christmas Carol (1997 animated) 63
Christmas Carol: The Movie (2001 animated) 63
A Christmas Carol: The Musical (2004) 66, 201
A Christmas Carol (2009 animated) 66, 201
A Christmas Carol (2019 miniseries) 66, 201, 209
A Christmas Carol (2020 film) 67, 201
Christmas Night (1946 ballet) 208
Cilento, Diane 43, 167
Circolo Pickwick, Il (1968 series) 16
Citizen Kane 208
Clarke, Warren 163
A Clockwork Orange 163
Coates, Albert 14
Collier, Constance 108
Collins, Alf 32, 53
Collins, Charles 175, 214
Collins, Wilkie 130, 172, 2013, 214, 218
Colman, Ronald 133, 193, 215
Coltrane, Robbie 155
Columbus, Christopher 77
Compton, Juliette 91
Connor, Kevin 154
Conte, John 5
Coogan, Jackie 20, 24
Cooke, Alistair 15
Cooke, Ethel 33
Cooper, Gary 82
Coriolanus 187
Cornwallis, Lord 50
Cossins, James 92
Courtenay, Margaret 44
Courtenay, Tom 37, 45, 127
Cox, Constance 26, 43, 46, 74, 99, 109, 134, 207, 213
Coyne, Susan 84, 188
Craft, Joan 43, 74, 91, 98–99, 134
Crewe, Francis 50
Crewe, John 50
Crewson, Wendy 64
The Cricket 85
The Cricket on the Hearth (1896 opera) 211
The Cricket on the Hearth (1908 opera) 211
The Cricket on the Hearth (1909 film) 6, 78, 81, 194, 197

The Cricket on the Hearth (1914 Johnston film) 82
The Cricket on the Hearth (1914 Marston film) 81, 198
The Cricket on the Hearth (1923 film) 81, 198
The Cricket on the Hearth (1949 TV special) 82
The Cricket on the Hearth (1952 TV special) 82, 199
The Cricket on the Hearth (1967 animated) 82–83, 199
The Cricket on the Hearth (novella) 2, 80–84, 86, 211
Cromwell, John 90
Cross, John Keir 178
The Crown 127
Cruikshank, Andrew 109
Cruikshank, George 4, 21–22, 203, 205, 208
Crutchley, Rosalie 117, 119
Cuarón, Alfonso 154, 194
Cukor, George 97
Cummings, Alan 37
Currie, Finlay 151
Curry, Tim 27, 209
Curtis, Simon 101
Cusack, Cyril 99
Cusack, Sinéad 99

Dahwan, Sacha 180
Dailey News 85
Dance, Charles 36, 110
Dancy, Hugh 102
Daniel, Jennifer 55
Darabont, Frank 65
D'Arcy, James 36
Darkest Hour 209
Darrow, Paul 94
Davenport, Nigel 102
David Copperfield (1913 film) 31, 53, 97, 198, 210, 212
David Copperfield (1922 film) 97, 150, 162, 198, 214
David Copperfield (1935 film) 60, 96–98, 133, 193, 198
David Copperfield (1954 miniseries) 98, 151, 199
David Copperfield (1956 miniseries) 98, 109, 199
David Copperfield (1966 miniseries) 98, 127, 199
David Copperfield (1969 film) 99–100, 199, 213
David Copperfield (1974 miniseries) 99–100, 200
David Copperfield (1983 animated) 100, 200
David Copperfield (1986 miniseries) 100–101, 200, 212, 217
David Copperfield (1993 animated) 100–101
David Copperfield (1999 miniseries) 101–102, 214, 219

David Copperfield (novel) 6–7, 35, 38, 50, 67, 76, 90, 93–105, 113, 137, 146, 148–149, 182, 184, 189–190, 211, 216
David Copperfield (2000 film) 102, 193, 206
Davies, Andrew 110, 127, 171
Davies, John Howard 25
Davis, Carl 44, 163
Davis, Jefferson 209, 216
Davis, Paul B. 208, 221
Davis, Sammy, Jr. 16
The Day of the Jackal 117
Deak, Jon 208
Dearman, Glyn 60
The Death of Nancy Sykes (1897 film) 22, 73, 195, 197, 203
The Death of Poor Joe (1901 film) 1, 107, 197, 203
The Death of Stalin 102
Dee, Frances 91
Defence of Poesie 217
Deluc, Xavier 136
DeLuise, Dom 27
DeMunn, Jeffrey 65
DeNiro, Robert 154
Dennehy, Ned 46
Dickens, Augustus (brother) 141, 166, 215–216
Dickens, Catherine, *née* Hogarth (wife) 130–131, 140, 184, 206
Dickens, Charles *passim*
Dickens, Charley (son) 168
Dickens, Elizabeth (grandmother) 50
Dickens, Elizabeth (mother) 120
Dickens, Fanny (sister) 87, 211
Dickens, Francis (son) 80, 141, 216
Dickens, Henry Fielding (son) 87, 89, 183–185, 218–219
Dickens, John (father) 50, 72, 84–85, 96, 106, 120, 144–145, 185
Dickens, William (grandfather) 50
Dickens and Little Nell (statue) 40, 47
Dickens Before Sound (2006 documentary) 185, 201, 204, 212
Dickens in America (2005 documentary) 145, 186, 201
Dickens of London (1976 miniseries) 144–145, 163, 185–186, 200, 220
Dickens on Film (2012 documentary) 3, 187, 201, 203
Dickensian (miniseries) 46, 195, 201
Dicks, Terrance 101, 212
Dobie, Alan 117
Doctor Marigold's Prescriptions (series) 169
Doctor Who 34, 36, 43, 92, 99, 101, 134, 207
Doctor Zhivago 211
Dog Day Afternoon 135
Dolly Varden (1906 film) 53, 197
Dolly Varden (1913 film) 53
Dolly Varden (painting) 49

Dolly Varden: The Musical Delicacy (1901 stage musical) 53
Dombey and Son (1917 film) 90–91, 108, 198
Dombey and Son (1969 miniseries) 91–92, 199
Dombey and Son (1983 miniseries) 92–93, 200, 212, 217
Dombey and Son (novel) 6, 85–93, 105, 108–109, 169
Donald, James 134
Donner, Clive 27, 63, 209
Donsky, Seth Michael 205
Doro, Marie 23–24
Dotheboys Hall; or Nicholas Nickleby (1903 film) 22, 32, 53, 169, 197
Dotrice, Ray 144–145, 185
Double Indemnity 54
Downhill 211
Downton Abbey 46, 84, 180, 188
Doyle, Patrick 154
Doyle, Richard 210
Dracula 219
Dreyfuss, Richard 28
Dunbar, Adrian 37

Easton, Sheena 100
The Early Life of David Copperfield (1911 film) 97, 124, 169, 197
Ebbie (1995 TV special) 64–65, 201
Ebert, Roger 209
Edgar, David 35
Edwards, Greg 215
Edwards, Julian 53
Edzard, Christine 125–127, 193, 214
Eisenstein, Sergei 7, 203, 221
Ekland, Britt 208
El Cid 109
Eleazar, Rosalind 103
Elfman, Danny 64
Eline, Mary 42
Eliot, T.S. 172
Elliott, Denholm 109, 171
Elton, Edward 106
Elvey, Maurice 90, 108
Elwell, Francis Edwin 40, 47
The Empire Strikes Back 92
Enchanted April 118
L'enfance d'Oliver Twist (1910 film) 205
The English Patient 220
Eugene Wrayburn (1911 film) 161, 197
Evans, Edith 99
Evita 172

Fagin (1922 film) 23
Fahrenheit 451 (1966 film) 94, 99, 211
Faires, Imogen 46
Fairfax, Diana 109
Farino, Julian 163
Farnum, William 132, 135
Fealy, Maude 124

Index

Felton, Norman 98
Ferris, Pam 163, 217
Field, Sally 102
Fielding, Henry 74, 183
Fielding, J.K. 218
Fields, W.C. 96–98, 193
Fiennes, Ralph 2, 155, 187, 220
Fildes, Lucas 175, 218
Finney, Albert 61
Firth, Colin 66
Flint, Kate 211
A Flintstones Christmas Carol (1994 animated) 63
Folliott, Doria 98
For Your Eyes Only 92
Forster, John 85, 188, 210, 216, 221
Forsythe, John 64
Four Weddings and a Funeral 217
Fox, Charles James 50
Fox, Edward 28, 37, 117
Fox, Freddie 180
Fox, James 45
Foy, Claire 127, 192
Francis, Derek 206
Frankenstein 218–219
Franklin, Pamela 99
Frasier 66
Fredric March Presents Tales from Dickens (TV series) 15–16, 99
Freeman, Martin 67
Friel, Anna 163
Frith, William Powell 52
The Frozen Deep (1857 play) 129–130, 132, 138, 172, 187, 203, 214, 218
The Full Monty 76, 101, 192

Gabriel Grub the Surly Sexton (1904 film) 13
Game of Thrones 29, 101, 193
Gaskell, Elizabeth 113, 213
Gatiss, Mark 172
Gazzara, Ben 208
Gibbon, Edward 161
Giedroyc, Coky 28
Gilbert, Arthur 176
Gilligan's Island 210
Gish sisters (Lillian and Dorothy) 215
Glover, Julian 92–93
Goddard, Jim 135
Goethe, Johan Wolfgang von 83
Goldberg, Whoopi 209
Goldmark, Karl 211
Goldsmith, John 154
Goldsmith, Oliver 207
Goodwin, Nat C. 23
Goodwin, Richard B. 125, 214
Gordon, George 207
Gordon, Serena 136
Gorman, Burn 110
Goulet, Robert 16
Grainger, Holliday 155

Grammer, Kelsey 66
Grandfather Smallweed (1928 film) 108–109, 198, 213
Grant, Marshall 82
Grant, Richard E. 65, 119
Grant, Ulysses S. 71, 142, 160, 216
Graves, Robert 144, 163
Graves, Taylor 20
Great Expectations (aka *Store Forventninger*; 1922 film) 150, 162, 198, 214
Great Expectations (1917 film) 149–150, 198
Great Expectations (1934 film) 150, 177
Great Expectations (1939 stage play) 150–151, 194
Great Expectations (1946 film) 5, 25, 34, 62, 71, 75, 98, 136, 148, 150–153, 156, 170, 177, 192, 194, 198, 216, 219–220
Great Expectations (1954 miniseries) 98, 199
Great Expectations (1959 miniseries) 151, 199
Great Expectations (1967 miniseries) 151, 199
Great Expectations (1974 film) 152–153, 156, 162, 200, 217
Great Expectations (1981 miniseries) 92, 152, 200
Great Expectations (1983 animated) 100, 153, 200
Great Expectations (1989 miniseries) 71, 153, 200, 217, 220
Great Expectations (1998 film) 154, 198, 201
Great Expectations (1999 miniseries) 154, 194, 201
Great Expectations (novel) 6–7, 35, 38, 67, 96, 146–156, 158, 184, 189–190, 219
Great Expectations: The Untold Story (1987 film) 153
Great Expectations (2011 miniseries) 155, 201, 217
Great Expectations (2012 film) 155–156, 179–180, 193, 201
The Great Train Robbery (1903) 33
The Great Ziegfeld 215
Green, Charles 169, 218
Green, Henry Towneley 169
Greenwood, Joan 126
Griffith, D.W. 6–7, 53–54, 78, 81–82, 194, 210, 218
Gruffudd, Ioan 154–155
Guest, Al 17
Guinness, Alec 3, 24–25, 27, 34, 62, 126–127, 150–151, 153, 155, 192–193, 205, 220
Gunga Din 177

Hale, Alan, Jr. 210
Hale, Alan, Sr. 74, 81, 210
Hall, James Andrew 92, 101, 152, 212, 217
Hammond, Peter 163
Hampshire, Susan 99
Handel, George Frideric 177
Hanna, William 205
Happy Days 209

228 Index

Hard Times (1915 film) 115–116, 198
Hard Times (1977 miniseries) 116–117, 125, 136, 200, 213
Hard Times (1994 miniseries) 118–119, 201, 213
Hard Times (novel) 105, 112–120, 130, 213
Harden, Jonathan 37
Hardie, Russell 82
Hardwicke, Cecil 33, 206
Hardwicke, Edward 33, 102, 102, 205–206
Hardy, Joseph 152
Hardy, Robert 98
Hardy, Thomas 218
Harper, Heather 215
Harris, Jonathan 64, 144, 220
Harrison, Rex 25, 204
Harry Potter and the Philosopher's Stone 220
Harvey, John Martin 133
Harvey, Laurence 43, 167
Hathaway, Anne 37
"The Haunted House" (short story) 168, 203
The Haunted Man (1862 stage play) 211
The Haunted Man (novella) 83–84, 212
Havers, Nigel 34
Hawes, Keeley 163
Hawke, Ethan 154
Hawthorne, Nigel 135
Hayden, Sterling 208
Haynes, Stanley 25
Hayter, James 15, 34
Headey, Lena 29, 193
Hedlund, Guy 73
Helmond, Katherine 65
Hemingway, Ernest 139
Henry IV, Part I 123
Henry IV, Part II 78
Hepworth, Cecil 23, 31, 53–54, 97, 170, 210
Herrmann, Bernard 61, 211
Hickey, William 205
Hicks, Barbara 92
Hicks, Seymour 59–60
Hickson, Joan 55, 152
Hiddleston, Tom 36
High Noon 82
Hill, Bernard 154
Hitchcock, Alfred 211, 219
Hobson, Valerie 151, 177
Hodges, Adrian 101
Hogarth, Georgina 96, 105, 131, 206
Hogarth, Mary 40, 206
Holloway, Stanley 33
Holm, Ian 171
Holman, Roger 34
Holmes, Rupert 178
Hopcraft, Arthur 116, 136, 213
Hopkins, Anthony 153–154
Hordern, Michael 62
Hoskins, Bob 66, 101
Household Words 5, 113, 130, 203

How Bella Was Won (1911 film) 159, 161, 197
Howard, Leslie 204
Howe, George 15
Hughes, Gwyneth 179
Hugo, Victor 136–137
Humphreys, William J. 23
Humphries, Barry 37
Hunnam, Charlies 37
Hunt, Leigh 106
Hunt, Martita 150, 155, 194
Hunted Down (1952 TV episode) 170, 178, 199
Hunted Down (1989 TV episode) 171, 200, 218
"Hunted Down" (short story) 168, 174, 218
Huntley, Raymond 55

I, Claudius 99, 126, 144, 163, 186
Iannucci, Armando 1, 102–103, 140, 193–194, 203, 212, 218
Inslee, Charles 78
The Invisible Man 177, 194, 219
The Invisible Woman (2013 film) 2, 155, 187–188, 201, 203
The Iron Lady 221
Irvin, John 116
Irvine, Jeremy 155
Isaacs, Mark 135
Ishiguro, Kazuo 213
It's a Wonderful Life 208

Jacobi, Derek 46, 80, 126–127, 186, 193
James, Emrys 92
James, M.R. 171–172
James, Pedr 75
James, Sid 25
Jarre, Maurice 152, 216
Jarrold, Julian 154
Jarvis, Martin 34, 100
Jeffrey, Francis 80
Jesus of Nazareth 179
Jo the Crossing Sweeper (1910 film) 108
Jo the Crossing Sweeper (1918 film) 108
Joel, Billy 27
Johansen, David 64
Johns, Stratford 152
Johnson, Edgar 218, 221
Johnson, Lamont 5
Johnston, Joseph 217
Johnston, Lorimer 81
Jones, Davy 27
Jones, David 65
Jones, Felicity 187
Jones, Toby 46
Jones, Tom 16
Joseph and the Amazing Technicolor Dreamcoat 151
Julian, Rupert 69
Jurassic Park 118

Index

Kaluuya, Daniel 67
Kane, Carol 64
Karloff, Boris 170, 218
Karr, Darwin 161
Kelly, Grace 82
Kendall, Jo 204
The Kid 23–24
Kidd, Barbara 36
King Lear 32, 122
Kingsford, Walter 177
Kingsley, Ben 28
Kinnear, Rory 180
Kipling, Rudyard 103
Kirby, Vanessa 155
Kirk, Brian 155
Kirkwood, James, Sr. 124
Klein Doortje (1917 film) 214
Kleine Dorrit (1934 film) 125
Knight, Steven 66
A Knight for a Night (1909 film) 13
Knightley, Keira 28
Korty, John 65
Krakowski, Jane 66
Krige, Alice 135
Kubrick, Stanley 163

Lamač, Karel 125
Landi, Lamberto 43
Lane, Nathan 37
Langley, Noel 15, 204
Lansbury, Angela 102
Lasky, Jesse L. 23
Laughton, Charles 97
Laurie, Hugh 103, 140
Law, Jude 29
Law, Rafferty 29
Lawrence, Diarmuid 179
Laws & Bass (songwriters) 82
Lawson, Denis 110
Lawton, Frank 98
Laye, Dilys 119
Lean, David 3, 5, 7, 22, 24–26, 34, 62, 71, 75, 98, 134, 150–153, 156, 162, 170, 177, 192–194, 205, 220
Lee, Robert E. 160
Leech, John 59, 62, 83–84, 208, 210
Leigh, Mike 209
Leighton, Margaret 152
Lennon, John 100
Lennon, Julian 100
Leonard, Bill 64
Leonard, Hugh 34, 91, 151, 171, 218
Leslie, Rolf 108
Lesser, Anton 46
Letts, Barry 92, 101, 134, 152, 212
Lewis, Emma 119
Leyda, Jay 203, 221
The Life and Adventures of Nicholas Nickleby (1947 film) 33–34, 36, 198, 206, 212
The Life and Adventures of Nicholas Nickleby (1982 stage play) 35, 63, 109, 200
The Life and Adventures of Nicholas Nickleby (2001 film) 36–37, 201
The Life and Adventures of Nick Nickleby (2012 TV series) 37, 179, 201
Lifeboat 219
Lincoln, Abraham 216
Lingstrom, Freda 162
Little Dorrit (novel) 6, 38, 105, 120–128, 143
Little Dorrit (1913 film) 124, 198
Little Dorrit (1920 film) 124
Little Dorrit (aka *Lille Dorrit*; 1924 film) 124–125, 150, 162, 198, 214
Little Dorrit (1987 film) 125–127, 193, 200, 216,
Little Dorrit (2008 miniseries) 126–127, 179, 201, 214, 219
Little Emily (1912 film) 97
Little Em'ly and David Copperfield (1911 film) 97, 124, 169, 197
Little Nell (1906 film) 41, 176, 197
Live and Let Die 163
Lloyd, Frank 20, 24, 132–133
Lloyd Webber, Andrew 151, 172, 212
Lockhart family 60
Lodge, David 75
Lodge, Guy 3–4, 221
Logan, Campbell 91, 98, 134
Loggia, Robert 27
Lonergan, Lloyd 124
Lord of the Rings 28
Lost in Space 144
Love and the Law (1910 film) 97
The Loves of David Copperfield (1911 film) 97, 124, 169, 197
Lowe, Arthur 100
Lucas, George 220
Lucci, Susan 64
Lunn, John 180, 219
Lyndhurst, Nicholas 101

Macfadyen, Matthew 127
MacKay, George 46, 207
Mackintosh, Steven 163
Maclise, Daniel 31–32, 80, 83, 206, 210
Macready, William 31–32
Macrone, John 4, 207
Magwitch (2012 film) 156, 217
Malone, William H. 14
Malthus, Thomas 115, 213
The Man from U.N.C.L.E. 162
The Man Who Invented Christmas (2017 film) 2, 84, 188–189, 201
Mancini, Henry 208
Manik (1961 film) 205
Mankiewicz, Herman 208
Mankiewicz, Joseph 60, 208
Mankowitz, Wolf 16, 185, 216
Mann, Delbert 99

230 Index

Mannering, Cecil 31
Manners, David 177
Manville, Lesley 66, 209
March, Fredric 61
Marchant, Tony 154
Marcus, James A. 24
Margolyes, Miriam 126, 145, 186, 188, 194, 215–216
Marre, Jeremy 16
Marsh, Joss 3, 53, 64, 126, 133, 150, 203
Marshall, Tully 23
Marston, Lawrence 81
Marston, Theodore 97
Martin, Anna Maxwell 110
Martin, Jesse L. 66
Martin Chuzzlewit (novel) 8, 59, 67, 69–77, 84, 86, 141–142, 188, 209, 214
Martin Chuzzlewit (1912 film) 73, 161, 197
Martin Chuzzlewit (1914 film) 73–74, 81, 198
Martin Chuzzlewit (1964 miniseries) 74, 91, 199, 213
Martin Chuzzlewit (1994 miniseries) 75–76, 136, 192, 201
"Martin's Close" (2019 TV episode) 172
Marx, Karl 19
Mason, James 152
Master Humphrey's Clock 39, 48
Mathieson, Jean 17
The Mating of Watkins Tottle (1956 TV episode) 4–5, 199
Matthau, Walter 61
Matz, B.W. 125
Maughan, Sharon 92
Maurice, Mary 170
May, Edna 31
May, Simon 34
Mayer, Louis B. 97
McAnally, Ray 154
McCallum, David 162
McCowan, Alec 218
McDermott, Marc 59
McDowall, Roddy 82, 151
McEnery, John 163
McGann, Paul 163
McGrath, Douglas 36
McKellan, Ian 98, 101
McKenna, T.P. 109
McKern, Leo 163
McKinnel, Norman 90, 211
McMenamin, Ciarán 101
Medak, Peter 102
Memoirs of Joseph Grimaldi (short story) 22
Mendes, Sam 46, 207
Menken, Alan 66
Merchant, Tamzin 180
Merchant, Vivian 135
Merchant and Ivory 119
Merrick, David 16
Mersereau, Violet 78

Micawber (2001 comedy series) 212
Mickey's Christmas Carol (1983 animated) 63
Middlemass, Frank 154
Miles, Bernard 151
Miles, Sarah 152, 217
Milford, Bliss 161
Mill, John Stuart 114–115, 213
Miller, Irene 108
Mills, John 5, 75, 136, 151
Mills, Juliet 5
Les Misérables 136–137
Miss Marple 152
Mr. Bumble the Beadle (1898 film) 22, 197
Mr. Dickens of London (1967 TV special) 5, 199
Mr. Guppy's Tale (1969 TV episode) 213
Mr. Horatio Sparkins (1913 film) 4, 198
Mister Magoo's Christmas Carol (1962 animated) 209
Mr. Pickwick (1963 TV teleplay) 16
Mr. Pickwick in a Double-Bedded Room (1913 film) 13
Mr. Pickwick's Christmas at Wardle's (1901 film) 12, 197
Mr. Pickwick's Dilemma (1959 TV episode) 16
Mr. Pickwick's Predicament (1912 film) 13
Mister Quilp (1975 musical) 43–44, 200
Mitchum, Robert 64
A Modern Day Fagin (1905 film) 205
The Modern Oliver Twist: or the Life of a Pickpocket (1906 film) 22
Montaigne 219
Montgomery, Douglass 177
Montgomery, Robert 98, 151
Moody, Ron 25, 99
Moon, H. Paul 208
Moore, Dickie 24
Moore, Owen 78, 81, 210
Moorehead, Agnes 134
More, Unity 108
Morgan, Abi 220
Morgan, Joan 124
Morgan, Sidney 124
Morley, Robert 152
Morris, David 67
Morris, Edna 15
Morris, Jacqui 67
Morrissey, David 164, 217
Morse, Barry 5
Moscheles, Ignaz 211
Mrs. Lirriper's Legacy (1912 film) 4, 169–170, 197
Mrs. Lirriper's Legacy (short story) 169
Mrs. Lirriper's Lodgers (1912 film) 4, 169–170, 197
Mrs. Lirriper's Lodgers (short story) 169
Ms. Scrooge (1997 film) 65, 201
The Mudfog Papers (short story) 22

Index 231

Mugby Junction (collection) 169
Mulligan, Carey 67, 110
Mulligan, Robert 134, 215
The Mummy 219
The Muppet Christmas Carol (1992 film) 58, 64, 200
Murder on the Orient Express 152, 217
Murders in the Rue Morgue 107, 174, 207, 219
Murray, Bill 63, 209
Myles, Eva 214
Myles, Sophia 36
The Mystery of Edwin Drood (1909 film) 176, 197
The Mystery of Edwin Drood (1914 film) 79–80, 175–176, 198
The Mystery of Edwin Drood (1935 film) 177, 180, 194, 198
The Mystery of Edwin Drood (1952 TV episode) 178
The Mystery of Edwin Drood (1960 miniseries) 178, 199
The Mystery of Edwin Drood (1985 stage musical) 178–179
The Mystery of Edwin Drood (1993 miniseries) 179, 200
The Mystery of Edwin Drood (novel) 76, 174–182, 190–191
The Mystery of Edwin Drood (2012 miniseries) 179–180, 201

Nalluri, Bharat 84, 188
Nancy (1922 film) 23
Neame, Ronald 62
Nelly (1947 opera) 43
New York Telegraph 168
Newell, Mike 155, 217
Newley, Anthony 49
Nicholas Nickleby (1912 film) 33, 124, 197
Nicholas Nickleby (1957 miniseries) 34, 199
Nicholas Nickleby (1968 miniseries) 34, 91, 199, 206
Nicholas Nickleby (1977 miniseries) 34–35, 200, 206
Nicholas Nickleby (1985 animated film) 17, 35, 200
Nicholas Nickleby (novel) 6, 30–39, 41, 53, 108, 188
Nicholas Nickleby (2002 film) 36–37, 127, 201, 205, 217
Nicholls, David 156
1917 46, 207
Nisbet, Ada 170, 221
North and South 113
Noy, Wilfred 13, 204
Nunn, Trevor 35
Nureyev: Lifting the Curtain 67

O Sinaleiro (2015 film) 172

Ockrent, Mike 209
Ogle, Charles Stanton 59, 73
Okonedo, Sophie 28
The Old Curiosity Shop (1909 film) 41–42, 169, 197
The Old Curiosity Shop (1911 film) 42, 109, 197
The Old Curiosity Shop (1912 film) 42, 124, 169
The Old Curiosity Shop (1914 film) 53, 198, 210
The Old Curiosity Shop (1921 film) 42, 198
The Old Curiosity Shop (1930 film) 206
The Old Curiosity Shop (1934 film) 42, 198
The Old Curiosity Shop (1962–1963 miniseries) 43, 74, 199, 213
The Old Curiosity Shop (1979 miniseries) 44, 200, 217
The Old Curiosity Shop (1984 animated) 44, 200
The Old Curiosity Shop (1995 miniseries) 45, 201
The Old Curiosity Shop (novel) 6–7, 39–48, 67, 108, 167, 176, 188, 218
The Old Curiosity Shop (2007 film) 46, 181, 201, 207
Oldman, Gary 66, 209
Oliver! (1960 musical) 16, 25–27, 43, 64, 93, 151, 178–179, 193
Oliver! (1968 film) 26–27, 61, 99, 137, 152, 199, 205
Oliver, Edna May 98, 133
Oliver & Company (1988 animated) 27, 100, 153, 200
Oliver and the Artful Dodger (1972 animated) 205
Oliver Twist (1906 film) 22, 169, 197
Oliver Twist (1909 film) 22, 169, 197
Oliver Twist (1912 American film) 23, 169
Oliver Twist (1912 British film) 23, 169, 197, 210
Oliver Twist (1916 film) 23, 198
Oliver Twist (1922 film) 20, 24, 133, 198
Oliver Twist (1933 film) 24, 91, 198
Oliver Twist (1948 film) 24–25, 62, 98, 150, 170, 177, 199
Oliver Twist (1959 TV special) 26
Oliver Twist (1961 miniseries) 26, 43, 74, 162, 199, 213
Oliver Twist (1974 animated) 27
Oliver Twist (1982 animated) 27, 100, 200
Oliver Twist (1982 TV series) 27, 63, 200
Oliver Twist (1985 miniseries) 26–28, 92, 200, 216
Oliver Twist (1986 animated) 27, 200
Oliver Twist (1997 film) 28, 201, 205
Oliver Twist (1999 miniseries) 28, 36, 201
Oliver Twist (novel) 6, 9, 16, 19–31, 38, 40, 51, 58–59, 67, 73, 146, 177, 179, 188, 194, 203, 205, 208

Oliver Twist (2005 film) 28, 201, 206, 214
Oliver Twist (2007 miniseries) 28, 201, 206, 217
Oliver Twist, Jr. (1921 film) 23
Olivier, Laurence 99
Ondra, Anny 125
O'Neil, Barry 42
O'Neill, Eugene 207
The Only Way (1899 play) 133, 215
The Only Way (1926 film) 133, 198, 215
The Only Way (1948 film) 134, 199, 215
Ora, Rita 29
Ornadel, Cyril 16
Orphans of the Storm 218
O'Sullivan, Maureen 98
Otis, Elita Proctor 23
Our Mutual Friend (aka *Vor Faelles Ven*; 1921 film) 162, 164, 198, 214, 217
Our Mutual Friend (1958–1959 miniseries) 162, 199
Our Mutual Friend (1976 miniseries) 144, 162, 200, 220
Our Mutual Friend (1998 miniseries) 164, 163, 201
Our Mutual Friend (novel) 6–7, 157–166, 175–176, 184, 217, 219
Owen, Martin 29
Owen, Reginald 60, 133

Packer, Peter 144
Palmer, Lilli 204
Palmer, Samuel 216
Paltrow, Gwyneth 154
Parfitt, Judy 127, 135
Parker, Molly 64
Parkinson, Henry Boughton 133
The Passion of Scrooge (2018 chamber opera) 208
Patel, Dev 102, 140, 193
Paterson, Bill 119
Patten, Robert L. 30, 206
Patton 209
Paul, Robert W. 12, 22, 59–60
Peacock, Trevor 44
Peake, Maxine 127
Peaky Blinders 66
Pearce, Guy 66
Peck, Bob 118
Penn, Robin Wright 66
Pepper, John Henry 211
The Personal History of David Copperfield (2019 film) 1, 4, 102–103, 140, 194, 201, 203, 218
Percival, Brian 46
Perugini, Carlo 183
Perugini (*née* Dickens; daughter), Kate 37, 87, 89–90, 92, 129, 158, 175, 182–185, 211, 214, 218
Petrie, Hay 42
Phelps, Sarah 28, 155, 217

Phillips, Jonathan 179
Phillips, Robin 99
Phillips, Siân 67
Pichel, Irving 24
Pickering, Sarah 126
Pickford, Jack 149
Pickford, Mary 81, 210
Pickwick (1889 operetta) 204
Pickwick (1936 opera) 14
Pickwick (1963 musical) 16, 62, 204
Pickwick (1969 TV special) 16, 199
The Pickwick Papers (1913 film) 10, 13, 198
The Pickwick Papers (1952 film) 15, 34, 199
The Pickwick Papers (1952–1953 miniseries) 15, 199
The Pickwick Papers (1985 miniseries) 17, 54, 200, 215
The Pickwick Papers (1985 animated film) 17–18, 35, 200
The Pickwick Papers (novel) 2, 6, 8–19, 21–22, 30, 32, 40–41, 67, 94, 121, 140, 181, 188–189, 191–192, 203, 206
Pickwick Theatre 14
Pickwick Versus Bardell (1913 film) 13
Pictures from Italy (travelogue) 77–78, 142–143, 216
A Pilgrim's Progress 205
Pip! (musical) 43, 152
Pithey, Wensley 44
Planet of the Apes 82
Plummer, Christopher 36, 84, 188, 193
Plutarch 191
Poe, Edgar Allan 51, 58, 84, 107, 141, 145, 168, 173–174, 177, 180, 185, 190, 207, 218–219, 217
Pointer, Michael 3, 5, 26–27, 91, 205, 215, 221
Polanski, Roman 22, 28–29
Pollard, Michael J. 64
Portman, Rachel 28, 36, 205
Postlethwaite, Pete 75, 210
Powell, Robert 179
Powell, William 49
Powers, Tom 54, 207
Pride & Prejudice 127
Prince (artist) 100
The Princess Diaries 37
Prior, Herbert 78
Pryce, Jonathan 84, 188
Public Life of Mr. Tulrumble—Once Mayor of Mudfog (short story) 21
Pulman, Jack 99, 144

Quayle, Anthony 152
Quiz Show 75

Radcliffe, Daniel 101, 192
Rains, Claude 177, 194, 219
Rampling, Charlotte 154
Rankin & Bass (producers) 61, 82–83, 209
The Rat Patrol 91
Rathbone, Basil 61, 98, 133, 208

Index

The Raven 51
Raymond, Gary 91
Rea, Stephen 46
Redford, Robert 75
Redgrave, Corin 99
Redgrave, Michael 5, 62, 99
Reed, Carol 26
Reed, Oliver 26
Rees, Roger 35, 63
Reid, Anne 109
Remains of the Day 119, 213
Rent 66
Revah, Amber Rose 180
Rhys, Matthew 180, 192, 219
Rhys, Paul 126
Rhys-Davies, John 154
Rich Man's Folly (1931 film) 90–91, 109, 198
Richard, Jean-Louis 211
Richards, Michael 102
Richardson, Ralph 99, 210
Richardson, Tony 74, 92
Ricketts, Thomas 208
The Riddle 186, 201
Rigg, Diana 109, 213
The Right to Be Happy (1916 film) 59–60, 208
The Robe 216
Roberts, Rachel 162, 217
Robson, Flora 135
Roma 154
Romeo and Juliet 32
Rosenberg, Edgar 216
Ross, Diana 16
Rowling, J.K. 155, 217
Rubin, Stanley 82
Rudolph the Red-Nosed Reindeer 82, 209
Russell, John 130
Russell, William 34, 99
Ryan, John 150
Ryan's Daughter 216

Saint, Eva Marie 208
Salaman, Merula Silvia 150
Sam Weller and His Father (1959 TV episode) 16
Sandberg, Anders Wilhelm 97, 125, 150, 162, 214
Santoriello, Jill 137
Sarandon, Chris 135
Sarandon, Susan 135
Sawalha, Julia 75
Schlesinger, John 36
Schmeling, Max 125
Schönberg, Claude-Michel 136
Scofield, Paul 74–76, 193
Scorsese, Martin 119
Scott, George C. 27, 63–65, 134, 209
Scott, Ridley 218
Scott, Walter 48–49, 51
Scott Thomas, Kristin 187, 220
Scroggie, Ebenezer 58, 84, 213

Scrooge (1913 film) 59
Scrooge (1928 film) 60, 109, 198
Scrooge (1935 film) 59
Scrooge (1951 film) 27, 60–61, 63, 199, 208–209, 218
Scrooge (1970 musical) 61–62, 199
Scrooge: or Marley's Ghost (1901 film) 12, 59, 65, 88, 107, 197
Scrooged (1988 film) 63, 200, 209
Searle, James 73
Secombe, Harry 16, 204
Seidelman, Arthur Allan 66
Seinfeld 66, 102
Sellers, Peter 25, 208
Selznick, David O. 97, 133, 219
Selznick, Louis J. 219
Sennett, Mack 81
Serkis, Andy 67
Serling, Rod 209
The Seven Poor Travellers 5, 203
Sewell, Danny 25
Seymour, Jane 163
Seymour, Robert 121, 203
Shakespeare, William 32, 77–78, 95, 122–123, 186–187, 204, 207, 218–219
"Sharpe's Company" 210
"Sharpe's Enemy" 210
Shaw, George Bernard 91, 182, 207, 211
Shaw, Harold 73
Shaw, Robert 208
Shaw, Sebastian 44
Shaw, William 31
Shelley, Paul 134
Sheridan, Philip H. 216
Sheridan, Richard Brinsley 50
Sherlock Holmes (TV series) 204–205
Sherman, William T. 216–217
Sidney, Philip 159, 161, 217
"The Signal-Man" (short story) 166, 169, 172
The Signalman (1953 TV episode) 170, 199
The Signalman (1976 TV episode) 171–172, 200
The Signalman (1996 TV episode) 172
Silence of the Lambs 154
Silvestri, Alan 66
Sim, Alistair 27, 60–62
Simmons, Jean 71, 151, 153, 192–193, 216, 220
The Simpsons (animated TV show) 204
Sinden, Donald 178
Sketches by "Boz" 4–6, 21, 140, 190–191, 203
The Small Servant (1955 TV special) 43, 167
Smike! (1973 musical) 34–35, 43, 200
Smiley, Jane 58, 208, 221
Smith, Adam 115, 213
Smith, Daniel 88
Smith, George Albert 1, 108, 203
Smith, Maggie 101
Spall, Timothy 28, 37, 164, 194, 217
Spencer, George Soule 161
Spielberg, Steven 118
Spielman & Torre (songwriters) 61

234 Index

Spriggs, Elizabeth 75, 210
Standiford, Les 84
Stanfield, Clarkson 210
Stangé, Stanislaus 53
Star Trek: The Next Generation 65
Star Wars 126, 151, 192–193, 220
Staunton, Imelda 101
Sternberg, Josef von 90
Stevens, Dan 2, 84, 188
Stevens, Robert 178
Stewart, James 208
Stewart, Patrick 65, 118
The Stingiest Man in Town (1956 musical) 61, 199
The Stingiest Man in Town (1978 animated) 61
Stock, Nigel 17, 135, 193, 204–205, 215
Stone, Marcus 158
Storey, Gladys 91, 182, 184, 211, 218, 221
Storia di un orfano (1911 film) 205
Story, Edith 23
Story of the Bagman's Uncle (excerpt) 13
Stothart, Herbert 133
Streep, Meryl 220
Strong, Mary Pearson 96
Styne & Merrill (songwriters) 209
Suchet, David 135, 155
Sullivan, Francis L. 25, 150–151, 177
Sullivan, John 212
Sunquist, Gerry 152
Supple, Samuel 217
Susskind, David 26, 134
Sutherland, Hal 27
Swift, Jonathan 102
Swinton, Tilda 103, 140

Taft, Lorado 47, 207
A Tale of Two Cities (1908 film) 132, 169
A Tale of Two Cities (1911 film) 53–54, 130, 132, 169, 197, 215
A Tale of Two Cities (1917 film) 132, 198
A Tale of Two Cities (1922 film) 133, 198
A Tale of Two Cities (1935 film) 60, 133–134, 136, 193, 198, 215
A Tale of Two Cities (1950 opera) 137, 218
A Tale of Two Cities (1953 miniseries) 134, 199
A Tale of Two Cities (1957 miniseries) 134, 199
A Tale of Two Cities (1958 film) 134, 199
A Tale of Two Cities (1958 TV special) 134
A Tale of Two Cities (1965 miniseries) 74, 99, 134, 199, 213
A Tale of Two Cities (1980 film) 135, 200
A Tale of Two Cities (1980 miniseries) 127, 134–135, 200
A Tale of Two Cities (1984 animated) 135, 200
A Tale of Two Cities (1989 miniseries) 136, 200
A Tale of Two Cities (novel) 6, 56, 67, 128–139, 146, 168, 204, 215
A Tale of Two Cities (2007 stage musical) 137
Tayler, Eric 162
Taymor, Julie 219
Teale, Owen 101
Tell Me on a Sunday 172
Tempos Difíceis (1988 film) 117–118, 200
Tenniel, John 83
Ternan, Nelly 129–131, 145, 158, 160, 172, 185, 187, 211, 214, 217–219
Terriss, Tom 79, 175–176, 219
Thackeray, William Makepeace 130, 204
Thanhouser, Edwin 33, 42, 46, 97, 124, 161, 170
That Girl 210
Thatcher, Margaret 220
Thewlis, David 126
30 Rock 66
Thomas, Danny 82, 210
Thomas, Marlo 82, 210
Thomson, Kim 154
Thorndike, Sybil 33, 108
Thug Notes 215
Tilsley, Vincent 98
Tiomkin, Dimitri 134
Titanic 179
Titus 219
To Kill a Mockingbird 215
Tocqueville, Alexis de 141
Tom Jones 74, 92
Tomalin, Claire 3, 39, 49, 51, 70, 86, 105, 107, 114, 122–123, 129, 147, 174, 187, 203, 211–212, 220–221
Tong, Jacqueline 117
Towers, Harry Alan 15
Trebaol, Edouard 20
Trevor, William 44
The Trial for Murder (1974 TV episode) 171
"The Trial for Murder" (short story) 169, 172
The Trial of Mr. Pickwick (1952 TV episode) 15
Trimble, Laurence 13
Twist (2020 film) 29, 193, 201, 220
Twisted (1996 film) 205
Troughton, Patrick 43–44
Truffaut, François 99, 211
Tyler, John 218
Tyson, Cicely 65

Uncle John (1857 stage play) 130
The Uncommercial Traveller 139, 143–144, 216
Uneasy Dreams: The Life of Mr. Pickwick (1970 film) 16, 199, 204
Upstairs, Downstairs 74, 117
Ustinov, Peter 45

Vale, Travers 74
Van Blerk, Lindsay 80
Van Doren, Mark 75

Index 235

Vanity Fair (novel) 204
Varley, Sarah-Jane 152
Vaughan, Peter 109, 163, 217
Vaughan Williams, Ralph 208
Vavasseur, Sophie 46
The Vicar of Wakefield 207
Victoria, Queen 4, 9, 214
Vignola, Robert G. 149
Voysey, Michael 54

Waddell, Justine 154
Wager, Anthony 151
Walker, Stuart 150, 177
Wall, Anthony 3
Wall, Max 126
Walpole, Hugh 98
Walsh, Kay 150
Walter, Harriet 119
Wanamaker, Zoë 46, 101
Watts, George Frederick 105
The Wealth of Nations 213
Webb, Alan 218
Webster, Ben 42
Welch, Sandy 163
Welles, Halsted 178
Welles, Orson 171, 208
Wellesley, Arthur 213
Werner, Oskar 211
West, Timothy 27, 110, 117
Wharton, Edith 119
Whishaw, Ben 103
White, Chrissie 54, 207
White, James Henry 32
White, Susanna 110
Whitelaw, Billie 135
Whitemore, Hugh 99
Whiting, Leonard 35
Whittaker, Stephen 36
Who Framed Roger Rabbit 62
Wilby, James 136

Wilcox, Herbert 133
Wild, Jack 163
Wilkinson, Tom 76, 101, 192
William IV, King 205
Williams, Bransby 60, 109, 115
Williams, Richard 62
Williamson, James A. 13
Wills & Longbridge (playwrights) 215
Wilson, Nancy 16
Winkler, Henry 209
Winslet, Kate 209
Winstone, Ray 155
Winton, Dora de 108
Winwood, Estelle 151
The Wizard of Oz (film) 133, 204, 215
Wolf Hall 127
Wolfit, Donald 15
The Woman in White 172
Wonder, Stevie 16
Wong, Benedict 103
Wood, Elijah 28
Wood, John 134
Woodard, Alfre 84
Woods, Frank 81
Wright, Thomas 211, 218–219, 221

X-Files 110, 155, 220

Yelland, David 100
York, Michael 100, 152, 209, 217, 221
A Yorkshire School (1910 film) 32
Young, Freddy 152
Yurka, Blanche 133

Zandonai, Riccardo 211
Zeffirelli, Franco 35, 125, 179
Zemeckis, Robert 66
Zook, McCaughey, & Iannelli (architects) 14

www.ingramcontent.com/pod-product-compliance
Lightning Source LLC
Chambersburg PA
CBHW032039300426
44117CB00009B/1118